Social Enterpri

Wang offers an empirically based exploration into work-integration social enterprises as a means for delivering social services in China.

Focusing on the political economy of social enterprise development in China, Wang examines the nature of the relationship between the state and social enterprises and the implications of such relationships for their institutional effectiveness. She adopts a bottom-up approach that investigates indigenous practices embedded within the local political context. Common ground has been established internationally that the social enterprise model provides new ways of social service delivery that could potentially change and restructure the social welfare economy. However, the development path differs across social contexts, especially in an authoritarian country like China. This study provides insights into China's efforts to develop its social welfare sector and reinvigorate customary ideas about how public services could be better offered given the country's political economy.

This book will be of great interest to both scholars of China's political economy and those with an interest in the development of the social enterprise sector looking to see how this works in a Chinese context.

Echo Lei Wang is currently Assistant Professor at the Department of China Studies, Xi'an Jiaotong-Liverpool University. She was a postdoctoral fellow at the Asia Research Institute, National University of Singapore during the writing of this book.

Routledge Contemporary China Series

For more information about this series, please visit: https://www.routledge.com/Routledge-Contemporary-China-Series/book-series/SE0768

Social Enterprise in China

State-Third Sector Relations and Institutional
Effectiveness

Echo Lei Wang

LONDON AND NEW YORK

First published 2024
by Routledge
4 Park Square, Milton Park, Abingdon, Oxon OX14 4RN

and by Routledge
605 Third Avenue, New York, NY 10158

Routledge is an imprint of the Taylor & Francis Group, an informa business

British Library Cataloguing-in-Publication Data
A catalogue record for this book is available from the British Library

Library of Congress Cataloging-in-Publication Data
Names: Wang, Echo Lei, author.
Title: Social enterprise in China : state-third sector relations and institutional effectiveness / Echo Lei Wang.
Description: Abingdon, Oxon ; New York, NY : Routledge, 2023. | Series: Routledge contemporary China series | Includes bibliographical references and index.
Identifiers: LCCN 2023006531 (print) | LCCN 2023006532 (ebook) | ISBN 9781032139586 (hardback) | ISBN 9781032139593 (paperback) | ISBN 9781003231677 (ebook)
Subjects: LCSH: China--Social conditions--2000- | Social services--China. | Social entrepreneurship--China.
Classification: LCC HN733.5 .W36228 2023 (print) | LCC HN733.5 (ebook) | DDC 306.0951--dc23/eng/20230303
LC record available at https://lccn.loc.gov/2023006531
LC ebook record available at https://lccn.loc.gov/2023006532

ISBN: 978-1-032-13958-6 (hbk)
ISBN: 978-1-032-13959-3 (pbk)
ISBN: 978-1-003-23167-7 (ebk)

DOI: 10.4324/9781003231677

Typeset in Galliard
by SPi Technologies India Pvt Ltd (Straive)

Contents

Illustrations

Figures

Tables

1 Introduction

1.1 Background of Study

The social enterprise model can be loosely defined as using market-based models to tackle obstinate and complex social problems that traditional non-profits fail to solve (Kerlin, 2010). To be qualified as a social enterprise, the organisation must possess two characteristics—some form of commercial activities that generate sustainable revenues and the concurrent pursuit of social goals (Doherty et al., 2014).

Social enterprise originated as a concept in Europe in the 1980s alongside the rapid expansion of the third sector as a response to the diminishing role of the welfare state regime (Poon, 2011). In the past three decades, in line with political decentralisation, marketisation, and the rise of the third sector, social enterprises have become an emerging global phenomenon (Kerlin, 2010; Hazenberg, Bajwa-Patel, Roy, Mazzei, & Baglioni, 2016). The benefits of involving the market and the social sector simultaneously in addressing social issues have been greeted by countries across the world (Defourny & Nyssens, 2010). As public budget deficits become more severe, the social enterprise model is adopted as an innovative approach for resolving labour unemployment and addressing social inclusion issues. Social enterprise as a topic increasingly gains attention as socially conscious individuals become interested in applying innovative enterprise models to address social problems that could not be easily tackled by a single sector alone (Zahra, Gedajlovic, Neubaum, & Shulman, 2009; Nyssens, 2006).

At the macro-level, this signifies a social service provision that helps reduce transaction costs (Borzaga & Defourny, 2001) and prevents single-sector failure (Salamon, 1987). Borzaga and Defourny (2001) argue that the social enterprise model particularly contributes to areas such as public goods and services, employment creation, social cohesion, and third-sector development. In practice, the social enterprise model has been adopted by various governments and policy makers with the aim to use commercial means to solve social problems. The social enterprise models, especially those with a work-integration purpose that aims to address social unemployment, urban poverty, and inequality issues, have proved their effectiveness across Europe and North America (Davister,

DOI: 10.4324/9781003231677-1

Defourny, & Gregoire, 2004; Bode, Evers, & Schulz, 2006; Laville, Lemaître, & Nyssens, 2006; Nyssens, 2006; Cooney, 2015). At the same time, there are also concerns regarding how their commercial nature would affect their missions and social effectiveness (Williamson & Sawhill, 2001; Ebrahim, Battilana, & Mair, 2014; Maier, Meyer, & Steinbereithner, 2014; Jeter, 2017).

Studies on social enterprises, especially in developing countries, are still lacking both depth and breadth. Being a new form of third-sector organisations (TSOs) with both positive features and downsides, it is crucial for one to investigate deeper into the conceptualisation, mechanisms, roles, and impact of social enterprises. A common question to ponder is how factors in the socio-political domain affect the construction of social enterprises. As Kerlin (2012) points out, still little is known about how political, institutional, and socio-political factors shape or define social enterprise models. Scholars observe that across countries, the institutional forms and practices of social enterprises vary significantly (Kerlin, 2010, 2012). Defourny and Nyssens (2008) and Hazenberg (2016) point to differences in origins as the reason for different social enterprise forms across Europe. Some studies identify the nature of the government as a common factor causing the variety in social enterprises (Kerlin, 2010; Nyssens, 2006).

The potential of social enterprises is not constrained to the developed world. During the past decade, social enterprises have been increasingly recognised as one of the key actors forging third-sector development among the less-developed countries (Etchart & Comolli, 2013; Kerlin, 2010). Social enterprises in Asia are still at their primary stage of development (Defourny, Kuan, Chan, & Kuan, 2011). The heterogeneous societies in this region give rise to diverse organisational forms and missions (Defourny, Kuan, Chan, & Kuan, 2011; Tan & Prakash, 2014). Asian countries, including China, have their own traditions and standards when it comes to defining what organisations should be classified as social enterprises.[1] Since a unified theory has yet to be conceived among developing economies, studies based on these countries need to define their own objects of interest.

The study of social enterprise as a foreign concept requires skilful integration with the local reality. This is particularly relevant to the context of China. Common characteristics of the Western welfare regimes such as vibrant civil society, social welfare market and democratic participation in public services hardly exist in China. In terms of socio-economic context, China has gone through cycles of decentralisation of state power, rapid market transformation, and privatisation of the welfare system in the past few decades (Howell, 1995; Whiting, 1991; Yu, 2011). Parallel to this economic reform is the consistent authoritarian nature of the state and political dismissiveness towards civil society (Gilley, 2012; O'Brien, 2015). The country has developed its welfare system based on central planning and state corporatism (Hsu, 2010). This makes China a unique country to study indigenous social enterprise models.

The Chinese government shows a mixed attitude towards the development of social enterprises. A report in 2012 on social enterprises in China points out that opposite to non-governmental organisations (NGOs), which have always been a sensitive issue in China, the Chinese government shows a neutral attitude towards social enterprises (Zhao, 2012). As shown in reports and papers, the government takes a much more open approach towards concepts such as 'social enterprise', 'social entrepreneur' and 'social venture' by permitting discussions and the formation of social networks on these themes (Lee, 2009; Zhao, 2012; Zhou et al., 2013). For example, the Global Links Initiative and the China Non-Profit Organisations Network jointly launched the first social enterprise conference in China—the 'Sino-British Symposium on Social Enterprises/NPO' in 2004 (British Council, 2008). The Chinese government has also addressed the concept of social enterprise in its policy paper 'Suggestions by The CPC Beijing Municipal Committee on Strengthening and Innovating Social Management in order to Advance Social Construction' published in June 2011, which advises local governments to 'proactively support the development of social enterprises for social services'.[2] This is the first time the term *social enterprise* as a foreign concept is formally used in a policy document from Beijing. It reflects the approval of the government towards these new ideas.

The rest of this chapter introduces the political economy of social enterprise development in the global context, followed by a brief discussion of relevant concepts such as the 'third sector' and its nexus with social enterprises. It then moves on to articulate the aim, the theoretical foundation, and the research design of this study. Before proceeding, it is important to note that social enterprise is a conceptual rather than a legal term. The term *social enterprise* is used to describe institutions with a distinctive set of features. In reality, social enterprises may take the forms of NGOs, social businesses, cooperatives or any other organisational entities. As Galera and Borzaga (2009) point out, the lack of a common definition of social enterprises should not limit intellectual debates on the topic.

Most of the fieldwork was conducted during 2015 and 2016 for a period of two years. Some of the data cover historical development dating back to as early as 1996, and a few follow-up interviews were conducted in 2017. The reform of state-owned enterprises starts in 1995, which signifies the start of the privatisation of the social welfare system in China, while the Charity Law issued in late 2016 connotes a shift towards more stringent management of and a stronger political grip on the third sector. The period covered in this study is therefore adequate in representing the development of social enterprises in contemporary China before the effects of the political tightening fully surface.

1.2 The Political Economy of Social Enterprise Development

1.2.1 The Third Sector

Today, TSOs are increasingly empowered to become self-reliant partners of the state in social welfare provision (Brandsen, Pestoff, & Verschuere, 2014).

The third sector has been developed into a gigantic landscape that hosts a large diversity of institutions that sometimes are subtly distinguishable in characteristics and nature. The list of TSOs includes NGOs, voluntary-sector organisations (VSOs), community-based organisations (CBOs), informal-sector organisations (ISOs) and civil society organisations (CSOs; Ma, 2009). Adding further to this terminological complexity, these categories are not necessarily mutually exclusive. For example, VSOs, which often rely solely on voluntary workers and philanthropic contributions, are often classified as ISOs due to their informal nature, while ISOs also cover autonomous, spontaneous, and needs-based organisations (Turnham, Salomé, & Schwartz, 1990). CBOs and ISOs are originated by members of the communities and usually focus on enhancing the welfare of their own communities (Motes & Hess, 2013), while NGOs, CSOs, and non-profit organisations (NPOs) usually refer to relatively large bureaucratic bodies employing professional staff and skillful workers to perform a wide range of social activities with more general goals (Mercer, 2002). CSOs, by contrast, are a broader concept. They not only include NGOs (which are usually assumed to be not profit-pursuing) but also organisations that are profit-making and adopt for-profit legal forms, such as private foundations, cooperatives and private research institutes (Wagle, 1999). These organisations are not generally recognised as NGOs, but they share the common feature of pursuing social goals rather than maximising profits (Costa, Parker, & Andreaus, 2014).

1.2.2   *The Shift from NGO to Social Enterprise*

Defourny, Hulgård, and Pestoff (2014) once wrote that

> it is striking to see how the concept of social enterprise has been a major vehicle in recent years to revisit the role of TSOs in today's societies, although this concept sometimes goes beyond the borders of the Third Sector...

(p. 6)

Public services today encounter more severe budget constraints in the face of the hollowing-out of state power (Arnouts, van der Zouwen, & Arts, 2012; Rees, Mullins, & Bovaird, 2012). The global movement towards market liberalisation and privatisation invokes people's desire to find alternative solutions that improve non-profit performance and impact (Goerke, 2003). In developing economies, problems such as resource scarcity and political corruption have sincerely impeded the effectiveness of traditional NGOs in addressing their social needs (Zahra et al., 2009). The combination of these push-and-pull factors leads to growing interest among NGOs to seek innovative solutions from the private sector to deal with socio-economic constraints. Commercial practices such as strategic planning, independent financial auditing, quantitative evaluation, and performance measurement growingly become part of the daily operation of traditional NGOs (Ebrahim & Rangan, 2014).

Scholars from both European and American schools concord that social enterprise is a type of TSOs that places social objectives before commercial means (Aiken, 2006; Osborne, 2008; Poon, 2011). The combination of social objectives with commercial means is a major feature differentiating social enterprises from other non-profits as well as private institutions. Since social enterprises may adopt various organisational forms, some NGOs utilise this trend to establish or transform themselves into social enterprises to benefit from this strong commercial culture. Unlike private firms, social enterprises in most countries are required by law to have their assets held in trust for the constituency they serve and invest part or most of their surpluses into the businesses or the communities they serve (Defourny & Nyssens, 2010; Park & Wilding, 2012). Thus, it is natural for NGOs to incorporate the social enterprise model into their operation (Stevens et al., 2015; Moizer & Tracey, 2010). NPOs and NGOs are incentivised to take this 'business-like' approach to offset their budget shortfalls because of cuts in public donations and grants (Zahra et al., 2009).

Some argue that social network support has been the driving factor behind the rapid growth of social enterprises (Gardin, 2006; Nyssens, 2006). A direct observation is the involvement of multiple societal stakeholders such as social entrepreneurs, social workers, representatives of traditional TSOs, investors, and beneficiaries in service offerings (Kerlin, 2006; Zahra et al., 2009). In the United States, one major driving factor is the support from the private sector. For example, many business schools and private foundations in the country set up training courses and programs to attract socially cautious individuals to set up enterprises with a social purpose (Kerlin, 2006). The Social Enterprise Alliance identifies social enterprises as organisations with substantial and stable commercial revenue incomes that address stubborn social problems and serve the common good.[3]

1.3   Aim of Research

1.3.1   The Research Question

Social enterprises in the global North have exhibited commonalities in development trajectories and characteristics. This study focuses on the development and performance of social enterprises in China, where the situation is distinctively different. The country started building its market economy only after 1979 with authoritarian features and socialist ideologies (Zhou et al., 2017). The government controls all public resources and most of the social service channels (Wang & Yao, 2016). NGOs that want to obtain more resources and improve their conditions have to build strong bonds with the state (Hsu, 2010; Zhan & Tang, 2013). This means that social enterprises in China are developed under a different set of political-economy conditions. Studies reveal that the social enterprise sector in China shares some institutional features with its Western counterparts, such as hybridity and market-based innovation (Chan & Yuen, 2013), but how political factors impact their structure and performance and what their social roles are in the political economy reform process remain unknown. This study addresses these questions.

This study is exploratory in nature.[4] It aims to understand how the political economy context of China affects the development and performance of social enterprises. A specific type of social enterprise, the work-integration social enterprise (WISE), is picked as the object of study. These organisations are initially established as a state effort to alleviate employment difficulty and social exclusion of vulnerable groups (Davister et al., 2004; Nyssens, Defourny, Gardin, & Laville, 2012; Poon, 2011). The proposition is that the mode of relationship between the state and the WISEs has significant impacts on organisational performance. This proposition is used to guide the analytical process of this study.

This proposition can be divided into several questions to ponder:

a) Are there distinctive modes of relationship between the state and WISEs in China?
b) How can state–society relationship be related to the institutional features and performance (effectiveness) of the WISEs?
c) How do the findings contribute to our understanding of social enterprise development in China?

1.3.2   *Theoretical Background*

A premise of the study is that the state has the power to fully determine and steer the direction of the relationship with the organisations. A second premise is that WISEs are always interested in building alliances with the state as long as it does not threaten their autonomy and violate their missions. These premises have their roots in the state corporatist framework (Chen & Dickson, 2010; Hsu & Hasmath, 2013; Yu & Guo, 2012) and the resource-dependence theory (Hillman, Withers, & Collins, 2009; Nienhüser, 2008; Wang & Yao, 2016).

1.3.2.1   *Resource Dependency in State–WISE Relationships*

When the state is the dominant player, its strategies determine the nature and characteristics of the relationship. State corporatism is usually used to describe this relationship of absolute top-down control between the state and social organisations in China (Hsu & Hasmath, 2014; Hsu & Hasmath, 2013; Yep, 2000). State corporatism is defined as utilising vertical networks of political control and command to replace the development of horizontal social networks and self-ruling classes (Hsia & White, 2002).

It is evident that the Chinese state employs a list of monitoring tactics in its engagements with TSOs. According to the corporatist framework, the state adopts tactics of control such as monitoring, cooptation, and dissolution (Whiting, 1991). Hsu and Hasmath (2014) claim that as part of the corporatist strategy, the Chinese state is using selective 'tacit sanctioning' (Hasmath & Hsu, 2014:8) to manage social organisations. This means the state initiates, manipulates, and controls the organisations by giving them selectively the privilege to act on behalf of the interest of the state (Hsu & Hasmath, 2014). This includes both resources in tangible forms such as funds and exclusive rights to operate (Fowler, 1991; Khieng & Dahles, 2015; Weihua, 2005), and in intangible forms such as special connections and unwritten privileges (Ma, 2002; Najam, 1996).

A direct consequence of this relationship is the resource dependency of the WISEs on the state. Pfeffer and Salancik (2003) states that '[t]he key to organisational survival is the ability to acquire and maintain resources' (p. 2). The gist of the resource-dependent theory is that the organisation's reliance on external sources as vital inputs has a fundamental impact on the behaviour of the organisation, as it becomes adaptive and beholden to these providers for survival (Froelich, 1999). This theory lays the fundamental assumption of this study: that the Chinese state has full determinant power over its relationship with the WISEs since it has control over the essential resources.[5] Therefore, the state could fully affect the behaviours and performance of organisations.

The corporatist framework faces some criticisms with its application in China for over-simplifying the relationships between the state and TSOs. To overcome this shortcoming, this study has added to the analyses the adaptive strategies of WISEs by assuming that WISEs adopt strategies that would optimise resource mobilisation to maximise their chances of survival and social impact. This is based on the theories of organisational adaption and contingency management. All organisations can be viewed as rational systems that produce goods and services to fulfil customers' demand for consumption in exchange for the acquisition of resources and legitimacy (Cameron & Whetten, 1983). Organisations adopt strategies to overcome their contingencies by adjusting their structures and procedures to fit externalities (Chakravarthy, 1982; Donaldson, 2001; Kimberly & Zajac, 1985). With NGOs in China, this involves changes in organisational relationships, structures, and behaviours (Hasmath & Hsu, 2016; Saich, 2009; Sasser, Prakash, Cashore, & Auld, 2006; Xiumei, 2004). It is argued that NGOs adopt strategies in their dealings with the state to achieve their development and advocacy goals (Ramanath & Ebrahim, 2010; Wu, 2003). Studies also find that NGOs seek ways to form collaborative relationships with the state to tap into government resources; the challenge for them is doing so without compromising their organisational autonomy (Dimaggio, 1986; Heurlin, 2010; Sasser et al., 2006; Xiumei, 2004). Although NGOs in China face more stringent constraints and have less political space to operate, scholars believe that they have their own ways to negotiate for what they want (Lu, 2008).

1.3.3   *WISE as the Subject of Study*

The European Commission divides social enterprises into four categories based on the field they operate in (European Commission, 2017), these are

- WISEs that provide training, employment services, and social integration of people with disabilities and long-term unemployment.
- social enterprises that provide other personal social services such as health-care, education, childcare, services for the elderly, or disaster aid.
- social enterprises that focus on community and neighbourhood development.
- social enterprises that are created with a social niche, including environmental protection, sports and arts promotion, culture or historical preservation, and science and research.

Based on this classification, WISE is a specific type of social enterprise focusing on providing work-integration services to socially disadvantaged and marginalised groups. Ramus and Vaccaro (2014) define WISEs as social enterprises that 'commercialise products and services to pursue the socially oriented mission of providing job opportunities to marginalised workers such as low-income immigrants, people with alcohol and substance addictions, ex-inmates, and people with physical and psychological diseases' (p. 3). They can also be more narrowly defined at the practical level as social enterprises with the mission to provide values through vocational rehabilitation and deliver a range of services and goods that create employment opportunities for socially marginalised people through productive activities (Cooney, 2015; Campi et al., 2006).

WISEs as social enterprises have a relatively long history of development. The earliest form of WISEs can be traced back to sheltered workshops for the disabled back in the 19th century (Cooney, 2015). Over time, these workshops expanded into other forms such as business enterprises as the non-profit sector became more market-based. Subsequent generations of WISEs emerged under an entrepreneurship culture that champions private solutions to common social issues; thus, they often take the form of non-profit business ventures. They could adopt a diversity of models from providing subsidies and job training to sheltered employment. In general, WISEs are most strictly subjected to regulations on ownership and profit distribution because they deal with socially vulnerable groups.

A report covering Austria, Belgium, Finland, Italy, Malta, and Poland shows that in all these European countries, WISEs are officially recognised by the government as social enterprises.[6] In Italy and Finland, WISEs often exist in the form of social cooperatives, and in many other European countries, such as Austria, Belgium, Poland, Romania, and Spain, they adopt a diversity of legal statuses from NGOs, workshops, and cooperatives to limited liability companies. In the United States, they are in the form of sheltered workshops, worker cooperatives, benefit corporations, and low-profit limited liability companies. Their popular presence makes comparisons across countries possible.

Focusing on WISEs as the sector of study also reduces externalities. Unlike conventional companies, where the staff are employed to serve the organisations, providing employment is the main purpose of WISEs. This is why WISEs

> can be considered to be an economic sector in their own rights, characterised by the fact that they occupy a specific space which is defined not so much by what they produce, but by the way they produce it, and by the very specific characteristics of their workforce.[7]

Some may cast doubt on whether studies on a particular field of service can be used to generalise a set of institutions. Kramer (1981) defends this approach in her study of voluntary agencies and argues that a particular type of service, such as service delivery for the disabled group, is 'one cell within a larger matrix of voluntary organisations', and although 'one cannot hope to prove the validity of one's hypotheses rigorously, but where, by the marshalling of a variety of pieces of evidence, one can establish a probability which has some relevance to the major problems of social welfare' (Kramer, 1981:15). The same argument can be made on using WISEs as a lens to understand the social enterprise sector in China.

1.3.4 *Identifying WISEs in China*

The Chinese Social Enterprise Report (Zhao, 2012) states that a social enterprise must fulfil the following characteristics: it must have an institutional structure, it must rely part or all (ideally more than 30%) of its revenue on sustainable commercial sales, it re-invest more than 50% of its profit back into the social mission it supports, and the organisation must prioritise its social mission before profit pursuit. This standard is used in this study to evaluate if an organisation can be classified as a WISE. Considering that the overall development of social enterprises in China is still in its initial phrase, the 30% requirement of commercial revenue has been lifted in this study as long as the organisation demonstrates a clear and sustainable business model. Also, by this definition, NGOs that organise random charity sales for extra income, social responsibility programmes that have no fixed structure or staff, and cooperatives and industrial associations that do not involve a business model are excluded from this study.

Since social enterprises in China do not have a common legislative framework, they could take any organisational form or ownership structure (Zhu, 2009). WISEs could register either as businesses with a core mission of creating social benefits (Zhou et al., 2013), or social organisations that offer social services (Defourny et al., 2011). The former is supervised by the State Bureau of Industry and Commerce (SAIC) and the latter by the Ministry of Civil Affairs (MCA; Zhou et al., 2013). In addition, a great number of Chinese NGOs are registered as companies under the SAIC rather than as non-profits to circumvent the screening process (Hsu, 2010; Yu & Zhang, 2009). Depending on the weightage of their social functions, some of these private companies may also be classified as WISEs if they satisfy the preceding conditions. Considering that the development of social enterprises in China is still at its initial phase, the 30% requirement of commercial revenue has been lifted in this study as long as the organisation demonstrates a clear and sustainable business model. Also, by this definition, NGOs that organise random charity sales for extra income, social projects that have no fixed institutional structure and staff, and cooperatives and industrial associations that do not involve a business model are excluded from this study.

1.4 Research Design and Methodology

1.4.1 *Methodology and Data Collection*

This study has picked interviews as the data collection method to cover a wide range of participants so that abundant information could be collected to generate relevant themes. For this purpose, semi-structured interviews with follow-up questions whenever necessary have been conducted that allow the interviewees to disclose their views as much as possible.

The analysis is based on a cross-comparison between different modes of state–WISE relationship. The interviews provide details on how the WISEs interact with their external networks and resources to achieve their missions. It also assesses the beneficiaries' perspectives on whether the organisation has fulfilled its goals (refer to Appendix for interview questions).

Relevant stakeholders include

- government bureaucrats and officials who are responsible for regulating social organisations and civil affairs in the city or district where the WISE is located.[8]
- founder and senior-level managers of the social enterprise.
- beneficiaries, who are usually members of the WISEs.

In cases when direct conversations with the beneficiaries are inconvenient, this is replaced by directly observing their workplace and work procedures.[9]

1.4.2 *Sample Selection*

Interviews have been conducted in four cities in China: Beijing, Guangzhou, Shenzhen, and Foshan (Shunde) between 2015 and 2016, with follow-up interviews in 2017. Guangzhou, Shenzhen, and Foshan are in Guangdong Province in southern China, while Beijing is the capital city and is located in northern China. As a controlled factor, the four sites are comparable in their levels of economic development with a gross domestic product per capita (2015) between 1.0 million to 1.8 million Chinese Yuan.[10] This minimises market differences due to differences in economic levels. Some scholars argue that policy implementation depend on how local agents selectively react to the central policies (O'Brien & Li, 1999). However, since civil society is a politically sensitive issue in China, the impact of local power networks on political strategy is minimised across the cities. There is no evidence to believe that the local municipal governments considerably differ from one another in political strategy towards social organisations.

To accommodate variations in legal forms for WISEs, samples are selected based on four general criteria to suit the social context of China: the organisation must have a stable institutional structure, a guideline for profit earning and redistribution, clear and prioritised goals related to work integration, and a sustainable business model. In cases in which the organisation is not legally registered, it must have a fixed group of employed staff and must be active for no less than two accounting years. Some people argue that for social enterprises more than 50% of the revenue should be from the market (Defourny & Nyssens, 2010). However, as Defourny and Nyssens (2010) admit, this condition is hardly met in reality. Therefore, this standard is loosened in this study to accommodate social enterprises at their early development stage. Organisations qualify as long as a business model is present to generate consistent income from sales.

The background and activity of the WISEs were collected from news and reports, official websites, related journals, and relevant materials online. Organisations that fit the criteria for WISEs were contacted for interviews with their founders or senior-level managers and beneficiaries. Organisations were also asked to refer their social investor for interviews if possible. WISEs were recruited in the four fieldwork sites using the snowball sampling technique.[11] This means new candidates were continuously recruited in the process by asking interviewees for referrals.[12] The interviews were then transcribed and coded using data analysis software (NVivo). A total number of 70 interviews were conducted with 21 WISEs across the four cities, each lasting between 1 and 5 hours.[13] These include 31 founders and managers, 15 government officials and government-affiliated staff, 4 social investors, and 20 beneficiaries.

1.4.3 *Qualitative Data Analysis*

The interview transcripts are coded in the sequence of (a) major characteristics of the organisation and the services offered, (b) engagement with the state, and (c) their levels of mission achievement.

- Government Engagement
  During the interviews, the social entrepreneurs were invited to describe all forms of engagement with the government since the organisation was established. Questions on opinion questions such as 'How would you describe your relationship with the government' has also been included. The social entrepreneurs are also invited to describe their personal experience with the government and how it has contributed to the development and performance of the organisations.

- Mission Accomplishment

  A challenge of mission analysis is that the actual 'social value' of the mission is subjective and varies from one context to another (Stevens et al., 2015). This problem is dealt with by imposing a standard of measurement for social missions for all WISEs. During the interviews, the founders or managers of the WISEs were asked to describe the operation, programmes and activities, and achievements of the WISEs, especially those related to their organisational goals. During the coding process, descriptive labels are attached to these phrases as indications of missions achieved. These labels constitute the fundamental level of mission achievement that emerged from the data. The labels are categorised based on the mission-accomplishment measurement framework based on existing literature.

1.5   Significance of this Study

1.5.1   *New Insights into Cross-Sector Development*

As Defourny et al. (2011) rightfully point out that a major concern of social enterprise research on East Asia is to view it through the lens of literature developed based on the experiences of North America and Europe. Any research attempting to explain social enterprise development in Asia needs to keep in mind the cultural background and social transformation ongoing in this region. A typical debate is about the theoretical lacuna between the Western civil society framework and the context-specific development of the third sector in non-democratic countries (Büsgen, 2006).

The transnational concept of social enterprise points to the possibility of alternative third-sector development in China. There is an argument for an instrumental approach that focuses on organisational behaviours, the formation and reproduction of new institutions, and the efficient and effective delivery of social services (Bryson, Gibbons, & Shaye, 2001). In this respect, social enterprises stand out as tools falling under this category between traditional civil society and instruments. Scholars have noted that a unique feature of social enterprise is using market-based means to initiate social changes (Hulgård, 2011; Zahra et al., 2009). Do these organisations fulfil the same responsibilities in a state-corporatist environment and what are the dynamics involved are questions this study aims to answer.

1.5.2   *Bridging Two Strands of Literature*

Few studies link political economy factors with organisational studies, especially in the field of social enterprise research. As Mcloughlin (2011) points out, studies focus explicitly on

> the quality of services delivered to the end user rather than the dynamics of the relationship. ... The history and policy context of relationships,

how they are formally and informally organised and maintained and the effects on each organisation's identity and autonomy are rarely objectively studied.

(Mcloughlin, 2011:241)

This study bridges this gap by providing theoretical insights into how political factors impact organisational behaviours and performance against the macro socio-political context. This is also useful for a holistic view of the socio-economic development of the social service sector.

1.5.3 *Understanding Social Welfare Reform in China*

This study also enhances understanding of China's strategies in welfare policies and social reform. Methodologically speaking, China can be viewed as an enclosed system for social enterprise study. The strict regulation reduces the effect of foreign influence on the domestic non-profit sector, which is rare among emerging economies and gives the country's social welfare sector its unique characteristics. The fact that most of the TSOs have been developed within the past three decades since the country adopted the open-door policy in 1978 also minimises the effect of path dependency.

It is believed that the Chinese government promotes social enterprises for the pragmatic reason of filling the institutional void in welfare provision as the country opens its market and shifts toward a more service-oriented power structure (Chan & Yuen, 2013). As a report on social enterprises points out, NGOs in China are not able to fulfil their social responsibilities under the current political restraints. This means social enterprises, which rely less on donations and government support and more on the market, may play an increasingly dynamic role in China's social welfare economy (Zhou et al., 2013). By combining the political economy environment and social enterprise performance in China into one framework, this study provides an alternative angle in understanding third-sector institutions and social welfare development in China.

This research also fills a research gap in the current literature for social enterprises (Jay, 2012). Because of their conceptual fluidity (Nicholls, 2010), systematic empirical analyses on social enterprises are still rare (Jenkins, Thompson, & Darby, 2006). The comparative empirical analysis of this study hence provides valuable data that help evaluate arguments regarding social enterprise development in China.

1.5.4 *The Advantage of the Grounded Approach*

Social enterprises have become indispensably important in today's philanthropic discourse. However, the academic necessity of the concept is not one without debate. The dispute is aggravated by both theoretical and empirical difficulties in ratifying the concept (Nicholls, 2010), especially regarding its diverse configurations and applications across contexts and fields of research, and whether doing so would validate the development of specific theories and policies to understand and promote social enterprises as new institutions for the social economy. This lack of theoretical and empirical rigour raises doubts about whether the subject is worth being explored as a 'legitimate' academic discipline (Mair & Noboa, 2003).

Since social enterprises operate with the purpose of creating social value while generating income from business operations, they have the obvious strength of bridging multiple solutions, producing cost-efficient outputs, and enhancing financial independence. However, social enterprises also need to overcome the distinctive challenges of balancing their stakeholder groups and integrating their economic perspectives with social perspectives without causing conflicts between the two (Stevens et al., 2015). The lack of experience and knowledge in this field has added to the conceptual challenge. Because of this, studies working on social enterprises need to address their theoretical clarity and relevance. This means that such studies need to go beyond the general framework for social enterprises and provide analyses within specific contexts. The grounded theory approach provides an appropriate solution to this challenge by allowing theory building based on observed reality from the 'field'.

The subsequent chapters are arranged as follows. Chapter 2 illustrates the emergence of social enterprises in contemporary China with special reference to the role of the state and social welfare reform. The types of WISEs in China are also discussed. Chapter 3 presents the four modes of state–WISE relationship based on their political engagement. Chapter 4 illustrates how state–WISE relations are linked to their organisational effectiveness. Chapter 5 explains the performance and social roles of the WISEs in terms of resource transfer as a political strategy, and Chapter 6 summarises the limitations and policy implications of this study.

Notes

1 Some loosely define social enterprises in these regions as 'small enterprise concept that addresses the issue of poverty, providing needed services … without proper formation of legitimacy' (Zainon et al., 2014:153).
2 Retrieved from the official website of Office of Beijing Social Building (Beijing Shehui Jianshe), retrieved from http://www.bjshjs.gov.cn/, translated by author.
3 Retrieved from the SEA's website, https://www.se-alliance.org/why#whatsasocial enterprise
4 Exploratory research is suited in areas where few theories have been established (Lijphart, 1971).
5 This is confirmed in the interviews that all WISEs envisioned strengthening bonds with the state and none of them conveyed concerns about political autonomy (interviews with WISEs conducted between 2016 and 2017).
6 From 'A WISE Way of Working: Work Integration Social Enterprises and their role in European Policies, Guidelines for European Policy Makers', a policy report by Gruppo Cooperativo CGM (Co-operative Group of the National Consortium of Italian Social Co-operatives Gino Mattarelli), With the financial support of the

European Community Programme for Employment and Social Solidarity PROGRESS (2007–2013), available at www.wiseproject.eu

7 Ibid.

8 These include government officials working in local MCA offices and staff of GONGOs and public agencies that are responsible for managing and supervising the WISEs. However, it is not always possible to reach this group of people; therefore, their opinions are only included when applicable.

9 Although beneficiaries' opinions have been included in the interviews, it is difficult to measure user feedback in an objective manner with a small-N sample; therefore, their opinions are included only as supplementary evidence.

10 Data from the National Bureau of Statistics of China, retrieved from http://data. stats.gov.cn/

11 The author recognises the limitations of the snowballing technique, such as selection bias. However, there is no other viable form of sampling available for these organisations since there is no reliable formal record of them. As Hsu and Teets (2016) explain, the snowballing technique remains the best available data sampling method to study NGOs in China.

12 The validity of the samples is improved by performing background checks of the social enterprises from information published on social media platforms. Every referee was asked to recommend other local WISEs (after the criteria for WISEs were explained) that they knew at the end of the interview, and the list of WISEs was updated until the saturation point was reached.

13 Some of the interviews were conducted as group interviews with the beneficiaries and other relevant stakeholders. Therefore, they are not presented individually in this study but are used as supplementary information to assist the analysis process.

References

Aiken, M. (2006). How do social enterprises operating in commercial markets reproduce their organisational values? Presented in *The 3rd Third Annual UK Social Enterprise Research Conference*.

Arnouts, R., van der Zouwen, M., & Arts, B. (2012). Analysing governance modes and shifts—Governance arrangements in Dutch nature policy. *Forest Policy and Economics*, 16, 43–50.

Bode, I., Evers, A., & Schulz, A. (2006). 15 Work integration social enterprises in Europe: Can hybridization be sustainable? In Marthe Nyssens (Ed.), *Social Enterprise: At the Crossroads of Market, State, and Civil Society*. London and New York: Routledge.

Borzaga, C., & Defourny, J. (2001). Conclusions: Social enterprises in Europe: A diversity of initiatives and prospects. In Carlo Borzaga & Jacques Defourny (Eds.), *The Emergence of Social Enterprise*. Routledge.

Brandsen, T., Pestoff, V., & Verschuere, B. (2014). Co-production and the third sector: The state of the art in research. In L. H. Jacques Defourny, Victor Pestoff (Eds.), *Social Enterprise and the Third Sector: Changing European Landscapes in a Comparative Perspective*. Routledge.

British Council. (2008). The general report of social enterprise in China. [Electronic]. Available at http://Dsi.Britishcouncil.Org.Cn/Images/BC_China_Social_Enterprise_Research_Report.Pdf

Bryson, John M., Gibbons, Michael J., & Shaye, Gary. (2001). Enterprise schemes for nonprofit survival, growth, and effectiveness. *Nonprofit Management and Leadership*, 11(3), 271–288.

Büsgen, M. (2006). NGOs and the search for Chinese civil society environmental non-governmental organisations in the Nujiang campaign. ISS Working Paper Series/General Series.

Cameron, K. S., & Whetten, D. A. (1983). Some conclusions about organizational effectiveness. In Kim S. Cameron & David A. Whetten (Eds.),*Organizational Effectiveness* (pp. 261–277). Elsevier.

Campi, S., Defourny, J., & Grégoire, O. (2006). Multiple goals and multiple stakeholder structure: The governance of social enterprises. In Nyssens (Ed.), *Social Enterprises at the Crossroads of Market, Public Policies and Civil Society* (pp. 29–49), Routledge.

Chakravarthy, B. S. (1982). Adaptation: A promising metaphor for strategic management. *The Academy of Management Review*, 7(1), 35–44.

Chan, K. M., & Yuen, Y. K. T. (2013). An overview of social enterprise development in China and Hong Kong. *Journal of Ritsumeikan Social Sciences and Humanities*, 5, 165–178.

Chen, J., & Dickson, B. J. (2010). *Allies of the State: China's Private Entrepreneurs and Democratic Change*. Harvard University Press.

Cooney, K. (2015). Social Enterprise in the United States: WISEs and Other Worker-Focused Models. ICSEM Working Papers.

Costa, E., Parker, L., & Andreaus, M. (2014). *Accountability and Social Accounting for Social and Non-profit Organizations*. Emerald Group Publishing.

Davister, C., Defourny, J., & Gregoire, O. (2004). Work integration social enterprises in the European Union: an overview of existing models. *Revue Internationale de l'Économie Sociale: Recma*, 293, WP no. 04/04.

Defourny, J., Hulgård, L., & Pestoff, V. (Eds.). (2014). *Social Enterprise and the Third Sector Changing European Landscapes in a Comparative Perspective*. Routledge.

Defourny, J., & Nyssens, M. (2008). Social enterprise in Europe: Recent trends and developments. *Social Enterprise Journal*, 4(3), 202–228.

Defourny, J., & Nyssens, M. (2010). Conceptions of social enterprise and social entrepreneurship in Europe and the United States: Convergences and divergences. *Journal of Social Entrepreneurship*, 1(1), 32–53.

Defourny, J., Kuan, Y. Y., Chan, K. T., & Kuan, Y. Y. (2011). Similarities and divergences: Comparison of social enterprises in Hong Kong and Taiwan. *Social Enterprise Journal*, 7(1), 33–49.

Dimaggio, P. (Ed.). (1986). *Nonprofit Enterprise in the Arts: Studies in Mission and Constraint*. Oxford University Express.

Doherty, B., Haugh, H., & Lyon, F. (2014). Social enterprises as hybrid organizations: A review and research agenda. *International Journal of Management Reviews*, 16(4), 417–436.

Donaldson, L. (2001). *Foundations for Organizational Science: The Contingency Theory of Organizations*. SAGE Publications, Inc.

Ebrahim, A., & Rangan, V. (2014). What impact? A framework for measuring the scale and scope of social performance. *California Management Review*, 56(3), 118–141.

Ebrahim, A., Battilana, J., & Mair, J. (2014). The governance of social enterprises: Mission drift and accountability challenges in hybrid organizations. *Research in Organizational Behavior*, 34, 81–100.

Etchart, N., & Comolli, L. (2013). *Social Enterprise in Emerging Market Countries: No Free Ride*. Palgrave Macmillan US.

European Commission (2017). *Social enterprises*. Retrieved February 20, 2017, from http://ec.europa.eu/growth/sectors/social-economy/enterprises_en

Fowler, A. (1991). The role of NGOs in changing state-society relations: Perspectives from Eastern and Southern Africa. *Development Policy Review*, 9(1), 53–84.

Froelich, K. A. (1999). Diversification of revenue strategies: Evolving resource dependence in nonprofit organizations. *Nonprofit and Voluntary Sector Quarterly*, 28(3), 246–268.

Galera, G., & Borzaga, C. (2009). Social enterprise: An international overview of its conceptual evolution and legal implementation. *Social Enterprise Journal*, 5(3), 210–228.

Gardin, L. (2006). A variety of resource mixes inside social enterprises. In M. Nyssens (Ed.), *Social enterprise At the Crossroads of Market, Public Policies and Civil Society*. Routledge.

Gilley, B. (2012). Authoritarian environmentalism and China's response to climate change. *Environmental Politics*, 21(2), 287–307.

Goerke, J. (2003). Taking the quantum leap: Nonprofits are now in business. An Australian perspective. *International Journal of Nonprofit and Voluntary Sector Marketing*, 8(4), 317–327.

Hasmath, R., & Hsu, J. Y. J. (2014). Isomorphic pressures, epistemic communities and state–NGO collaboration in China. *The China Quarterly*, 220, 936–954.

Hasmath, R., & Hsu, J. Y. J. (2016). Conceptualizing Government-Organized Non-Governmental Organizations across Contexts. Presented at the *Development Studies Association Annual Meeting* (Oxford, UK).

Hazenberg, R., Bajwa-Patel, M., Roy, M. J., Mazzei, M., & Baglioni, S. (2016). A comparative overview of social enterprise "ecosystems" in Scotland and England: An evolutionary perspective. *International Review of Sociology*, 26(2), 205–222.

Heurlin, C. (2010). Governing civil society: The political logic of NGO–state relations under dictatorship. *Voluntas*, 21(2), 220–239.

Hillman, A. J., Withers, M. C., & Collins, B. J. (2009). Resource dependence theory: A review. *Journal of Management*, 35(6), 1404–1427.

Howell, J. (1995). Prospects for NGOs in China. *Development in Practice*, 5(1), 5–15.

Hsia, R. Y.-J., & White, L. T., III. (2002). Working amid corporatism and confusion: Foreign NGOs in China. *Nonprofit and Voluntary Sector Quarterly*, 31(3), 329–351.

Hsu, C. (2010). Beyond civil society: An organizational perspective on state–NGO relations in the People's Republic of China. *Journal of Civil Society*, 6(3), 259–277.

Hsu, C., & Teets, J. (2016). Is China's new overseas NGO management law sounding the death knell for civil society? Maybe not *The Asia-Pacific Journal*, 14(4), 1–22.

Hsu, J. Y. J., & Hasmath, R. (2014). The local corporatist state and NGO relations in China. *Journal of Contemporary China*, 23(87), 516–534.

Hsu, J., & Hasmath, R. (2013). *The Chinese Corporatist State: Adaption, Survival and Resistance*. Routledge.

Hulgård, L. (2011). Social economy and social enterprise: An emerging alternative to mainstream market economy? *China Journal of Social Work*, 4(3), 201–215.

Jay, J. (2012). Navigating paradox as a mechanism of change and innovation in hybrid organizations. *Academy of Management Journal*, 56(1), 137–159.

Jenkins, H., Thompson, J., & Darby, L. (2006). Applying sustainability indicators to the social enterprise business model: The development and application of an indicator set for Newport Waste savers. *Wales*, 33(5/6), 411–431.

Jeter, T. M. (2017). Exploring Mission Drift and Tension in a Nonprofit Work Integration Social Enterprise. Doctoral Thesis, Walden University, College of Social and Behavioral Sciences.

Kerlin, J. A. (2006). Social enterprise in the United States and Europe: Understanding and learning from the differences. *Voluntas: International Journal of Voluntary and Nonprofit Organizations*, 17(3), 246–262.

Kerlin, J. A. (2010). A comparative analysis of the global emergence of social enterprise. *Voluntas*, 21(2), 162–179.

Kerlin, J. A. (2012). Defining social enterprise across different contexts: A conceptual framework based on institutional factors. *Nonprofit and Voluntary Sector Quarterly*, 42(1), 84–108.

Khieng, S., & Dahles, H. (2015). Resource dependence and effects of funding diversification strategies among NGOs in Cambodia. *Voluntas*, 26(4), 1–26.

Kimberly, J. R., & Zajac, E. J. (1985). Strategic adaptation in Health Care Organizations: Implications for theory and research. *Medical Care Review*, 42(2), 267–302.

Kramer, R. M. (1981). *Voluntary Agencies in the Welfare State*. University of California Press.

Laville, J. L., Lemaître, A., & Nyssens, M. (2006). Public policies and social enterprises in Europe: The challenge of institutionalization. In M. Nyssens (Ed.), *Social Enterprise: At the Crossroads of Market, Public Policy and Civil Society*. Routledge.

Lee, R. (2009). The emergence of social enterprises in China: The quest for space and legitimacy. *Tsinghua China Law Review*, 2(79), 80–99.

Lijphart, A. (1971). Comparative politics and the comparative method. *American Political Science Review*, 65(3), 682–693.

Lu, Y. (2008). NGOs in China: Development dynamics and challenges. In Y. Zheng & J. Fewsmith (Eds.), *China's Opening Society: The Non-State Sector and Governance*. Routledge.

Ma, Q. (2002). Defining Chinese nongovernmental organizations – Springer. *Voluntas: International Journal of Voluntary and Nonprofit Organizations*, 13(2), 113–130.

Ma, Q. (2009). *Non-Governmental Organizations in Contemporary China*. Routledge.

Maier, F., Meyer, M., & Steinbereithner, M. (2014). Nonprofit organizations becoming business-like. *Nonprofit and Voluntary Sector Quarterly*, 45(1), 64–86.

Mair, J., & Noboa, E. (2003). Emergence of social enterprises and their place in the new organizational landscape. IESE Working Paper No. D/523.

Mcloughlin, C. (2011). Factors affecting state-non-governmental organisation relations in service provision: Key themes from the literature. *Public Administration and Development*, 31(4), 240–251.

Mercer, C. (2002). NGOs, civil society and democratization: A critical review of the literature. *Progress in Development Studies*, 2(1), 5–22.

Moizer, J., & Tracey, P. (2010). Strategy making in social enterprise: The role of resource allocation and its effects on organizational sustainability. *Systems Research and Behavioral Science*, 27(3), 252–266.

Motes, P. S., & Hess, P. M. (2013). *Collaborating with Community-Based Organizations Through Consultation and Technical Assistance*. Columbia University Press.

Najam, A. (1996). NGO accountability: A conceptual framework. *Development Policy Review*, 14(4), 339–354.

Nicholls, A. (2010). The legitimacy of social entrepreneurship: Reflexive isomorphism in a pre-paradigmatic field. *Entrepreneurship Theory and Practice*, 34(4), 611–633.

Nienhüser, W. (2008). Resource dependence theory – How well does it explain behavior of organizations? *Management Revue, Special Issue: Resources and Dependencies,* 19(1/2), 9–32.

Nyssens, M. (2006). *Social Enterprise at the Crossroads of Market, Public Policy and Civil Society.* Routledge.

Nyssens, M., Defourny, J., Gardin, L., & Laville, J. L. (2012). *Work Integration Social Enterprises and Public Policy: An Analysis of the European Situation.* EMES Research Network.

O'Brien, Kevin J, & Li, L. (1999). Selective policy implementation in rural China. *Comparative Politics,* 31(2), 167–186.

O'Brien, T. (2015). Civil society under authoritarianism: The China model, by Jessica Teets. *Democratization,* 23(3), 570–572.

Osborne, S. P. (2008). *The Third Sector in Europe.* Edward Elgar Publishing.

Park, C., & Wilding, M. (2012). Social enterprise policy design: Constructing social enterprise in the UK and Korea. *International Journal of Social Welfare,* 22(3), 236–247.

Pfeffer, J., & Salancik, G. R. (2003). *The External Control of Organizations: A Resource Dependence Perspective.* Stanford University Press (reprint, reissue).

Poon, D. (2011). The emergence and development of social enterprise sectors. *Social Impact Research Experience SIRE,* available at https://repository.upenn.edu/cgi/viewcontent.cgi?article=1010&context=sire

Ramanath, R., & Ebrahim, A. (2010). Strategies and tactics in NGO-government relations. *Nonprofit Management and Leadership,* 21(1), 21–42.

Ramus, T., & Vaccaro, A. (2014). Stakeholders matter: How social enterprises address mission drift. *Journal of Business Ethics,* 143(2), 307–322.

Rees, J., Mullins, D., & Bovaird, T. (2012). Third Sector partnerships for public service delivery: An evidence review. TSRC Working Paper Series, University of Birmingham, Birmingham.

Saich, T. (2009). Negotiating the state: The development of social organizations in China. *The China Quarterly,* 161, 124–141.

Salamon, L. M. (1987). Of market failure, voluntary failure, and third-party government: Toward a theory of government-nonprofit relations in the modern welfare state. *Nonprofit and Voluntary Sector Quarterly,* 16(1–2), 29–49.

Sasser, E. N., Prakash, A., Cashore, B., & Auld, G. (2006). Direct targeting as an NGO political strategy: Examining private authority regimes in the forestry sector. *Business and Politics,* 8(3), 1–32.

Stevens, R., Moray, N., & Bruneel, J. (2015). The social and economic mission of social enterprises: Dimensions, measurement, validation, and relation. *Entrepreneurship Theory and Practice,* 39(5), 1051–1082.

Tan, P., & Prakash, R. (2014). Landscape of Social Enterprises in Singapore. Social Entrepreneurship in Asia: Working Paper No. 1. Singapore: Asia Centre for Social Entrepreneurship and Philanthropy, NUS Business School. Retrieved from http://bschool.nus.edu/Portals/0/docs/Social-Entrepreneurship-in-Asia-Working%20

Turnham, D., Salomé, B., & Schwartz, A. (1990). *The Informal Sector Revisited.* OECD Development Centre Seminars.

Wagle, U. (1999). The civil society sector in the developing world. *Public Administration and Management: An Interactive Journal,* 4(4), 525–546.

Wang, Q., & Yao, Y. (2016). Resource dependence and government-NGO relationship in China. *The China Nonprofit Review,* 8(1), 27–51.

Weihua, Y. (2005). On the relationship between NGOs and Government—From the perspective of resource-inter-dependence theory. *Journal of Public Management*, 2, 32–39. (in Chinese)

Whiting, S. H. (1991). The politics of NGO development in China. *Voluntas*, 2(2), 16–48.

Williamson, D., & Sawhill, J. C. (2001). Mission impossible?: Measuring success in nonprofit organizations. *Nonprofit Management and Leadership*, 11(3), 371–386.

Wu, F. (2003). Environmental GONGO Autonomy: Unintended consequences of state strategies in China. *The Good Society*, 12(1), 35–45.

Xiumei, Z. (2004). The strategy of Chinese NGO in dealing with the government: An initial research. *Open Times*, 6, 002.

Yep, R. (2000). The limitations of corporatism for understanding reforming China: An empirical analysis in a rural county. *Journal of Contemporary China*, 9(25), 547–566.

Yu, J., & Guo, S. (2012). *Civil Society and Governance in China*. Palgrave Macmillan.

Yu, X. (2011). Social enterprise in China: Driving forces, development patterns and legal framework. *Social Enterprise Journal*, 7(1), 9–32.

Yu, X., & Zhang, Q. (2009, July 1–4). Development of social enterprises under China's market transition. *2nd EMES International Conference on Social Enterprise, Euricse, Italy*.

Zahra, S. A., Gedajlovic, E., Neubaum, D. O., & Shulman, J. M. (2009). A typology of social entrepreneurs: Motives, search processes and ethical challenges. *Journal of Business Venturing*, 24(5), 519–532.

Zainon, S., Ahmad, S. A., Atan, R., Wah, Y. B., & Bakar, Z. A. (2014). Legitimacy and sustainability of social enterprise: Governance and accountability. *Procedia - Social and Behavioral Sciences*, 145, 152–157.

Zhan, X., & Tang, S. (2013). Political opportunities, resource constraints and policy advocacy of environmental NGOs in China. *Public Administration*, 91(2), 381–399.

Zhao, M. (2012). The social enterprise emerges in China. *Stanford Social Innovation Review*, available at SSRN: https://ssrn.com/abstract=2006776

Zhou, W., Zhu, X., Qiu, T., Yuan, R., Chen, J., & Chen, T. (2013). China Social Enterprise and Impact Investment Report. Public Administration (Vol. 91, pp. 1–119). Shanghai University of Finance & Economics, Social Enterprise Research Center, Peking University Center for Civil Society Studies, the 21st Century Social Innovation Research Center, the University of Pennsylvania School of Social Policy & Practice.

Zhou, Y., Chow, N., & Xu, Y. (2017). *Socialist Welfare in a Market Economy: Social Security Reforms in Guangzhou, China*. Routledge.

Zhu, X. (2009). Analysis of YBC's 'rebuild our home entrepreneurship campaign' – A social enterprise perspective. *The China Nonprofit Review*, 1(2), 263–283.

2 A Theoretical Review

Introduction

This chapter provides a theoretical review of the related concepts and theories on social enterprises and performance measurement. Starting with the broader literature on the third sector, it explains the theoretical aspect of social enterprises and how the concept is related to organisational theories and institutional studies. Common measurements of the effectiveness of third-sector organisations (TSOs) and non-profits and the development of social enterprises in developing countries like China have also been addressed.

2.1 Conceptualising Social Enterprises in Literature

2.1.1 Defining Social Enterprises in a Global Context

An Organisation for Economic Co-operation and Development report in 1999 explicitly introduces the concept of 'social enterprise' for the first time in reference to organisations that use both market and non-market resources to re-integrate disadvantaged groups into the labour market and provide goods and services (Noya & Lecamp, 1999). The report refines the definition of social enterprises as '[entities] seeking a certain degree of self-financing through the production of goods and services as a complement to (variable) public subsidies, with the primary goal of assisting victims of social exclusion rather than generating profit for shareholders' (Noya & Lecamp, 1999: 20). However, the report also admits that social enterprises have 'no universal, commonly accepted definition' (Noya & Lecamp, 1999: 9). Teasdale calls social enterprise a 'fluid' construct (Teasdale, 2011) because different actors promote different discourses connected to multiple organisational models and concepts (Hasan & Onyx, 2008).

As a result of this diversity, countries dissent from a unified model of social enterprises (Grant, 2008; Park & Wilding, 2012; Chan & Yuen, 2013). The EMergence des Enterprises Sociales en Europe (EMES) research network on social enterprises was formed in 1996 under the European Commission to serve the purpose of studying the emergence of social enterprises as an

DOI: 10.4324/9781003231677-2

innovative response to unemployment and social exclusion issues across Europe (Noya & Lecamp, 1999). The EMES network highlights four basic dimensions of social enterprises: continuous activities that produce or sell goods or services, a high degree of autonomy, a significant level of economic risk (compared to traditional non-profits), and a predominantly voluntary-based workforce (Defourny & Nyssens, 2012). These criteria define the 'ideal type' of social enterprises in a way highly relevant to their European origin, which stresses their democratic value and participatory nature (Defourny & Nyssens, 2010a). As a result, popular social enterprise models in Europe are mostly innovative forms of civil society entities, which include cooperatives, work-integration workshops, mutual societies, associations, and foundations (Defourny & Nyssens, 2010a; Wilkinson et al., 2014).

In the United States, where the private sector plays a much bigger role, the focus of U.S. schools is on how social enterprises as profit-oriented organisations engage in innovative and socially beneficial activities and support their social missions (Kerlin, 2006). Social enterprises hence are defined by their organisational forms rather than their social roles as NPOs involved in commercial activities (Haugh, 2005; Dees & Anderson, 2006; Massarsky, 2006). Common forms of social enterprises in the United States are social businesses, social purpose organisations, and for-profit companies with a social mission (Dees, 2018; Kerlin, 2006, 2012). This approach is further extended in the 1990s by the 'earned income' school of thought to include for-profit firms with social-purpose ventures (Defourny & Nyssens, 2010b). Borzaga and Solari (2001) provide a common definition of social enterprises as a private undertaking committed to achieving a social purpose, one that incorporates 'traditional resources of non-profit organisations (donations and voluntary participation), commercial revenue (originated both from public and private customers and founders), and business activity' (Borzaga & Solari, 2001). This stress on social innovation and social venture is also reflected in the business and management studies oriented around topics on entrepreneurship and enterprise management (Pierre, Friedrichs, & Wincent, 2014; Keohane, 2013).

Studies that attempt to conceptualise social enterprises can be loosely organised into three major groups, where social enterprises are understood as social welfare providers, as hybrid institutions, and as a new approach to public governance.

2.1.1.1   *Social Enterprise as Efficient Social Service Provider*

This stance of literature is rooted in the concept of comparative advantage. The classical piece by Arrow (1950) provides a succinct illustration of how the non-profit sector covers segments of society that both public and private agents are inefficient or negligent in fulfilling needs and demands. The third sector has advantages over the government and the market in service offerings for small and powerless minorities (Salamon, 1987; Gidron, Kramer &

Salamon, 1992). By comparison, traditional NPOs suffer from voluntary failure due to their weaknesses in generating resources and maintaining self-autonomy (Salamon, 1987). A social enterprise differs from a commercial business because of its priority in social mission and from an NGO because of its business-driven activities and financial goals (Kirkman, 2012; Massetti, 2013; Cornforth, 2014; Ebrahim et al., 2014).

Under this construct, social enterprises are viewed as social welfare service providers that fulfil traditional social missions with innovative business models. Their main purpose is to find new ways, such as forming collaborative strategies, building networks, and promoting social innovations and partnership alliances, to raise the efficiency of the social service sector (Kerlin, 2006). Scholars believe that with the adoption of formalised market practices such as commercial trading, strategic planning, independent financial auditing, quantitative evaluation, and performance measurement, social enterprises are, in general, more financially sustainable and cost-efficient than conventional TSOs (Bull, 2007; Borzaga & Depedri, 2013; Ebrahim et al., 2014).

2.1.1.2 *Social Enterprise as a Hybrid Organisation*

Scholars argue that social enterprises are by nature hybrid organisations that have emerged through the blurring of traditional boundaries between sectors (Brandsen & Van de Donk, 2005; Ramanath, 2009; Pestoff, 2014). Hybridity can be understood as a mixture of characteristics on a continuum between two opposite poles (Brozek, 2009). As Bielefeld (2012) states, hybridity is a fundamental characteristic of a social enterprise: 'the hybrid nature of social enterprise is not a contingent and empirical fact about this institution; it is an analytical truth that follows from the composite term itself'. Social enterprises are by nature hybrid organisations that span across institutional boundaries (Brandsen & Karré, 2011). This can happen in various ways, such as by joining the means of for-profits and non-profits (Boyd, Henning, Reyna, Welch, & Wang, 2017; Brozek, 2009), mixing and combining institutions across sectors (Brandsen & Van de Donk, 2005; Billis, 2010a; Defourny & Nyssens, 2010b), integrating the commercial arm with the social arm within the same organisational entity (Nicholls & Cho, 2006; Alter, 2007), or mixing the nature of goods produced (Becchetti, Pelloni, & Rossetti, 2008) and ownerships (Boyd et al., 2017; Billis, 2010b).

A hybrid spectrum is commonly used to represent the continuum of organisations. Dahl and Lindblom (2017) and Alter (2007) plot a spectrum of organisations from private enterprises to public agencies, with for-profit enterprises on one end and traditional non-profits on the other, and different organisation forms fall in between the two ends differentiated by characteristics such as profit model, motivation, stakeholder interest, and profit distribution (Alter, 2007). The different combinations of missions and characteristics lead to different forms of hybrid organisations with social enterprise positioned at the centre of the spectrum (Figure 2.1).

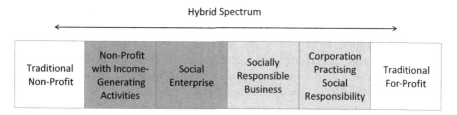

Figure 2.1 The Hybrid Spectrum (Alter, 2007)

The hybrid spectrum focuses on the private and the non-profit institutions and omits the role of the public sector. Some scholars consider the state as one of the three major social institutions that govern third-sector activities (the other two being the market and the third sector). Brandsen illustrates this point using the welfare triangle. The conjunction of two out of the three types of institutions leads to six sub-forms of hybrid organisations, namely informal and formal, public and private, non-profit and for-profit organisations (Brandsen et al., 2014). Interactions between and among these six types of hybrid organisations determine the nature of the activities involved.

2.1.1.3 Social Enterprises and Network Governance

The participative and multi-sectoral nature of social enterprises is a component of network governance (Ählström & Sjöström, 2005). The notion 'network governance' forms the basis of the New Public Governance (NPG) paradigm, with a special emphasis on increasing competition, contracting out, and power devolution. This usually happens in conjunction with the weakening and 'hollowing' of the state as a result of shifts in the public administration regime, which, in turn, fosters the role of the private and the third sector to replace the traditional role of the state as a service provider (Vamstad & Pestoff, 2006).

All of these imply a strong involvement of social enterprises in the co-production of public goods and services (Bode et al., 2006). When social enterprises are viewed as actors in a bigger political economy context, they must effectively balance the interests of stakeholders ranging from government officers, investors and donors, social entrepreneurs, and the beneficiaries and users. The literature on governance argues that the network of multiple stakeholders implies shared responsibilities that lead to welfare pluralism (Evers & Wintersberger, 1990; Kramer et al., 1993; Pestoff, 1998; Evers, 2005; Henriksen, Smith, & Zimmer, 2015).

2.1.2 Social Enterprises and the Third Sector

Social enterprises are viewed as situated at the junction of the public sector, the market, and the third sector (Nyssens, 2007; Hu, Zhang, & Niu, 2009; Meagher & Szebehely, 2013). The third sector is defined as the sector that is ruled neither by the market nor by the government. It is perceived to be volunteer-based, self-governing, and external to state control with non-profit or limited-profit distribution (Corry, 2010). To understand what the third sector constitutes, it is important to appreciate its fluid nature. As Borzaga and Defourny (2004) rightfully state, '*Much of the literature on the non-profit sector has been written from an explicitly or at least implicitly historical perspective … it is more often a matter of a posterior analysis than of studies of developments as they happen*' (Borzaga & Defourny, 2004: 19, emphasis in the original). The sector is an abstract community shaped by 'a particular form of communication' that plays the selective role of 'facilitating certain activities while obstructing others' (Corry, 2010). Two normative approaches have been identified. The institutional approach sees the third sector as a set of institutions with specific legal forms, such as charities, NGOs, cooperatives, mutual-help societies and groups, and social associations that exist beyond the public and the private sector (Corry, 2010; Hulgård, 2014; Wadongo et al., 2014). The systemic approach defines the third sector as a system that delivers and facilitates activities with specific normative logics based on shared values, social and community goals, and civil rights (Corry, 2010; Hall, 2012; Brandsen, Pestoff, & Verschuere, 2014). Under this approach, the third sector is a social process with its own internal logics that emphasize the ideological pursuit of symbolic rewards and shared values and idealism (Lewis, 2008).

Social enterprises are commonly viewed as TSOs. Salamon and Anheier (1997) conclude five common characteristics of TSOs: some institutional reality, non- or limited-profit distribution, self-governing, voluntary-based (at least partially), and private or civilian-based. Social enterprises certainly fit all these criteria. Some scholars conclude that social enterprises are unique TSOs that convey the important social values of encouraging citizens to participate in the co-production of public services and goods and that promote democratic governance and social innovation (Brandsen, Pestoff, & Verschuere, 2014; McColl Kennedy, 2012; Osborne et al., 2016). The 'uniqueness' of social enterprises as TSOs is reflected by their mixing and reshuffling of institutional logics and principles (Pestoff, 1992). This occurs when non-governmental organisations (NGOs) restructure themselves to incorporate additional commercial elements (Bryson et al., 2001) or when social businesses commit priorly to social missions (Duff, 2008; Bielefeld, 2012). Therefore, pinpointing the nexus between social enterprises and the third sector is helpful in understanding their features and activities in social contexts, including China.

2.1.3 *Models of Social Enterprise*

2.1.3.1 *Common Typologies*

It is challenging to categorise social enterprises because of their organisational diversity (Bielefeld, 2012). Spear et al. (2009) classify social enterprises in terms of their institutional forms and divide them into trading charities, public sector spin-offs, new-start social enterprises, and mutual societies. At the macro level, however, typologies based on organisational forms can be deceptive because they are context-dependent. Wang and Zhu (2011) propose classifying social enterprises based on the sort of socio-economic practices they are involved with, such as 'market practice-type social enterprises' (Wang & Zhu, 2011: 13) that are based on market practice, 'public-interest innovation-type social enterprises' (Wang & Zhu, 2011: 13) that are based on social innovation, 'policy support-type social enterprise' (Wang & Zhu, 2011: 14) based on the level of policy support, and 'ideals and values-type social enterprise' (Wang & Zhu, 2011: 14) based on ideas and values. An issue with this system is that the four categories are not mutually exclusive, as a social enterprise may be involved in more than one practice. This also causes confusion.

Another typology by Teasdale (2011) is based on organisational objectives, such as income earning, public services delivery, community development, or the collective goods of members. A few scholars arrange social enterprises into categories based on their other common qualities. For example, Alter (2007) classifies social enterprises by their level of business activities in social programmes, that is, whether they are mission-centric, mission-related, or unrelated to their missions. Moore (2000) and Nicholls and Cho (2006) divide social enterprises into three categories based on the relationship between their commercial and social units within the organisation. The two units may be embedded, mutually integrated, or external to each other depending on the extent to which their functions and goals overlap with each other.

Defourny and Kim (2011) provide the most comprehensive system for social enterprise classification. The five dimensions identified are development origins, social mission, organisational nature, legal status, and operational model. Under a combination of these dimensions, social enterprises can be classified into five types: commercialising non-profit organisations, work-integrated social enterprises (WISEs), non-profit or for-profit partnerships, non-profit cooperatives, and 'community development' enterprises. A variety of studies focus on one or more aspects of Defourny and Kim's categories. For example, Grassl (2011) derives a list of models based on different combinations of the hybrid components of social enterprises. Gordon (2015) highlights values and purposes as the differentiating factors for social enterprises that they may serve altruistic, public statist, private market, community, or mutual and ethical purposes, although these purposes can be again overlapping.

Last but not least, under the widely known EMES framework, Pestoff (2013) classifies social enterprises under two dimensions: social participation and the economic–social nature of organisational missions. Pestoff's work (2013) is unique in the sense that he relates social enterprises to a bundle of concepts including new public governance, co-production, and the 'welfare mix' model of social economy. However, as Pestoff establishes his work based on the European context, one needs to be extra cautious when one applies the previously mentioned concepts to developing countries.

2.1.3.2 The Tri-Sector Model

The tri-sector model provides an important framework that helps with understanding social enterprises at the macro-level (Salamon & Anheier, 1997; Salamon, Sokolowski, & Anheier, 2000; Brandsen, Pestoff, & Verschuere, 2014). Borzaga and Defourny (2001) define three elements, namely the structure of ownership, the kind of social capital mobilisation, and external economic relations, as the fundamental factors that differentiate the three sectors and call the tri-sector model 'a characteristic of social enterprises' (Borzaga & Defourny, 2001: 328). This is consolidated by Brandsen, Pestoff, and Verschuere (2014), who link the model to social enterprise typologies using the welfare triangle. The diagram in Figure 2.2 illustrates this institution mix, in which social enterprises are located at the centre of the plane (Evers & Laville, 2004a). Social enterprises are the result of overlapping features that causes tension in TSOs, which increases their complexity and provides the ground for social enterprises to emerge (Pestoff, 2014; Figure 2.2).

The study with the largest scale based on the tri-sector model is the International Comparative Social Enterprise Models project by Defourny and

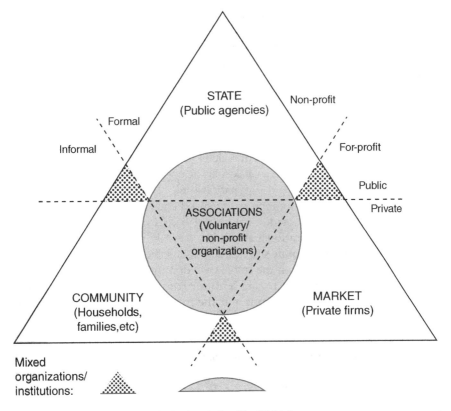

Figure 2.2 The welfare triangle (Evers & Laville, 2004a)

Nyssens, which covers about 50 countries with more than 200 researchers involved. It is based on the logics of action pertaining to individual sectors, what the authors refer to as 'matrix' (Defourny & Nyssens, 2017: 7). The study puts forward the 'principles of interest' and the 'resource mix' as two parameters defining the social enterprises in corresponding to the three sectors (Defourny & Nyssens, 2017). The model essentially concerns the missions of the organisation and the channels of resources to sustain those missions.

Salamon, Sokolowski, and Anheier (2000) construct a similar typology based on the size of civil society (in terms of the scale of the non-profit sector) and state capacity (in terms of government social welfare spending). Other factors such as governing regimes (Bode, 2011), market accessibility, and international aid (Salamon et al., 2000) have also been added. Nyssens (2007) tries to include the market as a third dimension, and his work is extended by Kerlin (2010), who constructs a social enterprise model with four fundamental elements: market performance, international aid, state capacity, and civil society. Different combinations of these four elements lead to diversity in social enterprise models.

Kerlin tests her model using seven countries and regions—the United States, Western Europe, Japan, East-Central Europe, Argentina, Zimbabwe/Zambia, and Southeast Asia (Kerlin, 2010, 2012). Based on this model, regions with strong market performance, such as the United States, Western Europe, and Japan, usually have a moderate to strong civil society, whilst in regions with weak market performance that suffer from weak civil society and state capacity, this has led to different patterns of social enterprises majoring on different sectoral elements. Kerlin's work links the social enterprise sector with political economy factors and suggests the possibilities of comparative analysis across regions. However, an obvious shortfall is the dichotomy nature of the model. The developed regions have strong capacities and abundant resources, and the developing countries are assumed to be lacking the fundamental elements to grow a strong social enterprise sector. Also, countries with a weak civil society give rise to social enterprises that rely heavily on market and international aid. These assumptions are not extensible to China, where both international aid and civil society are restricted.

The tri-sector model provides a universal basis for studying social enterprises beyond their organisational attributes. A weak link in the model is that it does not account for dynamic situations in which the three sectors are unbalanced in power. In cases when the state is the dominant sector, the autonomy of the market and the third sector are seriously compromised and the development and activity of social enterprises at the intersection of the three sectors will be affected as well.

2.1.4   Three Major Themes in Social Enterprise Research

2.1.4.1   Social Value and Mission

Social mission defines the intrinsic nature of social enterprises. The value of social enterprises is that they create both economic and social values with their dual-mission commitment. Although many NGOs today try to tap into private resources by charging the users for services and products they offer, they are still considered legally public-owned, as distributing profits among shareholders is strictly prohibited. In contrast, social enterprises face a 'double bottom line', with missions along both the social and economic dimensions. Defourny and Borzaga (2001) propose a list of social and economic criteria for social enterprises to corroborate their dual purposes. The economic criteria are continuous productive activities, degree of autonomy, level of economic risk, and amount of paid work (Borzaga & Defourny, 2001). For the social dimension, the organisation must be citizen-based with a share of rights, be participatory in nature, have limited profit distribution, and have an explicit social mission that benefits the community (Borzaga & Defourny, 2001). A direct implication of dual mission is that social enterprises are held accountable to both public and private stakeholders (Moizer & Tracey, 2010). Some scholars propose that to be qualified as social enterprises, these organisations must put their social missions before the pursuit of profit (Jenkins et al., 2006). This means a significant percentage of their profits must be reinvested back into their social activities or the organisations to be qualified as social enterprises. Overall, the rules are less restrictive with social enterprises than with traditional NPOs, but there is yet to be universal consensus over how much profit redistribution is appropriate for social enterprises. Therefore, the pursuit of dual missions is an important institutional characteristic of social enterprises, and its implications remain one of the key topics of research.

2.1.4.2   *Hybrid Institutions and the Cross-Sector Partnership Paradigm*

A group of studies emphasize the hybridity of social enterprises and focus on analysing the characteristics and performance of social enterprises as organisations. The notion of hybrid organisation starts with the evolution of institutional theories that view organisations as institutions with legitimacy sustained by shared values and rules, which could either be implemented internally or assigned externally (Powell, 1991; Jay, 2013; Kuosmanen, 2014). Hybrid organisations occur close to the boundaries of sectors, where different forms of organisations converge and integrate to form new and more complicated structures. This idea could be traced back to Bozeman (1988), who argues for a generic approach to organisations: that all organisations are public and should only be classified by their common nature of economic authority and political authority rather than conventional sectoral labels. Recent institutional theories attempt to incorporate multiple institutional logics under one roof (Reay & Hinings, 2009; Stark, 2010). Mair and Noboa (2003) point out that although at the macro-level sectors retain their individual terrains, there is a change in the institutional landscape at the micro-level, which results in hybridity as an important feature for social enterprises (Mahony & Bechky, 2008; Reay & Hinings, 2009).

The welfare triangle extends the research on social enterprises from organisational studies to sectoral analyses. Cross-sector partnerships (CSPs) are 'commitments by a corporation or a group of corporations to work with an organisation from a different economic sector (public or non-profit)' (Waddock, 1988), and they occur as 'the voluntary collaborative efforts of actors from organisations in two or more economic sectors' (Waddock, 1991). As issues within countries are becoming more complex today, it takes collaboration among sectors, especially participants from the third sector, to resolve new challenges (Pestoff, 2008). CSPs are formed when an array of institutions from various sectors form collaborative networks and commit their resources towards achieving common objectives and goals (Otiso, 2003).

Borzaga and Defourny (2001) argue that partnership is 'a characteristic of social enterprise'. Kindornay, Tissot, and Sheiban (2014) divide CSPs into four stages with increasing degrees of integration between the sectors. It starts with philanthropic partnerships that are solely about transferring resources in the form of partners' contributions to the NGOs to transactional partnerships that involve the exchange of resources between the partners to integrative partnerships when all partners interact and make decisions collectively in multi-stakeholder projects. The last stage called the transformational CSP is 'the most advanced collaborative stage that a partnership can reach' (Kindornay et al., 2014). This is the stage when hybrid institutions emerge to reform and introduce new practices and impacts. Social innovation occurs at this stage as a key feature. Therefore, social enterprises can be viewed as a form of partnership between or among the three sectors (Kwong et al., 2017). This leads to further research on their composition, stakeholder relations, and network analyses.

2.1.4.2.1   SOCIAL INNOVATION AND SOCIAL ENTREPRENEURSHIP

According to the American schools, social entrepreneurship is at the heart of social enterprise (Vurro & Perrini, 2006; Chell, 2007). Scholars argue that what differentiates social enterprises from private businesses is their innovative and social nature (Mair & Noboa, 2003; Sullivan Mort, Carnegie, & Weerawardena, 2003; Haugh, 2005; Austin, Stevenson, & Wei Skillern, 2006). Social enterprises introduce novel ideas by creating new social networks and practices, new services, and methods of production and institutions (Mair & Noboa, 2003; Fowler, 2010; Hussain, Ishaq, & Ullah, 2014). Social innovation, however, is defined as novel solutions that are more effective and efficient than existing solutions to social problems and hence create higher social value (Phillips, Alexander, & Lee, 2017). This innovation process requires social entrepreneurs to see new possibilities, play leading roles in breaking old rules, and eventually brings social change through the social enterprises established (Chan et al., 2019; Monroe-White & Zook, 2018; Phillips et al., 2017).

2.2   Assessing Institutional Effectiveness

Performance measurement is ambiguous about defining the outcome of an organisation when it has dual missions (Jay, 2013). A hybrid organisation can be seen as either effective or non-effective depending on the standard it is measured against. However, different measurement frameworks have different emphases that may lead to opposite conclusions. Therefore, clarifying the measurement standard is extremely important where institutional effectiveness is concerned.

2.2.1   *Theories on Effectiveness*

2.2.1.1   *The Early Organisational Theories*

The early organisational theories can be traced to Max Weber's conception of rationality and bureaucratic control in organisations (Weber, 1946). Theories around the same period stress formal rationality, scientific management, human relations, and decision-making within the institutional structures. Among all, the decision-making theorists focused on effectiveness argue that decisions are determined by the effectiveness of programmes developed as control systems that improve workers' discretion and flexibility, hence the organisation's overall ability to access and control outcomes can be improved (Vaughan, 1998).

The key issues of rationality, efficiency and effectiveness of organisations have been continuously addressed by organisational studies. Multiple studies have acknowledged the complexity of constructing what is termed effective performance (Hannan & Freeman, 1977). In the field of management, the most universal measure for effectiveness is how well the organisation's profitability is compatible with the company's target, followed by measurements of growth data and sometimes additional measures such as customer satisfaction, leadership, management process, human resources, and culture (Steers, 1975).

2.2.1.2   *Diversity in Measurement Standards*

The evaluation criteria for the effectiveness of NGOs are broader than those for private enterprises in the sense that input–output analyses for NGOs extend beyond financial factors (Willems, Boenigk, & Jegers, 2014). While it is generally agreed that the 'effectiveness' of an NGO is correlated to its social impacts, there still lacks a common baseline, especially for social enterprises (Bagnoli & Megali, 2009; Cordery & Sinclair, 2013; Millar & Hall, 2013). In general, the performance of TSOs is usually defined in terms of both economic efficiency and social effectiveness, where effectiveness usually refers to the level of outcomes accomplished while efficiency refers to the ratio of outputs to inputs (Berman, 1998). TSOs that are effective on the economic aspect might be considered ineffective when they are evaluated against the social benchmark (Ebrahim & Rangan, 2010; Lecy et al., 2012).

One way to measure the effectiveness of NGOs is through social impacts (Ho & Chan, 2010; Alvord, Brown, & Letts, 2016). A challenge is to differentiate the outcomes and outputs of projects. Some contest that efficiency is currently measured in terms of output but not outcome, as the latter admittedly concerns long-term effects that are difficult to access over a limited period (Berman, 1998). Here output refers to 'the direct, immediate consequences of strategies', while outcome is long-term, goal accomplishment (Berman, 1998: 53). Berman further argues that there could be multiple relationships between long-term outcomes and outputs, with which a single mechanism would be incapable to capture all (Berman, 1998). It is also difficult to measure the efficiency of an entire non-profit organisation, especially when the programme is operated as a sub-unit under the organisation—an arrangement that is not uncommon in the non-profit sector (Berman, 1998).

Another challenge is that NGOs usually disagree on what constitutes their own effectiveness. A series of face-to-face, in-depth interviews with NGO leaders in the United States reveal two distinctive perspectives of effectiveness. Based on a study by Mitchell (2012), a number of NGOs define effectiveness as outcome-based accountability, whereas some other defines it as output efficiency (Mitchell, 2012). Another survey with 152 NGO leaders in the United States ranks principles or strategies, the ability to attract resources and funding, inter-organisational collaborations, and quality of people as key attributes for organisational effectiveness (Mitchell, 2015). Research also shows that only one third of social enterprises in Britain use performance evaluation tools, while the majority still prefer to use their own customised methods for performance evaluation (Millar & Hall, 2013).

Studies approach the subject of NGO effectiveness from various angles, including project impact (Eisinger, 2002), progress towards achieving objectives and goals (Benjamin & Misra, 2006), board management effectiveness (Herman & Renz, 1997), and partnerships and networks (Candler & Dumont, 2010). However, Berman (1998) dismisses models that measure a single dimension of outcome as measuring *partial efficiency* (Berman, 1998:57). He argues that such measurement provides useful reference to certain key aspects of the organisations but fails to reveal the bigger picture of effectiveness (Berman, 1998).

Measuring the institutional effectiveness of social enterprises is challenging because of their multi-sector features and diversity in organisational forms. As Herman and Renz (1999) point out, effectiveness should be multidimensional. Studies incorporate multiple attributes at various levels to generate flexible measurement frameworks (Cameron & Whetten, 1983; Kendall & Knapp, 2000; Sowa, Selden & Sandfort, 2016). For example, Nanavati (2007) summarises six indicators that measure organisational effectiveness: financial resource management, human resource management, service delivery, organisational professionalism, external relations, and strategic management. Willems et al. (2014) identify four types of performance that assess non-profits: financial performance, which concerns the funding perspectives; stakeholder performance, which focuses on the balance of interests; market performance, which upholds the image, reputation, and service quality of the organisations; and mission performance, which measures the achievement of social targets. For Lecy et al. (2012), the four domains are organisational management, programs, operating environments, partnerships and networks.

2.2.2 *Debates over Effectiveness of Social Enterprises*

The literature on effectiveness measurement for NGOs is highly relevant to social enterprises because of the similarities between the two types of organisations in delivering services and achieving social impacts. In this sense, performance measurements for NGOs, especially those focusing on social missions, are also applicable to social enterprises. When NGOs have upward accountability to their donors (Jordan, 2005) and downward accountability to their beneficiaries (Kilby, 2006), social enterprises must be accountable to their multiple stakeholders (Ramus & Vaccaro, 2014). Lefroy and Tsarenko (2013) perform a statistical analysis based on 273 cases of corporate–NPO partnerships to understand how partners' reputations and financial and non-financial resources affect the effectiveness of the NPOs. This is one of a handful of studies that provide empirical analyses on social, financial, and non-financial capitals. Since the study only focuses on non-integrative, contract-based partnerships and contributions from the corporate to the social unit, it only provides a partial picture. Forsyth (2007) lists governance structure and diversity of actors as determinant factors, while Elizabeth Graddy (2009) names four additional factors—agreement on common goals, the relative size of the lead organisation in the network, the total size of the network, and the percentage of business institutions in the partnership—as being positively related to the effectiveness of CSPs. Lewis and Roehrich (2010) join this analysis by acknowledging the importance of both contractual governance and relational governance, but they also stress the importance of social capital, such as trust and reciprocity. Another informal factor brought up explicitly by Lewis and Roehrich (2010) is the role of good leaders in the transaction. This strand of study is relevant to social enterprises defined as CSPs.

A more comprehensive study explores how social capital and social network affect enterprise performance is done by Keeti Prajapati and Biswas (2011), who argue that both are crucial factors affecting enterprise effectiveness. Social capital encourages information diffusion and enhances mutual trust between actors and organisations, hence reducing opportunism and the cost of monitoring (Nahapiet & Ghoshal, 1998). The social network theory expands the notion of trust to include networks among organisations and argues that trust maintains inter-organisational cooperation. Organisational networks benefit from collective flexibility (Das, 1996) and the collective upholding of price and quality (Lechner, Welpe, & Dowling, 2006). Social networks also enhance both formal and informal user–producer relationships (Kingsley & Malecki, 2004). A few studies discuss the effectiveness of social enterprises from the angle of the organisational performance of hybrids. Under the organisational theory, scholars argue that developing an enterprise scheme is crucial for the effectiveness of TSOs (Bryson et al., 2001). The idea is that in complex modern societies, TSOs must be self-sustainable over the long term. The presence of an enterprise scheme demonstrates the organisation's ability for good management, innovation, and operation (Thompson & Doherty, 2006).

The differences between social enterprises and NGOs have been highlighted in the literature. Social enterprises are seen by many as being intrinsically more effective than traditional NGOs because of their business capabilities. As private enterprises are constantly driven by market competition to grow, people believe that this applies to social enterprises as well. Peredo and McLean (2006) discover that community-based social enterprises offer viable solutions for the economic development of resource-poor communities because these enterprises leverage local resources and social capital to promote economic efficiency. The business nature of these organisations plays an important role in forging economic benefits through technological advancements and job creation.

Another argument for effectiveness is based on the hybrid and innovative nature of social enterprises. According to the hybridity theory, social enterprises are hybrid organisations that incorporate resources, ways of financing, goals, and steering mechanisms from various sectors (Evers, 2005; Billis, 2010a). Their hybridity enables the integration of resources across sectors to provide cost-efficient, self-sustaining, and innovative social services. Ravichandran and Rajashree (2007) claim that innovative sources of funding enhance the sustainability of NPOs, and O'Cass and Ngo (2007) discover a positive correlation between market orientation and innovative culture. All these arguments point to the conclusion that social enterprises should be more effective than traditional NPOs in achieving social missions with the empowerment of the market.

While the preceding arguments focus on the economic advantages of social enterprises, another argument concerning the social aspect is the voluntary failure theory, which argues that the intrinsic weaknesses of the voluntary sector cause voluntary failure (Salamon, 1987). The state needs intervention from a 'third-party government', an elaborate system through which the government shares discretion power over the spending of public funds and the exercise of public authority with third-party implementers of social services (Salamon, 1981). However, the market or the voluntary sector alone cannot achieve this purpose, hence the strength of social enterprise in combining the advantages of the two.

Social enterprises are effective also in terms of portfolio diversification and sustainability-enhancing. The modern portfolio theory states that a diversified portfolio reduces volatility and financial instability (Farrell & Reinhart, 1997). The same arrangement can be applied to organisational sustainability (White,

1983). To test the previously mentioned theories, Deborah and Keely (2009) perform an empirical study on 990 NGOs in the United States during the period from 1991 to 2003 and discover that diversifying NPOs' financial portfolios by incorporating extra income streams lead to increased financial stability, hence better overall sustainability of the organisations. However, this conclusion is weak because NGOs reach out for multiple sources of revenue when they are already facing financial difficulty, in which cases diversity of revenue is not a good indicator of sustainability. What affects the social effectiveness of social enterprises therefore is still unclear from the empirical studies.

2.2.3 *Models for Organisational Effectiveness Measurement*

Cameron and Whetten (1983) conclude that 'there cannot be one universal model of organisational effectiveness' (p. 262), and 'there would be little utility in any model that tries to encompass them all' (p. 265). The solution to diversity in disciplinary frameworks is to identify the best measurement for a specific type of organisation by looking into its nature and constructing a particular set of situational factors, as 'all general theories of organisations have built into them implied criteria for measuring effectiveness' (p. 262).[1] As Cameron and Whetten (1983) further points out, 'it's more worthwhile to develop frameworks for assessing effectiveness than to try to develop theories of effectiveness' (p. 267).

One could identify three general frameworks for effectiveness measurement in the literature. The first group focuses on the mission-accomplishment or goal-achievement model (Spar & Dail, 2002), with the core idea that organisations 'deliberately construct and reconstruct to seek specific goals' (Etzioni, 1964: 3). Since all organisations are oriented towards attaining their goals, effectiveness is measured by their progress towards presumed goals.

A common shortfall of the mission-accomplishment model is that organisations sometimes have evolving or even contradictory goals rather than coherent goals (Salvato & Rerup, 2018). Whether these goals can be measured statistically is questionable. Moreover, the model does not pay sufficient attention to the type of organisations studied and the process mechanism, since the presence of goals does not necessarily mean they are realised (Child, 1974). It is also unclear how goals with different levels of complexity could be evaluated using a common set of standards. After all, organisations from the third sector perform a diversity of functions, some of which are difficult to measure by tangible outcomes (Lecy et al., 2012). A solution would be to define the goals carefully against a common benchmark if the mission-accomplishment model were to be used in empirical studies.

The second domain emphasises the systemic nature of organisations on resource mobilisation. The resource mobilisation model sees outcome as a major factor for effectiveness and emphasises the organisation's ability to provide services to clients (Hatry, 2016). These factors are measured in relation to the objectives, which vary from one organisation to another. This approach presumes that organisational performance is positively correlated with its ability to receive financial support and optimise economic efficiency (Lecy et al., 2012). Here the organisations, including the NPOs, are seen as competitors for resources in a free market.

The shortcoming of the resource mobilisation model is apparent: it assumes that non-profit organisations compete for bargaining positions as private companies do in the open market. No differentiation is made between for-profit and non-profit entities, despite that in reality, the two have different objectives and goals. Advocators of the resource mobilisation model try to redeem this by postulating that investors and donors are more willing to invest in organisations that fulfil their goals, therefore, the ability of an organisation to obtain resources is directly proportional to its goal achievement (Zammuto, 1984). However, this postulation is dubious when one contemplates how often market failures prevent resources from flowing to the neediest parties (Salamon, 1987).

The third domain measures effectiveness of organisations from the perspective of the participants and users (Pestoff, 2009). The reputational approach looks at two points: how organisations interact within and among themselves and how their judgement is shaped by the information and communication they receive. In other words, the effectiveness of non-profits is seen as a social construction based on the ongoing process of stakeholder judgement. An organisation is effective if it satisfies its stakeholders and maintains its legitimacy among all involved actors. The centre of judgement here is people's perceptions toward the organisation's social achievement. Social capital and reputation benefit the organisation by increasing its ability to operate in a given social environment (Moizer & Tracey, 2010), build networks (Welter & Kautonen, 2005), and enhance collaborations among actors (Evers, 2005). This approach is supported by a group of studies on the relationship between user satisfaction, accountability, and legitimacy (Pestoff, 2009).

The reputation model, coming from the social constructionists' conception, completely rebukes the notion of NPOs as private economic entities and accesses their effectiveness in terms of fulfilling their social roles, that is, how they respond to the needs and expectations of their stakeholders (Jobson & Schneck, 1982). However, the contextual-basing nature of stakeholder judgement means that the formulation of NPOs' effectiveness may not be consistent and intact.

As Willems et al. (2014) argue, all performance measurement frameworks face trade-offs. Because of the complications involved in their social missions, performance assessments of TSOs are always a matter of comparison (Herman & Renz, 2008). A major criticism is that there are no common criteria for measuring effectiveness across a variety of organisations forms (Steers, 1975); thus, they suffer from a 'criterion problem' (Jobson & Schneck, 1982: 26). Empirical research into any facet of effectiveness requires clear definitions and specificity regarding evaluation criteria (Jobson & Schneck, 1982). Rather than choosing the 'best' measurement, one should work one's objective preferences into the choice of parameters (Willems et al., 2014).

A complication of performance assessments for social enterprises is that they cannot be defined solely in economic or social terms. Performance measurement is complex for the non-profit sector because a broader spectrum of social goals needs to be included, and it is challenging to compare across organisations in terms of their achievement of goals. While the measurement of economic efficiency has already been well established in business and management studies, assessing social enterprises' performance still lacks standardisation and uniformity (Paton, 2002; Ebrahim & Rangan, 2010).

2.2.4   *Challenges with Effectiveness Measurement*

2.2.4.1   *Dimensions of Effectiveness*

Some of the common problems of effectiveness measurement include subjectivity (Mohr, 1982), incomparability between organisations (Lecy et al., 2012), and a lack of practicability (Herman & Renz, 1999). Researchers seek to mitigate these problems by developing proxies for organisational effectiveness (Liket & Maas, 2015), such as organisational growth (Kaplan & Norton, 2001), peer review (Purcell & Hawtin, 2010), or, as in the mission-accomplishment model, the extent to which the organisations achieve their goals (Mitchell, 2015).

Lecy et al. (2012) discuss three current shortfalls in operationalising the organisational effectiveness of NPOs that require careful attention. The first gap concerns effectiveness measurement beyond a single dimension. Exiting parameters that measure organisational effectiveness include impact analysis based on projects (Eisinger, 2002), financial efficiency, and managerial effectiveness (Smith & Lewis, 2011), and the effective formation of partnerships and networks (Salvato & Rerup, 2018). Lecy et al. (2012) point out that single-dimensional measurement of effectiveness is not particularly useful, as effectiveness usually requires more precise operationalisation that could reflect its multidimensional nature. The second gap is the lack of empirical data. The study reveals that out of the academic papers reviewed, only 14% have conducted empirical analysis (Lecy et al. 2012). The findings demonstrate a clear trend of 'lagging behind in providing theoretical and analytical insights' (Ebrahim & Rangan, 2010: 6) occurred at both theoretical and practical fronts. Last but not least, there is little consensus on the level of measurement of effectiveness, whether it should be measured at the project, organisational, or sectorial level (Lecy et al., 2012).

Diochon and Anderson (2009) defines social enterprise effectiveness using three dimensions: innovation, self-sufficiency, and sustainability. Here effectiveness refers to organisational capacity reflected by the extent to which the previously mentioned three components are congruently configured. These three dimensions define the basic needs for the survival, growth, and mission accomplishment capacities of the organisations (Diochon & Anderson, 2009). This approach focuses on effectiveness at the organisational level. An alternative method by Fowler measures effectiveness by the way the organisation engages its stakeholders, usually in terms of accountability, legitimacy, and organisational missions (Fowler, 2013). Advocators of this approach argue that indicators that reflect organisational missions and goals, the prominence of values, accountability, and public legitimacy are as important as those that reflect organisational capacity (Tai, 2014).

In practice, scholars usually combine both 'outcome' and 'process' measurements for optimal results. For example, Moore (2000) suggests three aspects that construct the strategic model of social enterprises: the extent of social missions, legitimacy and support among community members, and organisational efficiency in utilising its resources to deliver optimal and stable outputs. This strategic triangular model identifies three parameters that evaluate effectiveness: mission accomplishment, which concerns outcomes; participation, which concerns legitimacy; and operational capacity, which concerns process efficiency. These indicators vary across contextual situations. In the case of China, where most NGOs rely on the state for resources and funding support to a high extent, the NGOs have to succumb to state control and advocate government policy goals (Yu & Guo, 2012). In such cases, the indicators must be adjusted accordingly, which poses a challenge to studies that try to evaluate the effectiveness of social enterprises.

2.2.4.1.1   THE MISSION OF SOCIAL ENTERPRISE

This study uses mission accomplishment as the dimension to measure social enterprise effectiveness. The measurement will be explained in detail in Chapter 5. This section presents some of the challenges and debates from related studies. As mentioned, compared to traditional NPOs that rely on government subsidies and public donations, social enterprises are seen as more innovative and sustainable means to fund charitable activities. However, this claim assumes that the economic and social missions of social enterprises could be achieved concurrently, while the two could conflict with each other because of their 'double bottom line' (Dart, 2004: 413).

The dual economic and social nature of social enterprises means they have to fulfil both economic and social goals (Jäger & Schröer, 2014; Ramus & Vaccaro, 2014). It is a responsibility of social enterprises to balance among the beneficiaries, investors, and funders and clients who are paying for their services and products to satisfy the 'double bottom line' (Ebrahim et al., 2014). The social goals entail providing an effective solution to the problem and delivering impact, while the economic goals imply applying the most cost-effective business model to achieve the ends. Scholars argue that social enterprises constantly face conflicts between these missions (Strøm & Mersland, 2010; Ebrahim et al., 2014; Hishigsuren, 2016). When social enterprises compromise their social goals due to an excessive focus on commercial performance, 'mission drift' occurs (Hishigsuren, 2016). The off-balanced pursuit of economic rents increases tension and complexity within the organisation and may even impede its operational efficiency (Deborah & Keely, 2009).

Balancing the tension between economic and social goals is a big challenge for social enterprises (Christopher Cornforth, 2014; Ebrahim et al., 2014). Since social enterprises deliver blended values rather than exclusive financial returns, to accurately access their social values, techniques such as 'blended value accounting' and social return on investment have been developed (Manetti, 2012). However, these measures usually do not account for the different types of organisations constituting the third sector. Moreover, performance measurement tools that are applied on social enterprises are usually borrowed directly from the business world. They are created and designed to measure economic performance and focus mostly on strategy making, resource allocation, and financial returns (Bull, 2007). Social indicators tend to be under-expressed by these quantification tools. A different group of assessments developed under business and management studies view social enterprises as private enterprises with social objectives (Grassl, 2011; Zainon, Ahmad, Atan, Wah, Bakar, & Sarman, 2014), but these studies focus on the similarities and differences between social enterprises and commercial enterprises rather than those between social enterprises and traditional TSOs (Seelos & Mair, 2005; Austin et al., 2006).

Mission shift also affects organisational legitimacy. When an enterprise places itself in the competitive market, it is easy for it to prioritise service improvement and stakeholder interests as its primary strategies (Ebrahim et al., 2014). This forces social enterprises to set higher economic goals just to sustain their business units. Scholars debate the risk of social enterprises' losing sight of social missions to revenue optimisation as they try to balance their positions among multiple stakeholders (Freeman & Freeman, 2010). The requirement for more strategic stakeholder management and corporate engagement may pose a strain on the organisations' resources. Some scholars support the opposite argument that the double bottom line is an advantage because not-for-profit firms have an ethical advantage since they cannot distribute financial surpluses to shareholders and, therefore, are driven less by monetary incentives than private firms (Besley, 2006; Chaudhuri & Mujinja, 2011). However, little empirical evidence has been presented to support this argument.

2.3 The Role of the State in Social Enterprise Effectiveness

2.3.1 The 'Publicness' in Social Enterprises

It has long been established that effectiveness is a function of organisational externalities (Putterman & Dong, 2000; Chen et al., 2011). Similar arguments have been made on NPOs, where state intervention is seen as obstructing the performance of non-state actors (Deng, 2000; Wang & Yao, 2016). However, the application of the market mechanism is seen by some as enhancing allocative efficiency (Bai, Li, & Wang, 1997), which improves organisational performance.

Studying social enterprises merely as organisations may overlook the political economy nature of this phenomenon. The political embedment means the third sector is influenced by institutional factors especially related to the public sector, which affects the development of social enterprises (Evers & Laville, 2004b). Many see government support as crucial to social enterprises. Nyssens (2007) holds that public administration plays a crucial role in the development of social enterprises. Poon's (2011) study on Western Europe reveals that it is the active support of the state that facilitates the development of social enterprises.

Some scholars suggest a link between NPM and social enterprises. A common driving force behind social enterprises is the retrenchment of the welfare states alongside the devolution of management control, the rise of autonomous agencies, and the privatisation of public services. These measures are commonly recognised as under the NPM doctrine. With NPM becoming more popular worldwide, many TSOs that face funding depletion move away from government grants to build relationships with the private sector, either through forming partnerships or attracting direct investments (Defourny et al., 2014). This leads to a continuous and steady rationalisation and commercialisation of the social sector. This strand of theory suggests that a connection exists between public administration and social enterprises (Pestoff, 2014). Evers (2005) shows how broader institutional factors such as public administration reform may encourage the formation of hybrid organisations.

A stance of literature further relates the emergence of social enterprises to the concept of NPG (Pestoff, 2014). Among the three types of governance, political processes (politics), institutional structures (polity), and policy content (policy; Treib, Bähr, & Falkner, 2007), the 'politics' dimension is the most relevant to the social enterprise model. Relevant aspects on the 'politics' dimension include negotiations regarding power and resource distributions among state and non-state actors to balance multiple stakeholder interests and achieve collective actions (Lange et al., 2013).

2.3.2   *Frameworks of State–Society Relations*

Studies show that state–society relations, in particular the relationship between the state and social enterprises, is a crucial socio-political factor influencing the characteristics of the social enterprise sector. An analysis of social enterprises across 54 countries based on Kerlin's (2012) model confirms that the social enterprise model is affected directly by country-specific factors such as the role of the welfare state, the mode of governance, culture, and international aid. Acheson (2012) argues that how the government manages welfare provision in periods of falling budgets determines the options available for TSOs.

State–society relations with respect to the third sector can be divided into two groups. The first group discusses the different types of macro-level relationships and the nature of public administration systems and regimes. The second group focuses on the institutional environment by analysing the nature and behaviour of NGOs under different contexts.

2.3.2.1 *The Political Economy Approach*

A common state–third sector relationship model is Najam's four C's model of cooperation, confrontation, (functional) complementarity and co-optation (Najam, 2000). This work is extended by Coston (1998), who further includes the market into the state–NGO bipolar relationship into three forms of interactions—contracting, competition, and rivalry. This in a way connects state–society relations with the tri-sector social economy model. Acheson (2012) criticises Najam's model as being too simplistic, indicating that the model focuses on relations between sectors at the macro-level and fails to explain from the perspective of the NGOs why some manage to build up capacities on their own. A second question left unanswered by these studies is how the different state–society relations affect the actual performance of the organisations. Another study by Kerlin (2012) provides a conceptual framework for social enterprises based on macro-institutional factors. She argues that the social enterprise model is determined by political economy factors including culture and historical political economy development, which shape the form of government and civil society and eventually, social enterprise development. The implication of Kerlin's argument is that social enterprises are shaped by the political choices of the government. Her work explicitly shows that the social enterprise model is a function of its institutional environment, although it has provided little detail on how the mechanism works.

2.3.2.2 *The Institutional Analysis Approach*

The institutional analysis adopts a holistic approach towards social organisations and pays explicit attention to their mutual influence and context-based development (Powell, 1991). The institutionalists have long suggested that the forms and behaviours of organisations are a function of their institutional environment (Salamon & Sokolowski, 2010). This approach sees NGOs as political institutions that negotiate, bargain, and compromise with their donors to achieve their needs (Ghosh, 2009). Dependency on the state is usually viewed negatively. The dependent organisations are seen at best as passive players struggling to cope with changing externalities. As Evers (2005: 745) claims, 'shifts in welfare mix and hybridisation processes are not the outcome of strategic choices but rather of coping strategies of actors and organisations concerned under conditions of uncertainty'. Moreover, under such circumstances, organisations may shift their programmes to appeal to the interest of donors (Boris & Odendahl, 1990). With government financing, revenue volatility is less of a problem compared to those from philanthropic donations or commercial activities (Froelich, 1999). However, this is at the cost of greater goal displacement, as shown in social service contracting, such organisations may be driven by government priorities and be reduced to public agencies by proxy (Ferris, 1993).

All these studies are based on relationships between the state and traditional NGOs. State–social enterprise dynamics is a topic still being under-explored. While the state is still expected to play the dominant role, China is also undergoing a market reform that fosters private-sector competition. Social enterprises as hybrid organisations may face a unique set of economic and political concerns.

2.4   Social Enterprises in China

2.4.1   *State–Society Relations in China's Context*

Some scholars try to adjust the traditional civil society framework to suit the social context of China. Gold (1990) points out that civil society is not a dichotomous variable, it doesn't have to be wholly present or wholly absent. Since most of the potential beneficiaries and partners of NGOs still see social welfare as the state's sole responsibility, the government is still the source of legitimacy in China (Hsu, 2010). While the core theme is still power struggles between state and non-state actors—with the state in dominance, the actual tactics can be distinguished by a series of mixing measures of control and delegation (Farid & Li, 2021; Farid & Song, 2020; Weng & Zhang, 2019). This is explained by the top-down state-corporatism framework (Hsia & White, 2002; Hsu & Hasmath, 2013). The constituent units of such systems are described as 'singular, compulsory, non-competitive, hierarchically ordered and functionally differentiated categories ... recognised and licensed by the state' (Schmitter, 1974: 93). Under state corporatism, the state consistently resorts to authority and coercive means to retain civil society development (Saich, 2009). According to this theory, the success of the TSOs is fully dependent on their positive interactions with the local government (Hsu & Hasmath, 2013).

The corporatist framework alone lacks some explanatory power when it is applied to China (Gilley, 2011). Whiting (1991) argues that NGOs in China foster pluralism and offer alternative channels that articulate social interests to the government. Yep (2000) also argues that the corporatist framework assumes that the existence of alliance and solidarity among the social associations opposes the state, but his empirical study in China does not support this claim. In general, scholars agree that while the framework provides a general guideline, more explicit detail is needed to better understand state–society relations in contemporary China (Deng, 2010; Hasmath & Hsu, 2014). The state corporatists see the NGOs as dependents of the state, but some researchers argue that grassroots groups in China are capable of adopting measures 'with regards to different groups or spheres of activity' with a pragmatic approach that tones down its political nature (Whiting, 1991: 17).

2.4.2 *Typology of Social Enterprises in China*

A number of studies have tried to classify social enterprises in China. Some base the typology on the internal logic of operation. For example, Yu (2013) discusses the development patterns of major types of WISEs in China with several dimensions that could be used to classify WISEs, such as institutional origins, social functions, or social groups targeted. Yu (2013) classifies social enterprises in China into three categories based on the governance structure they adopt, which are government-supervised, shareholder-controlled, and member-regulated.[2] Zhou (2013) categorises social enterprises by key elements such as goal setting, operational model, and profit distribution.

Most studies still classify social enterprises in China based on their legal forms. Common forms of social enterprise under this typology include social welfare enterprises (SWEs) that focus on providing employment opportunities to disadvantaged people and minority groups (Wang & Zhu, 2011), Civilian-run non-enterprise units (CRNEUs) that offer privately-run social services, and social businesses (Chan & Yuen, 2013). Along this line, Lee (2009) divides Chinese social enterprises into four categories, namely NGOs and NPOs, SWEs, cooperatives, and community services centres (CSCs). Others see farmers' specialised cooperatives as a form of CRNEUs (Defourny & Kim, 2011). A similar categorisation by Lee (2009) bases the typology of social enterprise on organisational forms alone and divides social enterprises by their institutional origins as NGOs and NPOs, SWEs, cooperatives, and CSCs. These typologies by legal forms are easy to be recognised but are also ambiguous since not all organisations under these forms are social enterprises. Therefore, further criteria need to be imposed for empirical studies to differentiate social enterprises from other social organisations.

2.4.3 *Related Literature and Studies*

It is a common consensus that the development of the third sector in China has been impaired by the state (Schwartz, 2004; Lu, 2008; Hsu, 2010). Scholars apply different state–third sector relations frameworks to capture the increasingly nuanced methods the Chinese state adopts to manage social organisations. The concepts proposed include 'graduated control' (Wu & Chan, 2012: 9), 'consultative authoritarianism' (Teets, 2013: 19), 'contingent symbiosis' (Spires, 2011: 2), and 'embedded' control (Ni & Zhan, 2017: 731). Wei (2017) argues that state involvement in the third sector has shifted from direct to indirect control. In general, scholars agree that the codes of conduct of the Chinese state towards the independent NGOs can be summarised as a combination of tolerance with constraints and strict administrative control (Howell, 1995; Schwartz, 2004; Hsu, 2010; Hildebrandt, 2012; Wei, 2017).

Social enterprises appeared in China before the concept did (Wang & Zhu, 2011). Studies have provided comprehensive reviews of the background, development paths and operations of social enterprises in China, including their organisational models, governance, and relations to the broader social enterprise concept. A study by Chan & Yuen (2013) argues that China has gone through a widening income gap, degrading social equality and massive migration, which causes drastic changes in relationships between the state and the society and fulfils the conditions for social enterprises to emerge. Scholars believe that in China, hybrid institutions occur as a result of the social welfare reform through a top-down forceful 'splitting-up' of institutions from a centralised socialist state (Yu, 2013; Zhao, 2012). Social enterprises are called on in this social context to take care of the welfare needs of civil segments that are not covered by both the state and the market (Zhou et al., 2013).

In general, scholars agree that social welfare reform is an important factor driving and shaping social enterprises in China. Lee (2009) associates the growth of social enterprises with economic growth and market development, a reduction in government funding, and changes in political ideologies that occurred during the reform. Hu, Zhang, and Niu (2009) relate it to the civil society framework and explain the rise of social enterprises as the government's intention to empower the third sector in order to solve social problems that rise during the reform, such as urban–rural divide and social exclusion. Curtis (2011) discusses the historical connection between the work unit (*danwei*) system and social entrepreneurship and identifies the dismantlement of the state-led welfare system as the institutional factor that drives social entrepreneurship in China. Another study by Xiang and Luk (2011) analyses the institutional environment of NGOs and how they can be transformed into social enterprises in a post-socialist environment. Some experts have attempted to assess the current situation of social enterprises in China A few reports on the situation of social enterprises in China conclude that most social enterprises still face financial, talent and legislative constraints, and their development still depends on the sort of government support they receive (Zhou et al., 2013). However, both in-depth theoretical and empirical analyses of social enterprises in China are still lacking.

Notes

1 For example, models that focus explicitly on profits and outcomes rather than consumer sovereignty and suitable workforce, is a better option for commercial enterprises and *vice versa* for the non-profits.
2 Yu (2013) discovers that in terms of social enterprise governance, hybrid stewardship and stakeholder-controlled models are predominant in China. The first two categories usually take the form of organisations with control boards, while member-regulated social enterprises usually establish as cooperatives and communal groups.

References

Acheson, N. (2012). The co-construction of new policy-spaces for state third sector engagement: An exploration of third sector agency in austerity driven welfare states. Paper presented at the International Society for Third Sector Rersearch: Democratization, Marketization and the Third Sector.

Ählström, J., & Sjöström, E. (2005). CSOs and business partnerships: Strategies for interaction. *Business Strategy and the Environment, 14*(4), 230–240.

Alter, K. (2007). *Social enterprise typology.* Virtue Ventures LLC.

Alvord, S. H., Brown, L. D., & Letts, C. W. (2016, July 26). Social entrepreneurship and societal transformation. *The Journal of Applied Behavioral Science, 40*(3), 260–282. https://doi.org/10.1177/0021886304266847

Arrow, K. J. (1950). A difficulty in the concept of social welfare. *Journal of Political Economy, 58*(4), 328–346.

Austin, J., Stevenson, H., & Wei Skillern, J. (2006). Social and commercial entrepreneurship: Same, different, or both? *Entrepreneurship Theory and Practice, 30*(1), 1–22.

Bagnoli, L., & Megali, C. (2009). Measuring Performance in Social Enterprises. *Nonprofit and Voluntary Sector Quarterly, 40*(1), 149–165. https://doi.org/10.1177/0899764009351111

Bai, C.-E., Li, D. D., & Wang, Y. (1997). Enterprise productivity and efficiency: When is up really down? *Journal of Comparative Economics, 24*(3), 265–280. http://www.sciencedirect.com/science/article/pii/S0147596797914323

Becchetti, L., Pelloni, A., & Rossetti, F. (2008). Relational goods, sociability, and happiness. *Kyklos, 61*(3), 343–363.

Benjamin, L. M., & Misra, K. (2006). Doing good work: Implications of performance accountability for practice in the nonprofit sector. *International Journal of Rural Management, 2*(2), 147–162.

Berman, E. M. (1998). *Productivity in Public and Nonprofit Organisations.* SAGE Publications, Inc.

Besley, J. C. (2006). The role of entertainment television and its interactions with individual values in explaining political participation. *Press/Politics, 11*(2), 41–63.

Bielefeld, W. (2012). Business models of social enterprise: A design approach to hybridity [word document]. *ACRN Journal of Entrepreneurship Perspectives, 1*(1), 37–60. http://philpapers.org/rec/MULPWE

Billis, D. (2010a). *Hybrid Organizations and the Third Sector: Challenges for Practice, Theory and Policy.* Macmillan International Higher Education.

Billis, D. (2010b). Towards a theory of hybrid organizations. In *Hybrid Organizations and the Third Sector: Challenges for Practice, Theory and Policy* (pp. 46–69). Palgrave Macmillan.

Bode, I. (2011). Creeping marketization and post-corporatist governance: the transformation of state–nonprofit relations in continental Europe. In S. D. Phillips & S. R. Smith (Eds.), *Governance and Regulation in the Third Sector* (pp. 123–149). Routledge.

Bode, I., Evers, A., & Schulz, A. (2006). Work integration social enterprises in Europe: Can hybridization be sustainable? In M. Nyssens (Ed.), *Social enterprise: At the Crossroads of Market, Public Policies and Civil Society* (pp. 237–258). Taylor & Francis.

Boris, E. T., & Odendahl, T. J. (1990). Ethical issues in fund raising and philanthropy. *Critical Issues in American philanthropy*, 188–203.

Borzaga, C., & Defourny, J. (2001). *Conclusions: Social Enterprises in Europe: A Diversity of Initiatives and Prospects*. Routledge. https://www.researchgate.net/ profile/Jacques_Defourny/publication/264840316_CONCLUSIONS_SOCIAL_ ENTERPRISES_IN_EUROPE_A_DIVERSITY_OF_INITIATIVES_AND_ PROSPECTS/links/542006510cf2218008d4333a.pdf

Borzaga, C., & Defourny, J. (Eds.). (2004). *The Emergence of Social Enterprise* (Vol. 4). Routledge. http://www.worldcat.org/title/emergence-of-social-enterprise/oclc/ 879531133

Borzaga, C., & Depedri, S. (2013). When social enterprises do it better: Efficiency and efficacy of work integration in Italian social cooperatives. In C. Yang & F. Seddon (Eds.), *Social Enterprises, Accountability and Evaluation around the World* (pp. 85– 101). Routledge.

Borzaga, C., & Solari, L. (2001). Management challenges for social enterprises. In C. Bozaga & J. Defourny (Eds.) *The Emergence of Social Enterprise* (pp. 333–349). Routledge. http://www.worldcat.org/title/emergence-of-social-enterprise/oclc/ 901343217

Boyd, B., Henning, N., Reyna, E., Welch, M., & Wang, D. (2017). *Hybrid organizations: New business models for environmental leadership*. Routledge. http://books. google.com/books?hl=en&lr=&id=uCToEW9CO6gC& amp;oi=fnd&pg=PP1&dq=boyd+(Hybrid+Organizations+New+ Business+Models+for+Environmental+Leadership)&ots=qcGrVB9wpv& amp;amp;sig=rKo7LiZEBa7yDfKGSV_deeZE1FE

Bozeman, B. (1988). All Organizations Are Public: Bridging Public and Private Organization Theories. University of Michigan: Wiley.

Brandsen, T., & Karré, P. M. (2011). Hybrid organizations: No cause for concern? *International Journal of Public Administration, 34*(13), 827–836.

Brandsen, T., Pestoff, V., & Verschuere, B. (2014). Co-production and the third sector: The state of the art in research. In L. H. Jacques Defourny, & V. Pestoff (Ed.), *Social Enterprise and the Third Sector: Changing European Landscapes in a Comparative Perspective*. Routledge. https://doi.org/10.1007/s11266-014-9512-8

Brandsen, T., & Van de Donk, W. (2005). Griffins or chameleons? Hybridity as a permanent and inevitable characteristic of the third sector. *International Journal of Public Administration, 28*(9–10), 749–765. https://doi.org/10.1081/PAD- 200067320

Brozek, K. O. (2009). Exploring the continuum of social and financial returns: When does a nonprofit become a social enterprise? *Community Development Innovation Review, 5*(2), 7–17.

Bryson, J. M., Gibbons, M. J., & Shaye, G. (2001). Enterprise schemes for nonprofit survival, growth, and effectiveness. *Nonprofit Management and Leadership, 11*(3), 271–288. https://doi.org/10.1002/nml.11303

Bull, M. (2007). "Balance": The development of a social enterprise business performance analysis tool. *Social Enterprise Journal, 3*(1), 49–66. https://doi.org/10. 1108/17508610780000721

Cameron, K. S., & Whetten, D. A. (1983). Some conclusions about organizational effectiveness. In *Organizational Effectiveness: A Comparison of Multiple Models* (pp. 261– 277). Academic Press Inc. https://doi.org/10.1016/B978-0-12-157180-1.50017-3

Candler, G., & Dumont, G. (2010). A non-profit accountability framework. *Canadian Public Administration, 53*(2), 259–279. https://doi.org/10.1111/j.1754-7121. 2010.00126.x

Chan, C. H., Chui, C. H.-K., Chan, K. S. T., & Yip, P. S. F. (2019). The role of the social innovation and entrepreneurship development fund in fostering social entrepreneurship in Hong Kong: A study on public policy innovation. *Social Policy & Administration*, 53(6), 903–919. https://doi.org/10.1111/spol.12524

Chan, K. M., & Yuen, Y. K. T. (2013). An overview of social enterprise development in China and Hong Kong. *Journal of Ritsumeikan Social Sciences and Humanities*, 5, 165–178. http://www.ritsumei.ac.jp/acd/re/k-rsc/hss/book/pdf/vol05_12.pdf

Chell, E. (2007). Social Enterprise and entrepreneurship: Towards a convergent theory of the entrepreneurial process. *International Small Business Journal*, 25(1), 5–26. https://doi.org/10.1177/0266242607071779

Chen, S., Zheng, S., Song, T., & Wu, D. (2011). Government intervention and investment efficiency: Evidence from China. *Journal of Corporate Finance*, 17(2), 259–271. https://doi.org/10.1016/j.jcorpfin.2010.08.004

Child, J. (1974). Managerial and organizational factors associated with company performance. *Journal of Management Studies*, 11(3), 175–189. https://doi.org/10.1111/j.1467-6486.1974.tb00693.x

Cordery, C., & Sinclair, R. (2013). Measuring performance in the third sector. *Qualitative Research in Accounting and Management*, 10(3/4), 196–212. http://dx.doi.org/10.1108/QRAM-03-2013-0014

Cornforth, C. (2014). Understanding and combating mission drift in social enterprises. *Social Enterprise Journal*, 10(1), 3–20.

Corry, O. (2010). *Defining and Theorizing the Third Sector*. Springer. https://doi.org/10.1007/978-1-4419-5707-8_2

Coston, J. M. (1998). A model and typology of government-NGO relationships. *Nonprofit and Voluntary Sector Quarterly*, 27(3), 358–382. https://doi.org/10.1177/0899764098273006

Curtis, T. (2011). 'Newness' in social entrepreneurship discourses: The concept of 'Danwei' in the Chinese Experience. *Journal of Social Entrepreneurship*, 2(2), 198–217. https://doi.org/10.1080/19420676.2011.621444

Dahl, R. A., & Lindblom, C. E. (2017). *Politics, Economics, and Welfare*. Routledge.

Dart, R. (2004). The legitimacy of social enterprise. *Nonprofit Management and Leadership*, 14(4), 411–424.

Das, K. (1996). Flexibly together: Surviving and growing in a garment cluster, Ahmedabad, India. *The Journal of Entrepreneurship*, 5(2), 153–177. https://doi.org/10.1177/097135579600500201

Deborah, A., & Keely, J. (2009). The financially healthy organizations. *Journal of Public Administration Research and Theory*, 19(4), 947–966.

Dees, J. G. (2018). The meaning of social entrepreneurship. In J. Hamschmidt & M. Pirson (Eds.), *Case Studies in Social Entrepreneurship and Sustainability* (Vol. 2, pp. 22–30). Routledge.

Dees, J. G., & Anderson, B. B. (2006). Framing a theory of social entrepreneurship: Building on two schools of practice and thought. *ARNOVA Occasional Paper Series*, 1(3), 39–66.

Defourny, J., & Borzaga, C. (2001). *From Third Sector to Social Enterprise*. Routledge.

Defourny, J., Hulgård, L., & Pestoff, V. (2014). *Social Enterprise and the Third Sector: Changing European Landscapes in a Comparative Perspective*. Routledge.

Defourny, J., & Kim, S. Y. (2011). Emerging models of social enterprise in Eastern Asia: A cross-country analysis. *Social Enterprise Journal*, 7(1), 86–111. https://doi.org/10.1108/17508611111130176

Defourny, J., & Nyssens, M. (2010a, March 22). Conceptions of social enterprise and social entrepreneurship in Europe and the United States: Convergences and divergences. *Journal of Social Entrepreneurship, 1*(1), 32–53. https://doi.org/10.1080/19420670903442053

Defourny, J., & Nyssens, M. (2010b). Social enterprise in Europe: At the crossroads of market, public policies and third sector. *Policy and Society, 29*(3), 231–242. https://doi.org/10.1016/j.polsoc.2010.07.002

Defourny, J., & Nyssens, M. (2012). Conceptions of social enterprise in Europe: A comparative perspective with the United States. In B. Gidron & Y. Hasenfeld (Eds.), *Social Enterprises: An Organizational Perspective* (pp. 71–90). Palgrave Macmillan UK. https://doi.org/10.1057/9781137035301_4

Defourny, J., & Nyssens, M. (2017). Fundamentals for an International Typology of Social Enterprise Models. *VOLUNTAS: International Journal of Voluntary and Nonprofit Organizations, 28*(6), 2469–2497. https://doi.org/10.1007/s11266-017-9884-7

Deng, G. (2000). New environment for development of NGOS in China. *Global Economic Review, 29*(4), 43–61. https://doi.org/10.1080/12265080008449804

Deng, G. (2010). The hidden rules governing China's unregistered NGOs: Management and consequences. *China Review, 10*(1), 183–206. http://www.jstor.org/stable/23462247

Diochon, M., & Anderson, A. R. (2009). Social Enterprise and Effectiveness: A Process Typology. *Social Enterprise Journal, 5*(1), 7–29. https://doi.org/10.1108/17508610910956381

Duff, R. R. (2008). Social enterprise as a socially rational business. *International Journal of Entrepreneurial Behavior & Research, 14*(5), 291–312. https://doi.org/10.1108/13552550810897669

Ebrahim, A., Battilana, J., & Mair, J. (2014). The governance of social enterprises: Mission drift and accountability challenges in hybrid organizations. *Research in Organizational Behavior, 34*, 81–100. https://doi.org/10.1016/j.riob.2014.09.001

Ebrahim, A. S., & Rangan, V. K. (2010). The limits of nonprofit impact: A contingency framework for measuring social performance. *SSRN Electronic Journal.* https://doi.org/10.2139/ssrn.1611810

Eisinger, P. (2002). Organizational capacity and organizational effectiveness among street-level food assistance programs. *Nonprofit and Voluntary Sector Quarterly, 31*(1), 115–130.

Etzioni, A. (1964). *Modern Organizations.* Prentice-Hall.

Evers, A. (2005). Mixed welfare systems and hybrid organizations: Changes in the governance and provision of social services. *International Journal of Public Administration, 28*(9–10), 737–748. https://doi.org/10.1081/pad-200067318

Evers, A., & Laville, J.-L. (2004a). Defining the third sector in Europe. In A. Evers & J.-L. Laville (Eds.), *The Third Sector in Europe: globalization and welfare series.* Routledge.

Evers, A., & Laville, J.-L. (2004b). Social services by social enterprises: on the possible contributions of hybrid organizations and a civil society. In A. Evers & J.-L. Laville (Eds.), *The third sector in Europe* (pp. 237–255): Edward Elgar Publishing.

Evers, A., & Wintersberger, H. (1990). *Shifts in the Welfare Mix: Their Impact on Work, Social Services and Welfare Policies.* Westview Press.

Farid, M., & Li, H. (2021). Reciprocal engagement and NGO policy influence on the local state in China. *VOLUNTAS: International Journal of Voluntary and Nonprofit Organizations, 32*(3), 597–609.

Farid, M., & Song, C. (2020). Public trust as a driver of state-grassroots NGO collaboration in China. *Journal of Chinese Political Science, 25*(4), 591–613. https://doi.org/10.1007/s11366-020-09691-7

Farrell, J. L., & Reinhart, W. J. (1997). *Portfolio Management: Theory and Application.* McGraw-Hill.

Ferris, J. M. (1993). The double-edged sword of social service contracting: Public accountability versus nonprofit autonomy. *Nonprofit Management and Leadership, 3*(4), 363–376.

Forsyth, T. (2007). Promoting the "Development Dividend" of climate technology transfer: Can cross-sector partnerships help? *World Development, 35*(10), 1684–1698. https://doi.org/10.1016/j.worlddev.2007.06.001

Fowler, A. (2010). NGDOs as a moment in history: Beyond aid to social entrepreneurship or civic innovation? *Third World Quarterly, 21*(4), 637–654. http://www.tandfonline.com/doi/full/10.1080/713701063

Fowler, A. (2013). *Striking a Balance: A Guide to Enhancing the Effectiveness of Nongovernmental Organisations in International Development.* Routledge.

Freeman, M., & Freeman, A. (2010). *Bonding over Bushfires: Social Networks in Action.* 2010 IEEE International Symposium on Technology and Society. http://ieeexplore.ieee.org/document/5514611/

Froelich, K. A. (1999). Diversification of revenue strategies: Evolving resource dependence in nonprofit organizations. *Nonprofit and Voluntary Sector Quarterly, 28*(3), 246–268. https://doi.org/10.1177/0899764099283002

Ghosh, S. (2009). NGOs as Political Institutions. *Journal of Asian and African Studies, 44*(5), 475–495. https://doi.org/10.1177/0021909609340063

Gidron, B., Kramer, R. M., & Salamon, L. M. (1992). *Government and the Third Sector: Emerging Relationships in Welfare States.* Jossey-Bass Inc Pub. http://www.worldcat.org/title/government-and-the-third-sector-emerging-relationships-in-welfare-states/oclc/802791407

Gilley, B. (2011). Paradigms of Chinese Politics: Kicking society back out. *Journal of Contemporary China, 20*(70), 517–533. https://doi.org/10.1080/10670564.2011.565181

Gold, T. B. (1990). The resurgence of civil society in China. *Journal of Democracy, 1*(1), 18–31. http://muse.jhu.edu/journals/jod/summary/v001/1.1gold.html

Gordon, M. (2015). A Typology of Social Enterprise "Traditions". *International Comparative Social Enterprise Models Working Papers.* https://www.iap-socent.be/sites/default/files/Theory%20-%20Gordon.pdf

Graddy, E. A. (2009). Cross-sectoral governance and performance in service delivery. *International Review of Public Administration, 13*(sup. 1), 61–73. https://doi.org/10.1080/12294659.2009.10805140

Grant, S. (2008). Contextualising social enterprise in New Zealand. *Social Enterprise Journal, 4*(1), 9–23. https://doi.org/10.1108/17508610810877704

Grassl, W. (2011). Hybrid forms of business: The logic of gift in the commercial world. *Journal of Business Ethics, 100*(1), 109–123. https://doi.org/10.2139/ssrn.1776125

Hall, M. (2012). Evaluation logics in the third sector. *Voluntas, 25*(2), 307–336. https://doi.org/10.1007/s11266-012-9339-0

Hannan, M. T., & Freeman, J. (1977). Obstacles to comparative studies. *New Perspectives on Organizational Effectiveness,* 106–131.

Hasan, S., & Onyx, J. (Eds.). (2008). *Comparative Third Sector governance in Asia: Structure, process, and political economy.* Springer http://books.google.com/

books?hl=en&lr=&id=burJpVO7y5UC&oi=fnd&pg=PR5&dq=Comparative+Third+Sector+Governance+in+Asia&ots=JzDjtZNLIx-&sig=OQxYbiFG99MkyfxvLReB9V818EE

Hasmath, R., & Hsu, J. Y. J. (2014). Isomorphic pressures, epistemic communities and state–NGO collaboration in China. *The China Quarterly, 220*, 936–954. https://doi.org/10.1017/s0305741014001155

Hatry, H. P. (2016). Performance measurement. *Public Performance & Management Review, 25*(4), 352–358. https://doi.org/10.1080/15309576.2002.11643671

Haugh, H. (2005). A research agenda for social entrepreneurship. *Social Enterprise Journal, 1*(1), 1–12. https://doi.org/10.1108/17508610580000703

Henriksen, L. S., Smith, S. R., & Zimmer, A. (2015). Welfare mix and hybridity. Flexible adjustments to changed environments. Introduction to the special issue. *Voluntas, 26*(5), 1591–1600.

Herman, R. D., & Renz, D. O. (1997). Multiple constituencies and the social construction of nonprofit organization effectiveness. *Nonprofit and Voluntary Sector Quarterly, 26*(2), 185–206. https://doi.org/10.1177/0899764097262006

Herman, R. D., & Renz, D. O. (1999). Theses on nonprofit organizational effectiveness. *Nonprofit and Voluntary Sector Quarterly, 28*(2), 107–126. https://doi.org/10.1177/0899764099282001

Herman, R. D., & Renz, D. O. (2008). Advancing nonprofit organizational effectiveness research and theory: Nine theses. *Nonprofit Management and Leadership, 18*(4), 399–415. https://doi.org/10.1002/nml.195

Hildebrandt, T. (2012). The political economy of social organization registration in China. *The China Quarterly, 208*, 970–989. https://doi.org/10.1017/S0305741011001093

Hishigsuren, G. (2016). Evaluating mission drift in microfinance. *Evaluation Review, 31*(3), 203–260. https://doi.org/10.1177/0193841X06297886

Ho, A. P.-Y., & K.-T. Chan (2010). The social impact of work-integration social enterprise in Hong Kong. *International Social Work, 53*(1), 33–45.

Howell, J. (1995). Prospects for NGOs in China. *Development in Practice, 5*(1), 5–15. https://doi.org/10.1080/0961452951000156944

Hsia, R. Y. J., & White, L. T. (2002). Working amid corporatism and confusion: Foreign NGOs in China. *Nonprofit and Voluntary Sector Quarterly, 31*(3), 329–351. https://doi.org/10.1177/0899764002313002

Hsu, C. (2010). Beyond civil society: An organizational perspective on state–NGO relations in the People's Republic of China. *Journal of Civil Society, 6*(3), 259–277. https://doi.org/10.1080/17448689.2010.528949

Hsu, J., & Hasmath, R. (2013). *The Chinese Corporatist State: Adaption, Survival and Resistance*. Routledge. https://books.google.com.sg/books?id=_jlDx5XNmyEC

Hu, W., Zhang, Y., & Niu, F. (2009). The relationship among entrepreneurial orientation, dynamic capabilities and firm growth of new ventures in China. *China Soft Science, 4*, 107–118.

Hulgård, L. (2014). Social enterprise and the third sector: Innovative service delivery or a non-capitalist economy. In J. Defourney, L Hulgård, & V. Pestoff (Eds.), *Social Enterprise and the Third Sector: Changing European landscapes in a Comparative Perspective* (pp. 66–84). Routledge.

Hussain, N. M., Ishaq, M. I., & Ullah, A. (2014). Assessing social entrepreneurship initiatives. *Journey of Past, Present and Future, 1*(3), 215. http://scholarpublishing.org/index.php/ASSRJ/article/view/207

Jäger, U. P., & Schröer, A. (2014). Integrated organizational identity: A definition of hybrid organizations and a research agenda. *Voluntas, 25*(5), 1281–1306.

Jay, J. (2013). Navigating paradox as a mechanism of change and innovation in hybrid organizations. *Academy of Management Journal, 56*(1), 137–159. http://amj.aom.org/content/early/2012/07/20/amj.2010.0772.short

Jenkins, H., Thompson, J., & Darby, L. (2006). Applying sustainability indicators to the social enterprise business model: The development and application of an indicator set for Newport Wastesavers. *Wales, 33*(5/6), 411–431. https://doi.org/10.1108/03068290610660689

Jobson, J. D., & Schneck, R. (1982). Constituent views of organizational effectiveness: Evidence from police organizations. *Academy of Management Journal, 25*(1), 25–46. https://doi.org/10.2307/256022

Jordan, L. (2005). *Mechanisms for NGO accountability* (Vol. 3). Berlin: Global Public Policy Institute. http://scholar.google.com/scholar?q=related:FwXkucLmFdYJ:scholar.google.com/&hl=en&num=20&as_sdt=0,5

Kaplan, R. S., & Norton, D. P. (2001). Transforming the balanced scorecard from performance measurement to strategic management: Part I. *Accounting Horizons, 15*(1), 87–104. https://doi.org/10.2308/acch.2001.15.1.87

Kendall, J., & Knapp, M. (2000). Measuring the performance of voluntary organizations. *Public Management, 2*(1), 105–132. https://doi.org/10.1080/14616670360181

Keohane, G. L. (2013). *Social Entrepreneurship for the 21st century: Innovation Across the Nonprofit, Private, and Public Sectors*. McGraw Hill Professional.

Kerlin, J. A. (2006). Social enterprise in the United States and Europe: Understanding and learning from the differences. *VOLUNTAS: International Journal of Voluntary and Nonprofit Organizations, 17*(3), 246–262. https://doi.org/10.1007/s11266-006-9016-2

Kerlin, J. A. (2010). A Comparative Analysis of the Global Emergence of Social Enterprise. *VOLUNTAS: International Journal of Voluntary and Nonprofit Organizations, 21*(2), 162–179. doi:10.1007/s11266-010-9126-8

Kerlin, J. A. (2012). Defining social enterprise across different contexts: A conceptual framework based on institutional factors. In *Social Enterprises* (pp. 91–117). Springer.

Kilby, P. (2006). Accountability for empowerment: Dilemmas facing non-governmental organizations. *World Development, 34*(6), 951–963.

Kindornay, S., Tissot, S., & Sheiban, N. (2014). *The Value of Cross-Sector Development Partnerships*. North-South Institute.

Kingsley, G., & Malecki, E. J. (2004). Networking for competitiveness. *Small Business Economics, 23*(1), 71–84.

Kirkman, D. M. (2012). Social enterprises: An multi-level framework of the innovation adoption process. *Innovation Management, Policy & Practice, 14*(1), 143–155. https://doi.org/10.5172/impp.2012.14.1.143

Kramer, R. M., Lorentzen, H., Melief, W. B., & Pasquinelli, S. (1993). *Privatization in four European countries: comparative studies in government-third sector relationships*. M.E. Sharpe.

Kuosmanen, J. (2014). Care provision, empowerment, and market forces: The art of establishing legitimacy for Work Integration Social Enterprises (WISEs). *Voluntas: International Journal of Voluntary and Nonprofit Organisations, 25*(1), 248–269. https://doi.org/10.1007/s11266-012-9340-7

Kwong, C., Tasavori, M., & Wun-mei Cheung, C. (2017, June 5). Bricolage, collaboration and mission drift in social enterprises. *Entrepreneurship & Regional Development, 29*(7–8), 609–638. https://doi.org/10.1080/08985626.2017.1328904

Lange, P., Driessen, P. P. J., Sauer, A., Bornemann, B., & Burger, P. (2013). Governing towards sustainability—Conceptualizing modes of governance. *Journal of Environmental Policy & Planning*, *15*(3), 403–425. https://doi.org/10.1080/1523908X.2013.769414

Lechner, C., Welpe, I., & Dowling, M. (2006). Firm networks and firm development: The role of the relational mix. *Journal of Business Venturing*, *21*(4), 514–540.

Lecy, J. D., Schmitz, H. P., & Swedlund, H. (2012). Non-governmental and not-for-profit organizational effectiveness: A modern synthesis. *Voluntas: International Journal of Voluntary and Nonprofit Organizations*, *23*(2), 434–457. https://doi.org/10.1007/s11266-011-9204-6

Lee, R. (2009). The emergence of social enterprises in China: The quest for space and legitimacy. *Tsinghua China Law Review*, *2*(79), 80–99. http://heinonline.org/hol-cgi-bin/get_pdf.cgi?handle=hein.journals/tsinghua2&section=6

Lefroy, K., & Tsarenko, Y. (2013). From receiving to achieving: The role of relationship and dependence for nonprofit organisations in corporate partnerships. *European Journal of Marketing*, *47*(10), 1641–1666.

Lewis, D. (2008). Using Life Histories in Social Policy Research: The Case of Third Sector/Public Sector Boundary Crossing. *Journal of Social Policy*, *37*(04), 559–578.

Lewis, M. A., & Roehrich, J. K. (2010). Towards a model of governance in complex (product–service) inter-organizational systems. *Construction Management and Economics*, *28*(11), 1155–1164. https://doi.org/10.1080/01446191003762249

Liket, K. C., & Maas, K. (2015). Nonprofit organizational effectiveness: Analysis of best practices. *Nonprofit and Voluntary Sector Quarterly*, *44*(2), 268–296. https://doi.org/10.1177/0899764013510064

Lu, Y. (2008). NGOs in China: Development dynamics and challenges, in Y. Zheng and J. Fewsmith (ed.), *China's Opening Society: The Non-State Sector and Governance*, Routledge.

Mackintosh, M., et al. (2011). Can NGOs Regulate Medicines Markets? Social Enterprise in Wholesaling, and Access to Essential Medicines. *Globalization and Health*, *7*(1), 1–13.

Mair, J., & Noboa, E. (2003). Emergence of social enterprises and their place in the new organizational landscape. *IESE Working Paper No. D/523*.

Manetti, G. (2012). The role of blended value accounting in the evaluation of socio-economic impact of social enterprises. *Voluntas*, *25*(2), 443–464. https://doi.org/10.1007/s11266-012-9346-1

Massarsky, C. W. (2006). Coming of age: Social enterprise reaches its tipping point. *Research on Social Entrepreneurship*, *1*, 67–88.

Massetti, B. (2013). The duality of social enterprise: A framework for social action. *China Perspectives*, *33*(1), 50–64. http://search.proquest.com/openview/38f00f50f470fedabab2c9dde6a3b2ca/1?pq-origsite=gscholar&cbl=36534

McColl Kennedy, J. R. (2012). Engaging public sector clients: From service delivery to co-production by John Alford. *Australian journal of Public Administration*, *71*(1), 94–96.

Meagher, G., & Szebehely, M. E. (2013). *Marketisation in Nordic Eldercare*. Stockholm University: Department of Social Work. http://scholar.google.com/scholar?q=related:-AJ1TCz2GfYJ:scholar.google.com/&hl=en&num=20&as_sdt=0,5

Millar, R., & Hall, K. (2013). Social return on investment (SROI) and performance measurement: The opportunities and barriers for social enterprises in health and social care. *Public Management Review*, *15*(6), 923–941.

Mitchell, G. E. (2012). The construct of organizational effectiveness: Perspectives from leaders of international nonprofits in the United States. *Nonprofit and Voluntary Sector Quarterly, 42*(2), 324–345. https://doi.org/10.1177/0899764011434589

Mitchell, G. E. (2015). The attributes of effective NGOs and the leadership values associated with a reputation for organizational effectiveness. *Nonprofit Management and Leadership, 26*(1), 39–57. https://doi.org/10.1002/nml.21143

Mohr, L. B. (1982). *Explaining Organizational Behavior.* Jossey-Bass. http://www.worldcat.org/title/explaining-organizational-behavior/oclc/884699935

Moizer, J., & Tracey, P. (2010). Strategy making in social enterprise: The role of resource allocation and its effects on organizational sustainability. *Systems Research and Behavioral Science, 27*(3), 252–266. https://doi.org/10.1002/sres.1006

Monroe-White, T., & Zook, S. (2018). Social enterprise innovation: A quantitative analysis of global patterns. *VOLUNTAS: International Journal of Voluntary and Nonprofit Organizations, 29*(3), 496–510. https://doi.org/10.1007/s11266-018-9987-9

Moore, M. H. (2000). Managing for value: Organizational strategy in for-profit, nonprofit, and governmental organizations. *Nonprofit and Voluntary Sector Quarterly, 29*(suppl 1), 183–208. https://doi.org/10.1177/089976400773746391

Nahapiet, J., & Ghoshal, S. (1998). Social capital, intellectual capital, and the organizational source. *The Academy of Management Review, 23*(2), 242–266. http://scholar.google.com/scholar?q=related:z107EPSXrdQJ:scholar.google.com/&hl=en&num=20&as_sdt=0,5&as_ylo=1998&as_yhi=1998

Najam, A. (2000). The four C's of government third sector-government relations. *Nonprofit Management and Leadership, 10*(4), 375–396. https://doi.org/10.1002/nml.10403

Nanavati, A. (2007). Performance evaluation of non-government development organisations: A study in Vadodara, Gujarat. *Journal of Health Management, 9*(2), 275–299.

Ni, N., & X. Zhan (2017). Embedded Government Control and Nonprofit Revenue Growth. *Public Administration Review, 77*(5), 730–742.

Nicholls, A., & Cho, A. H. (2006). Social entrepreneurship: The structuration of a field. *Social Entrepreneurship: New Models of Sustainable Social Change, 34*(4), 99–118.

Noya, A., & Lecamp, G. (1999). *Social Enterprises* (9264170731). http://www.oecd-ilibrary.org/urban-rural-and-regional-development/social-enterprises_9789264182332-en

Nyssens, M. (2007). Social enterprise: Between market, public policies and civil society. In M. Nyssens (Ed.), *Social Enterprise at the Crossroads of Market, Public Policy and Civil Society* (pp. 329–344). Routledge.

O'Cass, A., & Ngo, L. V. (2007). Market orientation versus innovative culture: Two routes to superior brand performance. *European Journal of Marketing, 41*(7/8), 868–887.

O'Mahony, S., & B. A. Bechky (2008). Boundary Organizations: Enabling Collaboration among Unexpected Allies. *Administrative Science Quarterly, 53*(3), 422–459.

Osborne, S. P., Radnor, Z., & Strokosch, K. (2016). Co-production and the co-creation of value in public services: A suitable case for treatment? *Public Management Review, 18*(5), 639–653.

Otiso, K. M. (2003). State, voluntary and private sector partnerships for slum upgrading and basic service delivery in Nairobi City, Kenya. *Cities, 20*(4), 221–229. https://doi.org/10.1016/S0264-2751(03)00035-0

Park, C., & Wilding, M. (2012). Social enterprise policy design: Constructing social enterprise in the UK and Korea. *International Journal of Social Welfare*, *22*(3), 236–247. https://doi.org/10.1111/j.1468-2397.2012.00900.x

Paton, R. (2002). *Managing and Measuring Social Enterprises*. London: Sage.

Peredo, A. M., & McLean, M. (2006). Social entrepreneurship: A critical review of the concept. *Journal of World Business*, *41*(1), 56–65. https://doi.org/10.1016/j.jwb.2005.10.007

Pestoff, V. (1998). *Beyond the market and state: Social enterprises and civil democracy in a welfare society.* Ashgate.

Pestoff, V. A. (1992). Third sector and co-operative services—An alternative to privatization. *Journal of Consumer Policy*, *15*(1), 21–45. https://doi.org/10.1007/bf01016352

Pestoff, V. (2008). Citizens and co-production of welfare services: Childcare in eight European countries. In *Co-production. The Third Sector and the Delivery of Public Services*. Routledge.

Pestoff, V. (2009). Towards a paradigm of democratic participation: Citizen participation and co-production of personal social services in Sweden. *Annals of Public and Cooperative Economics*, *80*(2), 197–224. https://doi.org/10.1111/j.1467-8292.2009.00384.x

Pestoff, V. (2013). The role of participatory governance in the EMES approach to social enterprise. *Journal of Entrepreneurial and Organizational Diversity*, *2*(2), 48–60. https://doi.org/10.5947/jeod.2013.010

Pestoff, V. (2014). Hybridity, coproduction, and third sector social services in Europe. *American Behavioral Scientist*, *58*(11), 1412–1424. https://doi.org/10.1177/0002764214534670

Phillips, W., Alexander, E. A., & Lee, H. (2017). Going it alone won't work! The relational imperative for social innovation in social enterprises. *Journal of Business Ethics*, *14*(2), 1–17. https://doi.org/10.1007/s10551-017-3608-1

Pierre, A., Friedrichs, Y. V., & Wincent, J. (2014). A review of social entrepreneurship research. In A. Lundström, C. Zhou, Y. von Friedrichs, and E. Sundin (Eds.), *Social Entrepreneurship* (Vol. 29, pp. 43–69). Springer, Cham.

Poon, D. (2011). *The emergence and development of social enterprise sectors.* Social Impact Research Experience, 8. University of Pennsylvania.

Powell, W. W. (1991). Introduction. The new institutionalism in organizational analysis. In W. W. Powell & P. J. DiMaggio (Eds.), *The new institutionalism in organizational analysis*. University of Chicago Press.

Prajapati, K., & Biswas, S. N. (2011). Effect of entrepreneur network and entrepreneur self-efficacy on subjective performance: A study of handicraft and handloom cluster. *The Journal of Entrepreneurship*, *20*(2), 227–247. https://doi.org/10.1177/097135571102000204

Purcell, M. E., & Hawtin, M. (2010). Piloting external peer review as a model for performance improvement in third-sector organizations. *Nonprofit Management and Leadership*, *20*(3), 357–374.

Putterman, L., & Dong, X.-Y. (2000). China's state-owned enterprises: Their role, job creation, and efficiency in long-term perspective. *Modern China*, *26*(4), 403–447. http://www.jstor.org/stable/189426

Ramanath, R. (2009). Limits to institutional isomorphism: Examining internal processes in NGO—government interactions. *Nonprofit and Voluntary Sector Quarterly*, *38*(1), 51–76.

Ramus, T., & Vaccaro, A. (2014). Stakeholders matter: How social enterprises address mission drift. *Journal of Business Ethics, 143*(2), 307–322. https://doi.org/10.1007/s10551-014-2353-y

Ravichandran, N., & Rajashree, S. (2007). Financing sustainability and globalisation theory and research. *Journal of Health Management, 9*(2), 201–222. http://jhm.sagepub.com/content/9/2/201.short

Reay, T., & Hinings, C. R. (2009). Managing the rivalry of competing institutional logics. *Organization Studies, 30*(6), 629–652. https://doi.org/10.1177/0170840609104803

Saich, T. (2009). Negotiating the state: The development of social organizations in China. *The China Quarterly, 161*, 124–141. doi:10.1017/S0305741000003969

Salamon, L. M. (1981). Rethinking public management: Third-party government and the changing forms of government action. *Journal of Public Policy, 29*(3), 255–275.

Salamon, L. M. (1987). Of market failure, voluntary failure, and third-party government: Toward a theory of government-nonprofit relations in the modern welfare state. *Journal of Voluntary Action Research, 16*(1–2), 29–49.

Salamon, L. M., & Anheier, H. K. (1997). *Defining the nonprofit sector: A cross-national analysis*. Manchester University Press.

Salamon, L. M., Sokolowski, S. W., & Anheier, H. (2000). Social origins of civil society: An overview. In *Working Papers of the Johns Hopkins Comparative Nonprofit Sector Project*. Retrieved from http://ccss.jhu.edu/wp-content/uploads/downloads/2011/09/CNP_WP22_1996.pdf

Salamon, L., & Sokolowski, S. (2010). *The social origins of civil society: Explaining variations in the size and structure of the global civil society sector*. Paper presented at the 9th international conference of the international society for third sector research, Istanbul, Turkey.

Salvato, C., & Rerup, C. (2018). Routine regulation: Balancing conflicting goals in organizational routines. *Administrative Science Quarterly, 63*(1), 170–209. https://doi.org/10.1177/0001839217707738

Schmitter, P. C. (1974). Still the century of corporatism? *The Review of Politics, 36*(1), 85–131.

Schwartz, J. (2004). Environmental NGOs in China: roles and limits. *Pacific Affairs, 77*(1), 28–49. https://www.jstor.org/stable/40022273

Seelos, C., & Mair, J. (2005). Social entrepreneurship: Creating new business models to serve the poor. *Business Horizons, 48*(3), 241–246.

Smith, W. K., & Lewis, M. W. (2011). Toward a theory of paradox: A dynamic equilibrium model of organizing. *Academy of Management Review, 36*(2), 381–403. https://doi.org/10.5465/amr.2009.0223

Sowa, J. E., Selden, S. C., & Sandfort, J. R. (2016). No longer unmeasurable? A Multidimensional integrated model of nonprofit organizational effectiveness. *Nonprofit and Voluntary Sector Quarterly, 33*(4), 711–728. https://doi.org/10.1177/0899764004269146

Spar, D., & Dail, J. (2002). Of measurement and mission: Accounting for performance in non-governmental organizations. *Chicago Journal of International Law, 3*, 171–181. http://heinonline.org/hol-cgi-bin/get_pdf.cgi?handle=hein.journals/cjil3&section=17

Spear, R., Cornforth, C., & Aiken, M. (2009). The governance challenges of social enterprises: Evidence from A UK Empirical Study. *Annals of Public and Cooperative Economics, 80*(2), 247–273. https://doi.org/10.1111/j.1467–8292.2009.00386.x

Spires, A. (2011). Contingent symbiosis and civil society in an authoritarian state: Understanding the survival of China's grassroots NGOs. *American Journal of Sociology*, *117*(1), 1–45. http://www.journals.uchicago.edu/doi/10.1086/660741

Stark, A. (2010). The distinction between public, nonprofit, and for-profit: Revisiting the "Core Legal" approach. *Journal of Public Administration Research and Theory*, *21*(1), 3–26. https://doi.org/10.1093/jopart/muq008

Steers, R. M. (1975). Problems in the measurement of organizational effectiveness. *Administrative Science Quarterly*, *20*(4), 546–558. https://doi.org/10.2307/2392022

Strøm, R. Ø., & Mersland, R. (2010). Microfinance mission drift? *World Development*, *38*(1), 28–36. http://www.sciencedirect.com/science/article/pii/S0305750X09000990

Sullivan Mort, G., Carnegie, K., & Weerawardena, J. (2003). Social entrepreneurship: Towards conceptualisation. *International Journal of Nonprofit and Voluntary Sector Marketing*, *8*(1), 76–88. https://doi.org/10.1002/nvsm.202/abstract

Tai, J. W. (2014). *Building civil society in authoritarian China: Importance of leadership connections for establishing effective nongovernmental organizations in a non-democracy*, Springer.

Teasdale, S. (2011). What's in a name? Making sense of social enterprise discourses. *Public Policy and Administration*, *27*(2), 99–119. https://doi.org/10.1177/0952076711401466

Teets, J. C. (2013). Let many civil societies bloom: The rise of consultative authoritarianism in China. *The China Quarterly*, *213*, 19–38. https://doi.org/10.1017/s0305741012001269

Thompson, J., & Doherty, B. (2006). The diverse world of social enterprise. *International Journal of Social Economics*, *33*(5/6), 361–375. https://doi.org/10.1108/03068290610660643

Treib, O., Bähr, H., & Falkner, G. (2007). Modes of governance: Towards a conceptual clarification. *Journal of European Public Policy*, *14*(1), 1–20. https://doi.org/10.1080/13501760601071406

Vamstad, J., & Pestoff, V. (2006). *The Third Sector and Citizens as Co-Producers of Welfare Services: The Tenth International Research Symposium on Public Management*, Glasgow Caledonian University.

Vaughan, D. (1998). Rational choice, situated action, and the social control of organizations. *Law and Society Review*, *32*(1), 23–61. https://doi.org/10.2307/827748

Vurro, C., & Perrini, F. (2006). Social entrepreneurship: Innovation and social change across theory and practice. *Social Entrepreneurship*, *23*(1), 57–85.

Waddock, S. A. (1988). Building successful social partnerships. *MIT Sloan Management Review*, *29*(4), 17.

Waddock, S. A. (1991). A typology of social partnership organizations. *Administration & Society*, *22*(4), 480–515.

Wadongo, B., L. D. Huaccho Huatuco, D. C. D., & Abdel-Kader, M. (2014). Contingency theory, performance management and organisational effectiveness in the third sector. *International Journal of Productivity and Performance Management*, *63*(6), 680–703. https://doi.org/10.1108/ijppm-09-2013-0161

Wang, Q., & Yao, Y. (2016). Resource dependence and government-NGO relationship in China. *The China Nonprofit Review*, *8*(1), 27–51. https://doi.org/10.1163/18765149-12341304

Wang, M., & Zhu, X. (2011). An outline of social enterprises. *The China Nonprofit Review*, *3*(1), 3–31. https://doi.org/10.1163/187651411x566667

Weber, M. (1946). Essay on bureaucracy. In *From Max Weber: Essays in Sociology* (pp. 196–244). Routledge.

Wei, Q. (2017). From direct involvement to indirect control? A multilevel analysis of factors influencing chinese foundations' capacity for resource mobilization. *VOLUNTAS: International Journal of Voluntary and Nonprofit Organizations*, *26*(4), 1–17. https://doi.org/10.1007/s11266-017-9924-3

Welter, F., & Kautonen, T. (2005). Trust, social networks and enterprise development: Exploring evidence from East and West Germany. *The International Entrepreneurship and Management Journal*, *1*(3), 367–379. https://doi.org/10.1007/s11365-005-2601-9

Weng, S., & Zhang, Y. (2019). Coproduction of community public service: Evidence from China's community foundations. *Journal of Chinese Governance*, *5*(1), 90–109. https://doi.org/10.1080/23812346.2019.1710048

White, F. C. (1983). Trade-off in growth and stability in state taxes. *National Tax Journal*, *36*(1), 103–114.

Whiting, S. H. (1991). The politics of NGO development in China. *Voluntas*, *2*(2), 16–48. https://doi.org/10.1007/BF01398669

Wilkinson, C., Medhurst, J., Henry, N., Wihlborg, M., & Braithwaite, B. W. (2014). *A map of social enterprises and their eco-systems in Europe: Executive summary*, 1–16. ICF Consulting Services, European Commission.

Willems, J., Boenigk, S., & Jegers, M. (2014). Seven trade-offs in measuring nonprofit performance and effectiveness. *Voluntas: International Journal of Voluntary and Nonprofit Organizations*, *25*(6), 1648–1670. https://doi.org/10.1007/s11266-014-9446-1

Wu, F., & Chan, K.-M. (2012). Graduated control and beyond: The evolving government-NGO relations. *China Perspectives*, *3*, 9–17.

Xiang, R., & Luk, T.-C. (2011). Friends or foes? Social enterprise and women organizing in migrant communities of China. *China Journal of Social Work*, *4*(3), 255–270. https://doi.org/10.1080/17525098.2011.620698

Yep, R. (2000). The limitations of corporatism for understanding reforming China: An empirical analysis in a rural county. *Journal of Contemporary China*, *9*(25), 547–566. https://doi.org/10.1080/713675952

Yu, J., & Guo, S. (2012). *Civil Society and Governance in China*. Springer.

Yu, X. (2013). The governance of social enterprises in China. *Social Enterprise Journal*, *9*(3), 225–246.

Zainon, S., Ahmad, S. A., Atan, R., Wah, Y. B., Bakar, Z. A., & Sarman, S. R. (2014). Legitimacy and sustainability of social enterprise: Governance and accountability. *Procedia - Social and Behavioral Sciences*, *145*, 152–157. https://doi.org/10.1016/j.sbspro.2014.06.022

Zammuto, R. F. (1984). A comparison of multiple constituency models of organizational effectiveness. *Academy of Management Review*, *9*(4), 606–616. https://doi.org/10.2307/258484

Zhao, M. (2012). *The social enterprise emerges in China* (Stanford Social Innovation Review, Issue). http://papers.ssrn.com.libproxy1.nus.edu.sg/abstract=2006776

Zhou, W., Zhu, X., Qiu, T., Yuan, R., Chen, J., & Chen, T. (2013). *China Social Enterprise and Impact Investdment Report*. S. S. A. Press. http://onlinelibrary.wiley.com.libproxy1.nus.edu.sg/doi/10.1111/j.1467-9299.2011.02011.x/full

3 The Development of WISEs in China

Introduction

This chapter discusses the characteristics of indigenous social enterprises within the social context of China and examines the historical development, institutional background, and policy context of work-integration social enterprises (WISEs) in China. In particular, it examines the social welfare reform, the emergence of the Third Sector, and the forms, characteristics, and functions of WISEs as a new form of social welfare institutions in China. The institutional forms that could potentially be classified as WISEs in the Chinese context are discussed in detail and subsequently linked back to the Western social enterprise model in the last section in preparation for further empirical analysis in later chapters.

3.1 A Development Path for WISEs in China

3.1.1 Upward Trend for WISEs since the 1990s

WISEs registered as non-governmental organisations (NGOs) and private businesses are difficult to identify because there is a lack of a legal framework for social enterprises. Therefore, only figures for social welfare enterprises (SWEs) as one of the major forms of WISEs in China are presented. Nevertheless, the upward trend is indicated by growing SWE activity in China. These organisations are later joined by other varieties of social enterprises as the sector develops.

The statistics published by the National Bureau of Statistics from 1990 to 2012 show an increasing number of SWEs being established throughout the 1990s.

As shown in Figure 3.1, from 1990 to 2012, the number of SWEs reached its peak in 1995, the same year marking a new wave of state-owned enterprise (SOE) privatisation (Geng, Yang, & Janus, 2009). This trend continues into the 2000s. Although the number of SWEs has declined to 20,000 in 2012 at the national level, the number of employees with disabilities has stabilised at about 600,000 since 2000. This implies that the sector has remained consistent in size as the organisations are becoming more centralised.

DOI: 10.4324/9781003231677-3

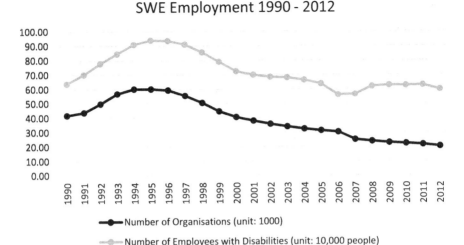

Figure 3.1 Social Welfare Enterprises (SWEs) Employment in China, 1990–2012

3.1.2   SOEs as Social Welfare Providers

The traditional Chinese SOEs, also known as 'work units' (*Danwei*; Bjorklund, 1986:19), are unique structures spanning China's early reform years. Curtis (2011) describes work units as an institutional space that helps mediate all functions of social security and employees' welfare (Curtis, 2011). As a structure, the work unit was a fundamental instrument of the state for social mobilisation and organisation in urban Chinese cities. The SOEs were not only commercial entities but also social welfare providers connecting the workers to specific welfare distribution and entitlements (Walder, 1989). In the three decades before the reform in 1979, workers had been receiving lifetime security and care for housing, health care, recreation, education, disability pensions, and even death benefits from the SOEs (Selden & You, 1997). The SOEs were also the principal tool for resource allocation and income redistribution for the state, as the organisations spent part of their profits on social infrastructure and public expenditure (Bjorklund, 1986).

Although these organisations provided stable employment, they also inhibited a free labour market, as movements between organisations were discouraged. Employees had to stay in the SOE to benefit from the social services it offered (Curtis, 2011). Scholars argue that the SOEs exerted control over people through the national welfare scheme (Guthrie, Lu, & Perry, 1999), which constructs small and enclosed communities integrating the work and social lives of its members by using employment benefits and social ties (Bjorklund 1986). The centralised scheme of linking social benefits and employment constituted the base of China's urban social welfare system before the country's economic reform (Huang, 2012; Selden & You, 1997).

3.1.3   *Dismantling Old Social Welfare System with Rising Pluralism*

The economic reform in the 1980s and 1990s have had changed the welfare system in urban cities significantly. The official policy of 'smashing the iron rice bowl' (Howell, 1995:7) in the late 1980s was symbolised by the unravelling of the old welfare system based on social merits. During the 15th Congress of the Chinese Communist Party in 1997, Party Secretary-General Jiang Zemin announced the reform of SOEs towards a more financially, competitive, politically independent, and self-reliant modern economy system (Chow, 2000). Subsequent reforms have slimmed down public bureaucracy at all administrative levels (Teets & Jagusztyn, 2013). The forty ministry-level departments were down to the size of twenty-nine within the State Council, with an employee cut from 33,000 to 16,000. Fifteen industrial ministries were abolished. Party bureaucracies were reduced by 48.2% in size at the provincial level and the township level by 19.4% (Yang, 2007), respectively.

Workers no longer enjoyed the lifelong benefits from the SOEs and huge lay-offs occurred with the colossal separation of the government from the SOEs. The central party was disconnected from 530 enterprises, including former army-owned enterprises, state-owned factories, and organisations attached to them. More than 300 state-controlled research and design institutes became private enterprises (Yang, 2007). As part of the reform, the Chinese government also urged the SOEs to diversify their revenue sources and unload most of their social responsibilities to small and private welfare-oriented institutions (Selden & You, 1997). The 'planned economy' system started to dismantle with social resources flowing into a more multifaceted social welfare structure (Deng, 2010; Teets & Jagusztyn, 2013).

The urban enterprise reform, the dismantling of the rural commune system, and the expansion of the socialist market economy in the 1990s led to the detachment of the State from the social welfare sector (Yu, 2011). The surging budget deficit before and during the reform due to a bulky administrative system and inefficient SOE performance (Howell, 1995) subsequently resulted in further decentralisation. More than 200 functions were then transferred from the central government to the SOEs, societal intermediary organisations, and local governments (Yang, 2007).

The rapid decentralisation of responsibilities for social services to private service providers has caused pervading changes across the social welfare system. The withdrawal of the state from the social welfare sector had created an institutional vacuum for intermediary agents to reconstruct a social safety net for ordinary citizens. Lee (2009) points out that the resulting dissociation and commodification of social goods and services gave rise to a certain 'welfare pluralism' in China: about 165,600 local social organisations and 700,000 civilian not-for-profit institutions were set up by enterprises, social groups, or entrepreneurs towards the end of 1998 as an outcome of downsizing the public administration (Yang, 2007). However, the deepening reform required a new national social welfare system incorporating both the private and the non-profit sectors.

3.1.4   *Social Organisations from an Inaugurating Third Sector*

The 1982 Constitution of the PRC stated that 'all citizens have the right to material assistance from the society when they are old, ill or disabled' (Chow, 2000). The labour Insurance Regulations were introduced at this time to strengthen the socialist ideology of working-class security (Chow, 2000). The Ministry of Civil Affairs (MCA) was established in 1978 as a functional department of the State Council to manage these socially functional groups, a leading role after the commencement of the social reform. The proposal put forward by the MCA suggested a new social security system with the sharing of responsibilities between the state, the enterprises, and the people (Chow, 2000). This marked the country's first step towards a social welfare system with pluralism, where the state was no longer the sole provider of social services and non-state actors were encouraged to participate actively.

The third sector started to emerge in the mid-1990s due to further economic and public administration reform (Yu, 2011). In response to increasingly diversified social needs, the Chinese government established NGO-like organisations that many referred to as 'GONGOs' in response to these needs while still maintaining a top-down government-controlled system (Deng, 2010; Hsu & Hasmath, 2014). Recognising the advantages of governing through social actors, these GONGOs concurrently function as the social arm of the state to address public issues (Hsu & Hasmath, 2014). Most of the founders of the first generation of NGOs were former party cadres or former SOE managers with political connections (Hsu, 2010). However, these public-sponsored NGOs are usually criticised as 'semi-governmental'(Deng, 2000:14) agencies and are deemed to be deficient in innovation, flexibility, efficiency, and management skills.

The first wave of bottom-up, privately run NGOs boomed in 1995 as a result of increasing interaction between the Chinese and the international community. Many Chinese citizens were exposed to the concept of NGOs for the first time (Deng, 2010). Grassroots NGOs started appearing to provide assistance in diverse areas such as women's rights, environmental protection, child protection, and so on (Deng, 2010). By the end of 2009, the total number of social organisations had reached 431,000, a significant number of them being social associations and civilian-run non-enterprise units (CRNEUs; Yu, 2011).

A new regulatory system has since been implemented to strengthen the policies on these newly emerged institutions. A policy paper named *Regulation and Management on Social Organisations* (*Shehui Tuanti Dengji Guanli Tiaoli*) and *Provisional Regulations on the Registration and Management of Civil, Non-Enterprise Institutions* (*Minban Feiqiye Danwei Dengji Guanli Zanxing Tiaoli*)[1] issued by the State Council in 1998 was implemented provide general regulatory guidelines for social organisations. The paper defined social organisations as 'voluntary groups formed by Chinese citizens in order to realise a shared objective according to their rules and to develop non-profit making activities'.[2] These voluntary groups include professional associations, chambers of commerce, charitable organisations, and all civilian-based organisations that fulfil the conditions stated in these documents, which specified the nature, rights, responsibilities, management structures, and activities these organisations may legitimately adopt. These policy documents marked the onset of legal legitimacy granted to NGOs in China.

It is within this context that the prospects of social organisations first appeared. The nature of these social organisations is very different from their Western counterparts. Under Chinese regulations, the organisation must be approved by the authorised department and register under the local Bureau of Civil Affairs (BCA) under the supervision of the MCA. The MCA system penetrates every administrative level and is in charge of registration and regulation of all official and independent civil organisations. It also interprets central policies and decides on practical measures to implement the policies locally (Hsu, 2010). As part of a dual management system, all organisations must be sponsored by a government or political agency, also known as a governing body, before they can be legally registered (Whiting, 1991).[3]

These requirements implied that the liberalisation of NGOs is off the political agenda right from the beginning, thus leaving little room for NGOs to expand their scope of influence (Howell, 1995). Since most people still see social welfare as the state's responsibility, it is difficult for NGOs without a government background to gain public trust and attain resources (Hsu, 2010). These grassroots NGOs lack human resources, knowledge, experience, and financial means to build their social impact successfully (Deng, 2010).[4] The NGOs also lack both experience and incentives to disengage from the state. Many NGOs, especially those with grassroots origins, still operate in a grey zone at the risk of state surveillance and sanction. Their vulnerability is reflected in the limited resources (Deng, 2010; Ma, 2009), accountability, and performance issues (Hasmath & Hsu, 2008) that they are facing.

This situation is further complicated by the diversity of social organisations formed within this institutional lacuna. A large number of organisations were developed within the old SOEs and needed no registration as a result of this connection (Huang et al., 2014). Some of them have to follow the double-registration policy, while other grassroots organisations have to register with State Administration for Industry and Commerce (SAIC) as private enterprises since they could not find a supervising unit (Lawrence & Nezhad, 2009; Xia, 2011). Moreover, since it was (and still is) difficult for NGOs with no political background to gain resources and trust under the political system, many social organisations adopt a pragmatic approach in their management and operation by prioritising measures that guarantee survival (Hsu, 2010). The combined effect of administrative uncertainty and the social service vacuum has nurtured the growth of institutions with mixed organisational identities and ownership structures (Hussain, 1994). This provides another route for grassroots-based social enterprises, usually in the form of social start-ups, to emerge in a bottom-up manner.

3.1.5   WISEs as a Solution for Social Unemployment

Chan and Yuen (2013) list four structural conditions for social enterprises to develop in an emerging economy—a shift in underlying welfare philosophy, the termination of a government-led welfare model, an economic crisis propagating changes in social relations, and, most important, the movement of the public sector toward the model of 'small government and big society' (Chan & Yuen, 2013). These four conditions have all been met in contemporary China. The country had shifted from the occupational welfare model prior to the 1979 reform, during which the communist state was the sole social welfare provider in the country (Whiting, 1991), to one that constitutes a socialist market with some degree of welfare pluralism (Lee, 2000).

This reform has created drastic impacts on the social welfare system. As the central government gradually withdrew financial support from the SOEs, their organisational obligations in terms of their social welfare functions incurred a heavy financial toll on their operations. In 1996, 66.7% of urban workers were working in these organisations. By the end of 1999, about 10.5 million workers were laid off by SOEs and urban collective enterprises. The economic crisis consequently surfaced as the urban unemployment rate peaked at around 13–15% (Ding & Warner, 2001) in 1998. The declined fiscal capacity created an institutional void that urged various social groups to fill up the gap. The disparity resulting from the socialist market system has therefore contributed to the emergence of private social welfare institutions (Deng, 2000).

Part of these changes occurred when the SOEs sold off their social welfare services at a price to private entities, organisations producing public goods, and services that were previously owned by these SOEs. These institutions were detached from the former SOEs to form companies with a social core (Deng, 2000). The separation of the social welfare functional units from the SOEs had led to an increasing number of 'mass-run' business units focusing on social service delivery. Social organisations developed from within the SOEs usually have commercial characteristics and resemble social enterprises more than NGOs because of their enterprise origins. These private enterprises with social missions, among them the SWEs, are seen by a group of scholars as the earliest social enterprises in China (Chan & Yuen, 2013; Hulgård, 2011; Xiaohong & Ming, 2011).

In order to tackle the growing problem of unemployment, the state introduced the Re-employment Project in 1993 by setting up Re-employment Service Centres (RSCs) to provide jobs to laid-off workers (Yu, 2011). These centres are seen by some Chinese scholars as the embryonic form of WISEs in China (Shi, 2005; Yu, 2011). These organisations switched their focus to assisting laid-off urban workers to return to work in communities after the SOE reform in 1998 by providing information, basic living allowances, and social insurance. Some of them were further converted to sheltered workshops to host people specifically with physical and psychological disparities and vocational training needs (Ran, Wen, Yonghe, & Honglu, 2009; Yip, 2005; Zhuo & Kun, 2009). This endeavour was subsequently joined by other forms of organisations serving similar purposes, such as enterprise-based sheltered workshops (Yip, 2005) and social start-ups (Zhao, 2012), as contemporary WISE models in China.

The SWEs, the public sector sheltered workshops, and the private social actors are the three stances supporting work-integration employment in China's social-economic reform. Although their characteristics are constantly modified to suit the need of the rapidly changing society, they still constitute the primary population of WISEs in China.[5]

3.2   The Socio-Political Context of WISEs

In order to resolve social problems caused by the reform measures, an unemployment insurance programme was introduced in 1986. Workers qualified as 'waiting for employment' (*Daiye*) were eligible for unemployment benefits from an unemployment insurance fund. This fund also covers training and employment assistance expenses and medical expenses, as well as other expenses to maintain the life quality of these unemployed workers (State Council Document No. 110[1993]). Starting in 1988, the state also initiated a series of Five-Year Plans with the aim to promote employment and improve life quality for the disabled, who were among those worst affected by the reform. A state agency named China Disabled Persons' Federation (CDPF) was established in 1988 to 'represent, manage, and serve' the disabled community.[6]

In terms of employment for people with disabilities, China has gone through a policy shift from employment of concentration to employment of dispersion since its market reform in 1979 (Jin Huang, Baorong Guo, & Bricout, 2009).[7] The concentration approach was compatible with the old central planned economy, where the objective was to employ disabled citizens under one roof for easy supervision and management. SWEs and sheltered workshops are examples of such arrangements. SWEs are commercial entities set up by or under the assistance of, the government with the specific objective of providing employment to people with disabilities (Hulgård, 2011). The concept of SWEs was particularly popular in the 1990s when close to 1,000,000 people with disabilities were employed by almost 60,000 SWEs across China (Jin Huang et al., 2009). Sheltered workshops, however, focus on providing training, usually on simple handicrafts, and remain under direct government control. They are completely dependent on the government for production and sales as well as subsidised fees and expenses (Jin Huang et al., 2009).

The establishment of the Law on the Protection of Disabled Persons (LPDP) at the beginning of the 1990s[8] symbolised the first shift of China's employment policy for people with disabilities from concentration towards

dispersion (Hampton, 2001).[9] Starting in 2015, the state revised its employment policy for the disabled and started to promote dispersive employment as
an alternative to the traditional concentration employment policy. The
*Administrative Measures for the Collection and Use of Employment Security for
Persons with Disabilities* (Fiscal [2015] 72) issued by the Ministry of Finance
(MOF) stated that companies with more than twenty employees must have
1.5% of their workforce made up of people with disabilities, and companies
that fail to comply will be subjected to a levy for each shortfall in headcount.
This levy is collectable by the local CDPF office. The wage for the disabled
person must also be above the local minimum wage with their social insurance
and pension scheme covered by their employers.[10] The adoption of the employment quota scheme implies it is now mandatory for the private sector to assist
the state in providing employment for people with disabilities. For organisations that failed to meet the quota, the levy collected is used to provide collective training services and support self-employment for the disabled under the
supervision of the local BCA and CDPF. Another document named *Notice on
Carrying out the Pilot Program by the Office of the Commission for the Disability
of the State Council* was also issued in 2015 to further promote the employment of the disabled. Policies that narrate and protect the labour rights of the
disabled were also introduced during the same period.[11]

The transition from concentration to dispersion approach to the employment of the disabled has resulted in a parallel 'double track' system in China
(Huang et al., 2009). It symbolises the transition of social welfare policy from
a central planned model to a socialist market model. From the micro-institu-
tional perspective, this transition leads to the emergence of various forms of
WISEs in China.

3.3 Types and Features of WISEs in China

Against the previously mentioned social background, four categories of WISEs
have been recognised in this study, namely SWEs, sheltered workshops,
CRNEUs, and a new type of social enterprise—social businesses and start-ups
based on the concept of social entrepreneurship.[12]

3.3.1 SWEs

SWEs are a form of indigenous for-profit social enterprises in China that
receive benefits from the government to host people with disabilities (Croll,
2009). SWEs are regulated by the *Temporary Regulations on the Management
of Social Welfare Enterprises* issued in 1990,[13] and they are defined as 'a special
form of organisation with the purpose of providing sheltered employment for
people with disabilities with social welfare as its core purpose'.[14] SWEs are
registered under the SAIC and supervised by the local BCA. According to the
regulation, at least 35% of the operational staff in an SWE must be either physically or mentally disabled workers (Zhao, 2012). It is also generally agreed

that to distinguish social enterprises from private firms, a certain percentage of the income earned by these organisations must be reinvested back into their activities. This percentage varies across cases but is usually no less than 50% for most SWEs (Yu and Zhang, 2009). Therefore, some scholars view SWEs as 'quasi-social enterprises' (Zhao, 2012:5). Many studies also see SWEs as an indigenous form of social enterprises in contemporary China (Lee, 2009; Yu, 2011).

The earliest institutions that resembled the Western WISEs could be traced back to the Mao era in the 1950s when welfare workshops were set up nationally to accommodate people with disabilities under the central planning of the government (Jin Huang et al., 2009). Urbanites relying on social security worked in these workshops to earn living expenses. These workshops were renamed 'Social Welfare Production Units' (*Shehui Shengchan Danwei*) since 1959 under the supervision of MCA as workstations for the disadvantaged and disabled workers (MOCA, 2008). These workshops were replaced by welfare enterprises after reform when the government changed its policy from unconditional support to tax incentives to encourage free-market competition in the sector (Jin Huang et al., 2009).

Although SWEs were initiated by the government, this was implemented alongside the introduction of private capital into the sector in the form of public–private partnerships since the 1990s (Yu, 2011). After this period, SWEs are divided into 'society-run' SWEs and 'government-run' SWEs, with most (about two thirds) of the SWEs belonging to the former category (Yu, 2011). The percentage of private capital increases significantly after 1998 as the 'society-run' model gains popularity for social welfare programmes. The number of SWEs increased from 920 to a significant amount of 32,410 over two decades from the 1980s to 2000, with privatised SWEs making up 85% of the total number of SWEs (Yu, 2011). The number of SWEs in the country has had increased five-fold from 1999 to 2000 and reached its peak of 38,000 with a workforce size of 699,000 disabled people in 2001.[15] Some of the SWEs even gained economy of scale and grew into big factories and franchises (Liao, 2014).

From 2006 onwards, a new tide of privatisation occurred in China. The state ceased to issue exclusive subsidies and benefits for these SWEs. The new tax policy in 2007 provided an income tax deduction based on the number of disabled workers hired in an organisation rather than its legal title. This caused a massive closing down of SWEs that relied heavily on government subsidies (Liao, 2014).[16] SWEs that survived were completely privatised into market-based institutions, with the distinction of a higher percentage (usually more than 25%) of disabled workers employed compared to standard private companies (Liao, 2014). In 2007, the MCA issued *Measures for Welfare Enterprise Accreditation of Qualification*, which further opened welfare enterprises to diversified investors and sped up their privatisation. Today, SWEs could be seen as a special type of company that employ disabled workers alongside their daily operations and economic pursuits. They enjoy wide-ranging tax exemptions of 50% to 100% income tax to 100% business tax, depending on the percentage of disabled workers employed. Limited profit distribution is allowed with no legal constraint (Yu, 2011).

Located at the frontier of public service delivery, the SWEs are examples of hybrid organisations combining public interest with the market mechanism. Lee (2009) argues that SWEs are the most common legal form of social enterprises in China. Other than giving dividends, these organisations fit the broad definition of social enterprises in terms of their composition, model, social functions, and goals; thus, they are included as social enterprises in this study.

3.3.2 State-Owned Sheltered Workshops

Sheltered workshops are a common traditional model for social enterprises in Europe and North America that provide employment and social and occupational integration for disabled or socially marginalised people (Defourny & Nyssens, 2008; Kerlin, 2006; Spear & Bidet, 2005). In the United States, sheltered workshops have been employing adults with mental and physical disabilities since the 19th century. Although this has since been converted to community-based employment programs over time as the traditional model of sheltered workshops becomes less popular, most studies still recognise sheltered workshops as a conventional form for WISEs (Cooney, 2015).

In China, the majority of the sheltered workshops are founded under the supervision of the CDPF. The GONGO has the same management structure as any public administrative unit, with a hierarchical system ranging from the national level down to the township and district level in almost every major city and county in China. The GONGO serves as 'the Secretariat of the State Council Working Committee on Disability'[17] and can be seen as the arm of the state bureau responsible for representing and safeguarding the interest of people with disabilities in China. As a measure to promote the functions of state-led social organisations at the community level, the local office of the CDPF and the subdistrict government under the local BCA have set up community service centres since the 1980s within individual subdistrict units to provide social services to vulnerable groups within the local community.[18] These subdistrict offices are important hubs for delivering public services, as they are the first line of contact for local residents and social organisations, and they report directly to higher levels of the bureau regarding all local affairs occurring within the subdistrict. These subdistrict offices can be seen as street-level bureaus in China (Leung & Nann, 1996).

Disabled people will receive training in sheltered workshops run by the CDPF collectively with these subdistrict offices. The early batches of sheltered workshops are a result of the urban commune movement alongside economic reform (Dixon, 1981). They were set up by the government bureau as communal workshops for the aged, the disabled, and sometimes unemployed adults and youths to reduce the burden of the local government in dispensing unemployment relief (Dixon, 1981). Today, state-founded sheltered workshops under the

CDPF are exclusively for the disabled, particularly individuals with mental disabilities. They play an important role in providing employment and rehabilitation. Some of these sheltered workshops are combined with community-based rehabilitations co-managed by the subdistrict BCA. Sometimes, these workshops are integrated with community-run enterprises for the workers to earn extra-occupational incomes (Stratford & Ng, 2000). These state-run sheltered workshops are also referred to as work-rehabilitation centres in China.

3.3.3   CRNEUs

For China's third-sector organisations, a CRNEU is the predominant legal option. (Yu, 2011). Most social organisations in China are registered under the MCA as CRNEUs (Lee, 2009). CRNEUs first appeared in the 1990s as private social service institutions. They could be schools, health care centres, culture or technology associations, or any general form of non-profit organisation. They are also referred to as 'Private Non-Enterprise Units' (Deng, 2010:6) or 'Civil Non-Enterprise Institutions' (Lee, 2009:9) by some individuals. This term was adopted in contrast with SOEs to emphasise the non-state and non-profit nature of these organisations. Together with social associations (*Shehui Tuanti*) and non-profit foundations, they are regarded as the main form of NGOs in China and qualify for tax reductions or government grants for the non-profit sector (Ming and Zhu, 2011).

These organisations are incorporated into the administrative system of civil organisations by the State Council in 1998. The Act of *Provisional Regulations for the Registration and Management of Civil Non-Enterprise Institutions* published in 1998 formalises the double registration of social organisations under the MCA, and any unregistered organisations that carry out social activities are considered illegal.[19] Under the 'dual management system', NGOs have to be sponsored by a government department or a government agency (Chen, 2012). According to the *Notice from the Ministry of Finance on Publishing and Distributing the Accounting System of Non-Profit Organisations* released by the Ministry of Finance (MOF) in 2004, a policy aimed to regulate the financial reporting of non-profit organisations (NPOs), to be qualified as a CRNEU, an organisation must fulfil three conditions: non-profit mission and goals, no economic gains by investors of the organisation, and the organisation must not be owned by any shareholders or investors.[20] WISEs registered as CRNEUs must also follow these legal guidelines.

The acceptance of public donations is another common challenge for CRNEUs. Before the implementation of the Charity Act 2016, only qualified NGOs could legally initiate fundraising campaigns and received public donations. The Charity Act 2016 has simplified the application process for the qualification, but it still requires social organisations to register as a 'charity organisation' for at least two years before it can apply to the MCA to be qualified for public fundraising. Under these strict regulations, some CRNEUs prefer to acquire income through operations by collecting appropriate fees for their socially beneficial activities or services for their members (Zhou et al., 2013). CRNEUs that contribute to employment and social integration and choose to self-finance via commercial operations fulfil two major conditions of social enterprises: they are self-sustainable, and their primary purpose is for public welfare. Furthermore, CRNEUs can accept charity donations, but by law, they cannot distribute dividends.[21] Therefore, in terms of organisational form and characteristics, CRNEUs in China operating as work-integration service providers are the closest to the Western ideals of WISEs.

3.3.4 Social Businesses and Social Start-Ups

Based on the Grameen Bank's model, Yunus et al. (2010) define a social business as 'a self-sustaining company that sells goods or services and repays its owners investments, but whose primary purpose is to serve society and improve the lives of the poor'(p.309). Social businesses started by proactive individual citizens in response to unmet social employment needs have been a common form of WISEs in Europe since the late 1970s, (Grégoire, Campi, & Defourny, 2006). The 'Social Purpose Company' in Belgium (Hulgard, Pestoff, & Defourny, 2014) and the 'Community Interest Company' in the United Kingdom (Hulgard et al., 2014) are examples of legal forms specifically created for social enterprises in the form of social businesses.

The social business model is consistent with the social innovation school of thought that stresses the concept of social entrepreneurship and the introduction of innovative and effective measures by individuals in addressing social problems (Dees and Anderson, 2006). A social business is usually run by social entrepreneurs and is operated like any 'regular' business, with the exception that the business model is designed to reinvest the profits into its operations to pass on the benefits to targeted beneficiaries. Compared to normal businesses, its primary motive and objective are for public interests rather than private interests (Bull, 2007). Studies and reports have included social businesses as a common form of market-based social enterprises in China (Xiaohong & Ming, 2011; FYSE, 2013; Chan & Yuen, 2013; Chandra & Wong, 2016; Zhou et al., 2013). However, few studies have analysed them in detail. Social businesses that satisfy the conditions of WISEs can be included as a form of WISEs in China.

Notes

1 Refer to the official website of Congressional-Executive Commission on China (CECC), retrieved from https://www.cecc.gov/resources/legal-provisions/temporary-regulations-on-the-registration-and-management-of-non-1#body-chinese
2 Details from the China Development Brief, June 23, 1998.
3 This system has been loosened since 2016 to allow NGOs that focus on charity, professional association and services, technology development and social services to register directly under the MCA without a governing body.
4 For example, in 1999, 8.7% NGOs in Beijing had no full-time staff, while 55.8% had no volunteers, and many NGOs were *de facto* 'rest-homes' for retirees and the jobless (Deng, 2000).

5 The MCA cancelled the qualification for all SWEs since October 2016. Since then, SWEs are no longer recognised as an official form of social welfare institution in China, although they may continue their operations and claim tax benefits based on the number of disabled workers they employ.

6 Programme supporting the Implementation of the 1995 'Plan and Legal System Construction', retrieved from http://www.cdpf.org.cn/ghjh/syfzgh/jw/201407/t20140725_387591.shtml

7 The purpose of concentration employment is to combine daily care, rehabilitation training, vocational skills training, and sheltered employment of people with disabilities under one organisational roof (Huang et al., 2009). SWEs and public-sector sheltered workshops are typical forms of institutions with this concept.

8 LPDP; National People's Congress of China (1990), retrieved from http://www.ilo.org/dyn/natlex/docs/WEBTEXT/31906/64869/E90CHN01.htmhttp://www.ilo.org/dyn/natlex/docs/WEBTEXT/31906/64869/E90CHN01.htm

9 The LPDP paper states that 'state organs, nongovernmental organisations, enterprises, institutions and urban and rural collective economic organisations should employ a certain proportion of disabled persons in appropriate types of jobs and posts', and 'governmental departments concerned shall encourage and assist disabled persons to obtain employment through voluntary organization or to open individual business'.

10 Ministry of Finance of the People's Republic of China, retrieved from http://szs.mof.gov.cn/bgtZaiXianFuWu_1_1_11/mlqd/201509/t20150914_1458276.html.

11 Ibid.

12 Some experts argue that the SWE and Non-Enterprise Civil-Run Unit does not fully adhere to the features and characteristics of social enterprises as defined by Western definitions (Lee, 2009). Nevertheless, these organisations still have similar structures and perform similar functions as their Western counterparts; therefore, they do provide a relevant reference for establishing a conceptual framework for social enterprises in China.

13 Retrieved from the official website of China Social Welfare at http://shfl.mca.gov.cn/article/bzgf/flqy/200807/20080700018559.shtml

14 Retrieved from the official website of China Social Welfare at http://shfl.mca.gov.cn/article/bzgf/flqy/200807/20080700018559.shtml, translated by the author.

15 Data from International Labour Office, Disability Compensation System—People's Republic of China, http://wallis.kezenfogva.iif.hu/eu_konyvtar/Projektek/Vocational_Rehabilitiation/china/chi_rap/comp.htm

16 State Administration of Taxation, retrieved from http://www.chinatax.gov.cn/n810219/n810744/n2048831/n2059355/c2138740/content.html

17 China's Disabled Persons' Federation, retrieved from http://www.cdpf.org.cn/english/About/overview_1793/

18 Subdistricts are the smallest public administrative units in urban China. A city is divided into a number of subdistricts, each subdistrict has its own set of administrative offices delivering a range of political services from security, urban management, and the economic management to civil affairs. Information retrieved from http://theory.people.com.cn/n1/2019/0626/c40531-31196857.html

19 Retrieved from the official website of the SAIC of the People's Republic of China at http://www.saic.gov.cn/fldyfbzdjz/zcfg/xzfg/200909/t20090927_233496.html

20 Refer to The Collection of Policies and Regulations on Social Organisations in Guangdong (Guangdong Sheng Shehui Zuzhi Zhengce Fagui Huibian), 1998–2008, edited and published by the Guangdong Civil Administration Bureau and the Guangdong General Committee of Social Organisations.

21 *Provisional Measures for Registration of Civilian-Run Non-Enterprise Units*, retrieved from http://www.gov.cn/gongbao/content/2000/content_60647.htm

References

Bjorklund, E. M. (1986). The Danwei: Socio-spatial characteristics of work units in China's urban society. *Economic Geography*, *62*(1), 19–29.

Bull, M. (2007). "Balance": The development of a social enterprise business performance analysis tool. *Social Enterprise Journal*, *3*(1), 49–66.

Chan, K. M., & Yuen, Y. K. T. (2013). An overview of social enterprise development in China and Hong Kong. *Journal of Ritsumeikan Social Sciences and Humanities*, 5, 165–178.

Chandra, Y., & Wong, L. (2016). *Social Entrepreneurship in the Greater China Region*. Routledge.

Chen, J. (2012). *Transnational Civil Society in China*. Edward Elgar Publishing.

Chow, N. W. S. (2000). *Socialist Welfare with Chinese Characteristics: The Reform of the Social Security System in China*. Centre of Asian Studies, the University of Hong Kong.

Cooney, K. (2015). Social Enterprise in the United States: WISEs and Other Worker-Focused Models. *ICSEM Working Papers*.

Croll, E. J. (2009). Social welfare reform: Trends and tensions. *The China Quarterly*, *159*, 684–699.

Curtis, Timothy. (2011). 'Newness' in social entrepreneurship discourses: The concept of 'Danwei' in the Chinese Experience. *Journal of Social Entrepreneurship*, *2*(2), 198–217.

Dees, J. G., & Anderson, B. B. (2006). Framing a theory of social entrepreneurship: Building on two schools of practice and thought. *Research on Social Entrepreneurship: Understanding and Contributing to an Emerging Field*, *1*(3), 39–66.

Defourny, J., & Nyssens, M. (2008). Social enterprise in Europe: Recent trends and developments. *Social Enterprise Journal*, *4*(3), 202–228.

Deng, G. (2000). New environment for development of NGOS in China. *Global Economic Review*, *29*(4), 43–61.

Deng, G. (2010). The hidden rules governing China's unregistered NGOs: Management and consequences. *China Review*, *10*(1), 183–206.

Ding, D. Z., & Warner, M. (2001). China's labour-management system reforms: Breaking the 'Three Old Irons' (1978–1999). *Asia Pacific Journal of Management*, *18*(3), 315–334.

Dixon, J. (1981). Community-based welfare support in China: 1949–1979. *Community Development Journal*, *16*(1), 1–9.

FYSE. (2013). China Social Enterprise Report 2012. Foundation for Youth and Social Entrepreneurship FYSE (pp. 1–4).

Geng, X., Yang, X., & Janus, A. (2009). State-owned enterprises in China reform dynamics and impacts. In R. Garnaut, L. Song, & L. T. Woo (Eds.), *China's New Place in a World Crisis: Economic, Geopolitical and Environmental Dimensions* (pp. 155–178). ANU Press.

Grégoire, O., Campi, S., & Defourny, J. (2006). Work integration social enterprises: Are they multiple-goal and multi-stakeholder organizations? In M. Nyssens (Ed.), *Social Enterprise: At the Crossroads of Market, Public Policies and Civil Society* (pp. 29–49). Routledge.

Guthrie, D., Lu, X., & Perry, E. J. (1999). Danwei: The changing Chinese workplace in historical and comparative perspective. *The China Journal*, *41*, 182–183.

Hampton, N. Z. (2001). An evolving rehabilitation service delivery system in the People's Republic of China. *Journal of Rehabilitation, 67*(3), 20.

Hasmath, R., & Hsu, J. (2008). NGOs in China: Issues of good governance and accountability. *Asia Pacific Journal of Public Administration, 30*(1), 29–39.

Howell, J. (1995). Prospects for NGOs in China. *Development in Practice, 5*(1), 5–15.

Hsu, C. (2010). Beyond civil society: An organizational perspective on state–NGO relations in the People's Republic of China. *Journal of Civil Society, 6*(3), 259–277.

Hsu, J. Y. J., & Hasmath, R. (2014). The local corporatist state and NGO relations in China. *Journal of Contemporary China, 23*(87), 516–534.

Huang, C. C., Deng, G., Wang, Z., & Edwards, R. L. (Eds.). (2014). *China's Nonprofit Sector: Progress and Challenges*. Volume 1 of Asian Studies, Transaction Publishers.

Huang, X. (2012). The politics of Social Welfare Reform in Urban China: Social welfare preferences and reform policies. *Journal of Chinese Political Science, 18*(1), 61–85.

Hulgard, L., Pestoff, V., & Defourny, J. (2014). *Social Enterprise and the Third Sector: Changing European Landscapes in a Comparative Perspective*. Taylor & Francis.

Hulgård, L. (2011). Social economy and social enterprise: An emerging alternative to mainstream market economy? *China Journal of Social Work, 4*(3), 201–215.

Hussain, A. (1994). Social security in present-day China and its reform. *The American Economic Review, 84*(2), 276–280.

Huang, J., Guo, B., & Bricout, J. C. (2009). From concentration to dispersion. *Journal of Disability Policy Studies, 20*(1), 46–54.

Kerlin, J. A. (2006). Social Enterprise in the United States and Europe: Understanding and Learning from the Differences. *Voluntas: International Journal of Voluntary and Nonprofit Organizations, 17*(3), 246–262.

Lawrence, P. G., & Nezhad, S. (2009). Accountability, transparency, and government co-option: A case study of four NGOs. *International NGO Journal, 4*(3), 76–83.

Lee, M. (2000). Chinese Occupational Welfare in Market transition. Springer.

Lee, R. (2009). The emergence of social enterprises in China: the quest for space and legitimacy. *Tsinghua China Law Review 2*(79), 80–99.

Leung, J. C. B., & Nann, R. C. (1996). *Authority and Benevolence: Social Welfare in China* (In Chinese, revised version). Chinese University Press.

Liao, H. (2014). *State, Market and Labour Rights for the Disabled*. China Social Sciences Press.

Ma, Qiusha. (2009). *Non-Governmental Organizations in Contemporary China*. Routledge.

Ming, W., & Zhu, X. (2011). An outline of social enterprises. *The China Nonprofit Review 3*(1): 3–31.

MOCA. (2008). *Policy Research on Development of Social Welfare Enterprise*. Policy Research Center of Ministry of Civil Affairs of the Peoples Republic of China (MOCA). Retrieved from http://zyzx.mca.gov.cn/article/yjcg/shfl/200808/2008 0800019219.shtml

Ran, C., Wen, S., Yonghe, W., & Honglu, M. (2009). A glimpse of community-based rehabilitation in China. *Disability and Rehabilitation, 14*(2), 103–107.

Selden, M., & You, L. (1997). The reform of social welfare in China. *World Development, 25*(10), 1667–1668.

Shi, L. R. (2005). From informal employment organizations to social enterprise. *Theoretical Journal, 139*, 42–44.

Teets, J. C., & Jagusztyn, M. (2013, May 23). The evolution of a collaborative governance model: Public-nonprofit partnerships in China. *RTI International and Pact Under USAID*.

Walder, A. G. (1989). Factory and manager in an era of reform. *The China Quarterly*, *118*, 242–264.

Whiting, S. H. (1991). The politics of NGO development in China. *Voluntas*, *2*(2), 16–48.

Xia, M. (2011). Social capital and rural grassroots governance in China. *Journal of Current Chinese Affairs*, *40*(2), 135–163.

Xiaohong, Z., & Ming, W. (2011). An outline of social enterprises*. *The China Nonprofit Review*, *3*(1), 3–31.

Spear, R., & Bidet, E. (2005). Social enterprise for work integration in 12 European countries: A descriptive analysis. *Annals of Public and Cooperative Economics*, *76*(2), 195–231.

Stratford, B., & Ng, H. (2000). People with Disabilities in China: Changing outlook—new solutions—growing problems. *International Journal of Disability, Development and Education*, *47*(1), 7–14.

Yang, K. (2007). China's 1998 Administrative Reform and New Public Management: Applying a Comparative Framework. *International Journal of Public Administration*, *30*(12–14), 1371–1392.

Yip, K.-S. (2005). Vocational Rehabilitation for Persons with Mental Illness in the People's Republic of China. *Administration and Policy in Mental Health and Mental Health Services Research*, *34*(1), 80–85.

Yu, X. (2011). Social enterprise in China: Driving forces, development patterns and legal framework. *Social Enterprise Journal*, *7*(1), 9–32.

Yu, X. & Zhang, Q. (2009). Development of social enterprises under China's market transition. *Presentation at the 2nd EMES International Conference on Social Enterprise*, University of Trento, Trento, Italy.

Yunus, M., Moingeon, B., & Lehmann-Ortega, L. (2010). Building social business models: Lessons from the Grameen experience. *Long Range Planning*, *43*(2–3), 308–325.

Zhao, M. (2012). The social enterprise emerges in China. *Stanford Social Innovation Review*, available at SSRN: https://ssrn.com/abstract=2006776

Zhou, W., Zhu, X., Qiu, T., Yuan, R., Chen, J., & Chen, T. (2013). *China Social Enterprise and Impact Investment Report*. *Public Administration* (Vol. 91, pp. 1–119). Shanghai University of Finance & Economics, Social Enterprise Research Center, Peking University Center for Civil Society Studies, the 21st Century Social Innovation Research Center, the University of Pennsylvania School of Social Policy & Practice.

Zhuo D, & Kun, N. D. (2009). Community-based rehabilitation in the People's Republic of China. *Disability and Rehabilitation*, *21*(10–11), 490–494.

4 Relationship between the State and WISEs

Introduction

This chapter presents four modes of relationship between the government and work-integrated social enterprises (WISEs) identified through this study's grounded theory approach—cooptation, cooperation, complementarity, and competition—with supporting evidence from the case studies. The model is based on data drawn from 21 WISEs across four major cities in China: Beijing, Guangzhou, Shenzhen, and Foshan. A similar pattern was found in all four cities, showing that geographical region is not a determinant factor for typology. The model also makes reference to state–third sector studies such as Najam's‘ 4C's model of government–third sector relations (Najam, 2000), Young's multilayered approach to government–non-profit relations (Young, 2000), and Conston's typology of government–non-governmental organisation (NGO) relationships based on power symmetry (Coston, 1998). The subsequent sections of this chapter illustrate the four modes of relationship and link them to existing literature. Each model is identified by formal (institutional) intervention and informal (personal) relationship. This chapter concludes with a discussion about the nature and characteristics of the four modes of relationship.

4.1 Theorising State–WISE Relations

4.1.1 Related Theories on State–Third Sector Relations

Najam's model explains how different types of state–third sector relations occur based on a means–ends analysis of the two parties, that is, cooperation when the means and ends are similar, confrontation when the two depart, complementarity when only the ends are similar, and cooptation when only the means are met (Najam, 2000). His model interprets state–NGO relationships as a continuous formation determined by the combined strategic choices of the state and the organisation during their respective pursuits. To some other scholars, NGOs are co-opted when they discord with but are still subordinated to the state (McFarlane, 2008), which means the two parties have different goals but still follow similar strategies.

DOI: 10.4324/9781003231677-4

The theorists also argue that cooperation is a more effective means to meet modern society's increasingly diverse service demands (Liu & Qiu, 2013). Cooperation is a typical relationship in state–NGO relations. NGOs and the state enter cooperation mode through various means of collaboration. This is usually an interdependent relationship in which the NGOs contribute skills and talents and the government provides a supportive network and funding. In ideal situations, one could expect balanced power between the NGO and the government.

Power asymmetry is a determining factor in this relationship (Coston, 1998). In her study, Coston differentiates collaboration from cooperation as a higher level of state–NGO relationship. The former is symbolised by favourable government policy, information and resource sharing, and a symmetrical relationship between the NGO and the government. Cooperation, however, entails neutral government policies towards the NGOs with low linkages and informal engagements (Coston, 1998). According to her classification, true collaboration is rare (Coston, 1998). While this statement is true, a distinction between collaboration and cooperation may not always be necessary. For example, the term *cooperation* is used by Najam to describe all circumstances in which the government and the organisation are working in synergy towards the same goals (Najam, 2000). Yu (2012) concludes that three factors determine organisational dependency: the significance of the resources being exchanged or provided to the organisation, the importance of the groups utilising these resources, and the availability of alternative resources. In cases when the state dominates the resources, the NGOs are reduced to the role of the implementer (Coston, 1998).

This dependency is sometimes mutual. As quoted in Coston (1998) by Gronbjerg (1987), complementarity is similar to a symbiotic relationship with a moderate to high linkage between the NGOs and the government with somewhat symmetrical power. The two are in mutual dependence based on comparative advantages (Kramer et al., 1981). This idea is echoed by Young (2000), who defines complementarity as a partnership or contractual relationship in which the government finances and the NGOs deliver (Young, 2000, 2006a, 2006b). This mutual dependency is not reflected in Najam's (2000) interest-based model. His means–ends argument contends that the objective ends serve as the means to define state–NGO relations. A complementary relationship is likely to emerge when the government and the organisation share convergent goals but prefer different strategies (Najam, 2000). The transfer of resources or interaction between the two parties is not necessary.

Last but not least, the notion of conflict between NGOs and the government has been discussed in various studies as rivalry between the state and NGOs. Studies based on the civil society framework use the term *confrontation* more often than 'competition' to emphasise the power struggle between the two (Gary, 1996; Skokova et al., 2018; Wu, 2019). In Najam's theory on 'institutional interests', confrontation is used in cases where the NGO and the state have dissimilar means and goals, or what Young (2000) calls an

'adversarial relationship' (p. 149), which is believed to be more likely in causing political coercion, repression, and harassment from the government
(Hasmath & Hsu, 2016; Lu, 2008). In some recent studies, confrontation is
interpreted as advocacy, where the NGOs attempt to change and influence the
behaviour and decision of the government (Franceschini & Nesossi, 2018;
Han, 2018; Liu, 2020). All these approaches imply a contesting relationship
between the parties.

The previously mentioned forms provide a useful theoretical reference for
articulating state–NGO relationships in the Chinese state. However, they do
not accurately describe social enterprises in China. As explained, social enterprises differ from NGOs in terms of their profit-making models and market
features. Many of the social enterprises studied focused on profiteering
through their social services and products and did not entirely rely on voluntary resources and donations as many NGOs do. Based on the empirical findings, this study enunciates four types of state–WISE relationships in China.

4.1.2   Two Attributes of State–WISE Relations

In this study, each state–WISE relationship is identified by two attributes: formal government intervention and informal network with individual governors. Formal institutions include 'rules' that are clearly defined and structured
(Lowndes, 2005). Formal involvement involves systematic institutional interactions between the government and the organisations, such as deliberate and
contractual arrangements (i.e., subsidies, incentives, legislative support, government procurement, partnership, joint venture, and so on). They are trace-
able channels for resources to flow from the government to the organisation.

Informal institutions span across government ties, and social norms to
non-contractual engagements (Lazzarini, 2004). These informal institutions
are created outside of officially sanctioned channels. According to Chen et al.
(2015) and Wiegel & Bamford (2015), these are usually not documented and
viewed as a personal relationship (*guanxi*), which plays a critical role in China,
especially with small and medium-sized enterprises (SMEs). Although their
effects are not necessarily observable, there is a general consensus that these
rules coexist with and sometimes even subvert formal institutions to become
game rules (Helmke, 2004). For example, a strong government connection is
believed to facilitate an NGO in terms of smooth registration, operation, and
access to political resources. These factors help it gain competitive advantages
over its peers (Hildebrandt, 2012; Hsu, 2010).

4.2   Co-Optation

In this study, a number of WISEs are found to be managed by the Chinese
state. This is different from how public-sector social enterprises (PSSEs) operate in Western democratic societies. In Western societies, many governments
face the pressure to reduce expenditure on public service provision. The 'Big

Society' agenda announced by the Cameron government is a typical example of how the government changes the way private capitals and traditional voluntary partners perform (Alcock, 2016). According to Defourny and Nyssens (2017), the transfer of public responsibilities to private entities has paved the way for social enterprises to emerge as 'public sector spin-offs' that drive state-led, in-house service provision towards more entrepreneurial activities (Defourny and Nyssens, 2017:6). Based on the tri-sector typology, PSSEs are defined as social enterprises with strong institutional linkages or are implemented directly by the public sector as administrative units (Defourny & Nyssens, 2017).

NGOs in China do not initially start off as civil groups but as institutions budding off from the state's apparatus as part of the country's state-led decentralisation reforms, during which the state creates social institutions as governing instruments (Frolic, 1997; Saich, 2010). In this study, social organisations organised or founded by the Chinese state are classified as co-opted organisations. These organizations result from the top-down political effort in the state-corporatist system, under which the Chinese state co-opts certain NGOs to extend its political arm within the society (Hsu & Hasmath, 2014). In Hasmath and Hsu's recent typology on NGOs, co-opted NGOs demonstrate non-governmental features with a strong political nature, such as having government representatives sitting on their directors' boards (Hasmath & Hsu, 2016).

4.2.1   *Profile of WISEs under Cooptation*

The public sector sheltered workshops for the disabled and the unemployed are usually embedded within local recreational service centres (RSCs). The MCA first raised the concept of RSCs in 1987. Most of the social service centres were set up in the first and second-tier cities in China in the 1990s and the 2000s. By the end of 1992, more than 70% of subdistricts in China had set up some form of community service.[1] The RSCs are considered public institutions and are usually managed by government-affiliated staff. They are usually set up collectively by the subdistrict government and the residents' committee in every neighbourhood as the standard government agency to attend to the daily affairs of local residents and to accommodate and serve the socially marginalised in the neighbourhood. RSCs that exclusively host people with disabilities are called work-rehabilitation centres (WRCs) and they provide 'concentration employment' (Huang et al., 2009) which combines routinary care, rehabilitation, vocational skills training, and sheltered employment for people with disabilities under one roof and supervised by programme coordinators and therapists. The WRCs create a special work environment that accommodates and trains people with special needs and no access to typical employment.

Since the WRCs are founded by the local subdistrict bureau, their locations and sizes are fully determined by the subdistrict officials, usually one in each subdistrict. Some of these centres exist in the form of government pro-grammes, and staff working in these centres are on the payroll of the China Disabled Persons' Federation (CDPF) or the subdistrict office. The staff per-forms operational duties such as agenda setting, employee recruitment, and project management for the centres. In order to be accepted by these work-shops, a person with a disability must be locally registered under the house-reg-istration system and has a 'certificate of disability' by the CDPF at the time of application. The CDPF will then assess the degree of disability and file a record for the person with a disability. A person with disability is only entitled to social security schemes and special benefits if they are registered as a local res-ident and is registered with the CDPF. Thus, the WRCs can be seen as admin-istrative units embedded within the local government's network for managing local residents with disabilities.

In the face of budget cuts, some local governments have changed their strategy to encourage independent NGOs to bid for long-term service con-tracts with the government. These NGOs offer work-rehabilitation services the way public-sector WISEs do on a contract basis. These NGOs are under the support and supervision of the local Bureau of Civil Affairs and subdistrict governments, which means their autonomies are compromised for the sup-port. In fact, the contract will usually be extended or granted to the same NGO upon completion due to the connection established (personal commu-nication, September 2015). In general, WISEs that operate in the public sec-tor are considered co-opted in this study because their operations are supervised and managed directly by the CDPF and are accountable mainly to the government.

4.2.1.1   Co-Opted WISEs Interviewed

This session includes four WRCs in three major Chinese cities across Beijing, Guangzhou, and Shenzhen. The centres were selected using snowballing sam-pling. Since all major cities have a similar administrative system for the disabled led by CDPF and the subdistrict bureau, the four cases represent the typical situation of public sector WISEs in China. Table 4.1 summarises information about the WISEs interviewed in this section.

CO1 to CO3 are established exclusively for adults with physical or mental disabilities above the age of 16, while CO4 accepts people of all ages, and more than 90% of the people accepted suffer from physical or mental disabili-ties. All WISEs are designed with similar structures, with one manager appointed by CDPF and two to three social workers or therapists assisting in the daily operations and specialised duties. Members of these WISEs perform simple manual tasks daily, such as handcrafting and painting, and those in a better state are trained to assemble simple product packaging for companies for extra pay. Membership is voluntary, but once being recruited, the members must report to the centre daily to complete their training and tasks. It is worth noting that regardless of the geographical region, all public-sector WISEs

Table 4.1 Basic Information of WISEs under Cooptation

WISE	Location	Organisational Status	Business Model	Social Model	Size (full-time staff)	Size (estimated number of beneficiaries)	Founding Year
CO1	Beijing	Not registered	Sheltered workshop	Provide work training and employment to people with mental disabilities	3	15	2012
CO2	Guangzhou	Not registered	Sheltered workshop	Provide work training and employment to people with various physical disabilities	3	21	2009
CO3	Guangzhou	Not registered	Sheltered workshop	Provide work training and employment to people with mental disabilities	3	24	2006
CO4	Shenzhen	Not registered	Welfare centre	Provide personal care and employment recommendation to people with various disabilities	NA	200	1992

Note: WISE = work-integrated social enterprise; NA = not applicable.

interviewed operate as affiliated units under the CDPF and the subdistrict government. Funded by CDPF, these units are financially stable. The co-opted organisations are not required to register officially as other WISEs do. However, they satisfy all the institutional features of WISEs, such as consistent operation, a fixed management team, and independent financial account, and providing job-related training and services to the disabled as their basic services.

4.2.1.2   *Organisational Characteristics*

The WRCs have a centrally designed organisational structure. It usually involves a managing director and two administrative staff responsible for the rehabilitation and training programmes. Each centre's capacity is capped at 30 members. Members attended workshop sessions during weekdays, and the ratio of members (i.e., beneficiaries) to staff is kept between 3:1 and 5:1 for effective management. All members must have local resident status under the house administration system in China and be certified by CDPF in order to apply to these programmes.

The internal management of the WISEs is inefficient due to the restrictions set forth by bureaucratic rules.[2] For example, projects cannot be implemented without clear instructions from the higher-level government, which usually results in a delayed market response. For example, the manager of CO1 was 'unclear on how to assess the ability of the members with disability since there were no guidelines from the CDPF (personal communication with the manager of CO1, November 2016). For the manager of CO4, she needed to write a report to the senior officer in order to collaborate with other organisations: 'timing [of the report] is important, you have to wait for [the right] conditions to be met' (personal communication, May 2016). Based on government policy, the WRCs only accept adults between 18 and 55 years old. Long-term plans wise, such as retirement schemes for the members, are beyond the scope of the WISEs. All the managers from CO1, CO2, and CO3 indicated that they were not aware of any future arrangement for the members or development for the organisation since 'there was no instruction [from the government] yet' (personal communication, 2016–2017). This shows that the WISEs' managers are more like the government's executive staff rather than decision-makers.

However, financial sustainability is clearly not an issue for the WISEs. All co-opted WISEs were fully subsidised by the government. Their annual budget and monthly stipend were set by the CDPF, which also provided them with physical assets, salaries, extra spending for activities, and any additional bursaries to their members. The WISEs also presented themselves like state agencies and were generally referred by their members as 'the government' (personal communication with the users of CO1 and CO3, November 2016). The WISEs collaborated with other agencies, such as the regional family service centres (FSCs), in their service offerings, with the government in between as the coordinator. The manager of CO1 called it a 'service network' constructed by the CDPF to access and stream the residents with different disabilities into different service agencies based on their health conditions and needs (personal communication, November 2016). Similar arrangements were implemented in all three sites, which suggests that this arrangement had been adopted universally in China.

In terms of social networks, the WISEs are completely isolated from their external environment. Outsiders were not allowed to enter the work centres and the CDPF directly managed all external communications. The beneficiaries were shielded from the local communities. The managers admitted that they did not know any other social service–sector organizations, nor were they in contact with any business partners. They liaised directly with CDPF (personal communication with managers of CO1, CO2, and CO3, November to December 2016). Local residents with disabilities would report to the subdistrict government or the local CDPF office and would be allocated to the corresponding centres. Companies interested in hiring these members with disabilities would also approach the subdistrict office, which then assisted in matching the members with suitable positions.

4.2.2 *Two Attributes of the Cooperation Relationship*

4.2.2.1 *Political Intervention*

Political intervention in the WISEs is scrupulous. All development strategies and agendas were designed and managed collectively by the CDPF and the subdistrict bureau. The management team only focused on executing the plans. The bureaucratic control over the WISEs is also reflected in their human resource management. Most of the staff in the WISEs were recruited directly by the CDPF, which was also responsible for screening their members as beneficiaries. For example, CO1 was converted from an activity centre in 2008, when the municipal government made it a policy that every subdistrict in Beijing must establish a WRC to serve local residents with disabilities. A staff of CO1 was posed to the centre by CDPF as a social worker, and she did not know how long she would stay there because 'it was all arranged by CDPF' (personal communication, November 2016).

A major characteristic of the co-opted WISEs is their lack of autonomy over their agenda and financial accounts. The top-down management structure means nobody in the organisation held any decision-making power; neither could they decide on any of the programmes or resources deployed. The manager of CO2 described their model as a government project; 'We are an affiliated unit under [the] CDPF ... the government purchases services from a social work agency [*Shegong Jigou*], then the social work agency sends someone to assist us to design and run the programmes' (personal communication, December 2016). All WISEs are entirely reliant on CDPF for capital and financial support. The manager of CO4, a government officer, commented that 'everything in our organisation is managed by the government ... including this building [we are in] … any change will depend on their arrangement' (personal communication, May 2016). The manager of CO1 had little knowledge about the operational costs of his organisation: 'I don't know what our expenses are' (personal communication, November 2016), although he admitted that the organisation was never lacking in money. The manager of CO3 complained, 'it [the budget] has not been changed for years' (personal communication, December 2016). The WISE had to report all operational expenses to the CDPF and any unused budget would be written off. The manager of CO3 detailed this process:

> 'Income earned from external projects are paid by the businesses to [the] CDPF directly … they negotiate the deals for us. We have no idea how much [the amount is]… . We receive money from CDPF every month anyway.'
>
> (personal communication, December 2016)

The manager of CO1 further explained how the organisation conducted its financial planning; 'We just report what we need to buy to [the] CDPF and they will appropriate funds to us' (personal communication, November 2016). Similarly, according to the manager of CO3, the organisation received a monthly budget from CDPF to cover staff salaries, social activities and essential equipment, but they 'had to think of ways to use up all the money (personal communication, December 2016), because the budget could not be used for any other purposes. As the manager of CO2 concluded their relationship with the CDPF, 'everything of us is from [the] CDPF … they are our big boss' (personal communication with the manager of CO2, December 2016). The manager of CO1 confirmed that this was also the case for all WRCs in their city, as all of them were managed by CDPF as part of its national employment programme for the disabled.

To sum up, all public-sector WISEs interviewed are completely dependent on the government for resources and sustainable operation. The CDPF also sets the agenda and makes strategic decisions for the organisations. Little power is delegated to the management team. The same features have been observed across all geographical locations, which confirms the complete dependency on the government as a general phenomenon for co-opted WISEs operating as public-sector sheltered workshops in urban China.

4.2.2.2   *Informal Network*

Since the WISEs report directly to the government bureau, separating formal and informal relationships is difficult. The fact that some of the WISEs provided re-employment to former retired government officers reveals the presence of informal connections in the system. For example, the manager of CO1 was working as a special committee member in CDPF before he was posted to the centre. He was re-employed after his retirement '*as a means to cover some expenses and spend time*' (personal communication, November 2016). Although the interpersonal relationship is harder to observe in this case, we can still conclude their presence because of these special arrangements.

4.2.2.3 Main Characteristics of the Cooptation Model

The co-opted WISEs fulfil Defourny and Nyssens' definition of public-sector social enterprise as 'social enterprises implemented by a local public service' (Defourny and Nyssens, 2017:20). These WISEs are integrated within the state administrative system and are managed like bureaucratic units, with a management style that is best known for top-down planning and control in the form of strict compliance with predetermined rules and protocols. The local government and CDPF as the state agency, give commands, determine their organisational structure and operational model, design work-rehabilitation programmes, provide both economic and political resources, and manage their budget and staff recruitment. Organisations have little autonomy in agenda-setting and strategic decision-making.

On the other hand, the government is a generous supplier for the WISEs, at least financially. Direct subsidies to the organisations included funds, human capital, business contracts, and social and rehabilitation programmes. The government also acted as a guarantor for these activities, which gave the organisations a firm base of public legitimacy. In terms of economic resources, the government provided a direct living allowance, basic insurance and extra personal income for the members as benefits. Overall, healthcare, security protection, training and employment were integrated under one shelter within the co-opted WISEs.

4.3 Cooperation

4.3.1 Profile of WISEs under Cooperation

This category includes eight WISEs, out of which four are registered under the Ministry of Civil Affairs (MCA) as CRNEUs, and four as private enterprises registered under the State Bureau of Industry and Commerce (SAIC). There is no direct linkage between organisational status and sectoral origin. Social enterprises may either register under the MCA as social organisations or under the SAIC as private companies. Since there are no official rules on social enterprise forms, WISEs usually register themselves based on political convenience and potential economic benefits. For example, some grassroots WISEs were registered as private ownership, but they relied mostly on community support and social capital rather than market resources, while others registered under the MCA in order to be qualified for government subsidies and public donations.[3] Therefore, the legal status of the WISEs did not necessarily indicate their nature.

WISEs registered as civilian-run non-enterprise units (CRNEUs) are considered NGOs. They were managed by a board of administrators and were not allowed to attain private assets or redistribute their profits.[4] These organisations usually made collective decisions and encouraged active participation among their members.

4.3.1.1   *WISEs Interviewed*

Table 4.2 summarises the WISEs interviewed under the category of cooperation.

CP1 is a sheltered workshop registered as a CRNEU in Shunde. The organisation was the first sheltered workshop in the area, and it tried to replicate the WISE model from Hong Kong to Shunde. It was founded as a department under the CDPF in 2000 as a vocational training centre and was subsequently converted to a social enterprise in 2010 with start-up capital from the subdistrict government and a private foundation in Hong Kong. The sheltered workshop hosts about 70 members; most are suffering from some form of mental disability. The organisation is divided into eight workshops involving handicrafts, sewing, printing, design, and car-washing to deliver employment-related training combined with rehabilitation through a work environment specially designed to suit the needs of workers with disability. People with certain work capabilities in the sheltered environment would be recommended to work in other companies.

CP2 is a social enterprise started in Shenzhen as a project by a social worker under the local branch of China Women's Federation (CWF), a GONGO set up in 1949 by the Communist Party to promote gender equality and women's rights. The project was registered as a CRNEU under the CWF in 2015. Its main purpose is to train single mothers in the area to work as surveyors for government agencies and private companies. These single mothers could work on a flexible basis that accommodates their schedules. The WISE serves the dual mission of reducing urban poverty and promoting personal development for women. Currently, the social enterprise is managed by two social workers from the CWF.

CP3 is a CRNEU established in Beijing back in 2003 under the guidance of CDPF as a labour training centre for students who had graduated from schools for the mentally disabled. Today, the organisation comprises a rehabilitation centre, a vocational training school, and a social service centre. The centre provides a range of services related to work integration, including work rehabilitation and on-the-job training for people with disabilities and training courses for social workers. The centre also runs a food store in a local food mall as a training base for its members with disabilities. The organisation has been actively seeking to develop and promote its new work-rehabilitation model among the parents of children with special needs. The organisation goes beyond providing essential caring and training-related services to advocate 'equality, respect, trust, care, practice, innovation' as its vision.[5]

CP4 is a market-based organisation based on an innovative model. The organisation is a maid agency in Beijing with its own training school and agency shops. The organisation was set up in 2002 by two economists as an

Table 4.2 Basic Information of WISEs under Cooperation

WISE	Location	Organisational Status	Business Model	Social Model	Size (full-time staff)	Size (estimated number of beneficiaries)	Founding Year
CP1	Shunde	non-profit (CRNEU)	Sheltered workshop	Provide work training and employment to people with mental disabilities	10	70	2000
CP2	Shenzhen	non-profit (CRNEU)	Social work organisation	Train single women to be surveyers	3	200	2015
CP3	Beijing	non-profit (CRNEU)	Rehabilitation centre	Provide job recommendation and on-job training for people with mental disabilities	31	400	2003
CP4	Beijing	Company (collective ownership)	Maid agency	Provide training and agency services to women from rural villages	60	200–300/ year	2002
CP5	Guangzhou	Private company	Bakery shop	Provide training and employment to people with mental disabilities	5	4	2015
CP6	Shenzhen	Corporation	Software development	Provide employment to people with physical disabilities	NA	5000	1997
CP7	Shunde	Private company	Business corporation with café and activity centre	people with physical and mental disabilities	NA	4	2013 (the WISE unit only)
CP8	Guangzhou	market-based	Car parts manufacture	Provide employment to people with physical disabilities	800	360	1996

Note: WISE = work-integrated social enterprise; CRNEU = civilian-run non-enterprise unit; NA = not applicable.

experimental project for their poverty-alleviation scheme. The organisation was set up to recruit, transport and train women from poverty-stricken rural villages in China to work as domestic helpers in Beijing. These women would attend school for two weeks before they were sent to individual urban households to work as domestic helpers. The social enterprise completely subsidised the services offered to these domestic workers. The WISE was also the first official domestic helper agency in Beijing that combined accommodation, training and referral into a standardised one-stop service. The training school was a registered non-profit while the agency shop was registered as a private company. Both organisations were managed by the same group of office staff. An average of 200–300 women are trained and recommended for individual positions annually (personal communication with CP4, November 2016).

CP5 is a bakery shop in Guangzhou specialising in training and hiring people who are physically and mentally disabled to work as kitchen staff. The bakery products were sold through its e-commerce store and through corporate orders. The social enterprise also organised baking workshops for the public and set up a foundation to manage the organisation's funding.

CP6 was initially set up by a group of five entrepreneurs with physical disabilities in 1997. The organisation started as a self-employed business and grew into a corporation with a foundation, listed companies, social organisations, and more than 5000 employees. The company only hires technicians and information technology developers with disabilities. It covers areas in software, animation, cultural design, system development, and e-commerce. As the business expanded, the company hired many employees with physical disabilities living and working together with their daily lives taken care of by professional social workers. Several social service centres were set up to fulfil this purpose. They provide services not only to the company's internal employees but also to other organisations with similar needs. Hence, the social service centres became the social arm of the company. A foundation was also set up to integrate the resources from individual organisations so that centralised strategies could be made to ensure the long-term development of the social enterprise. Resultantly, the company provided one-stop employment and care for its employees with disabilities.

CP7 is in the food and beverage sector as a coffee shop. Staff was trained to prepare simple food and drinks and serve customers. It was set up by a cooperation from the manufacturing industry. CP7 was set up as a social enterprise unit under the corporation, which used part of its commercial revenues to support the operations of the social enterprise. This started as corporate social responsibility but went one step ahead as the social unit became independent from its corporate body and became a private entity on its own. The social enterprise was founded with the collective support of the local office of China Youth League (CYL), a GONGO representing the young people, the CDPF, the subdistrict government, and the Shunde Social Innovation Centre as a government agency promoting social enterprise and social innovation. The purpose of CP7 was to offer employment, vocational training, and social integration for people with disabilities using the social enterprise model.

CP8 is a corporation founded in 1996 as a social welfare enterprise (SWE). The government had encouraged entrepreneurs to set up SWEs to hire people with special needs by offering subsidies for every worker with disabilities hired. The factory had since grown to a significant size and established itself firmly in the manufacturing industry, hiring over 1000 workers, with more than 35% of them having some form of disability. Besides the special employment policy, the factory was operated like any other factory in the private sector.

4.3.1.2 *Organisational Characteristics*

Most WISEs under this category have medium to large organisational size (with 70–1000 members or staff). Therefore, effective management is necessary for them to support their social and economic functional units concurrently. Since WISEs under cooperation adopt a diversity of organisational forms ranging from business enterprise to traditional non-profit, their managerial structure and style vary across organisations, from central committee teams with participative decision-making to hierarchical management by a board of directors.

Many WISEs have adopted a hybrid structure that combines the social and the business units under one roof. This means that the social enterprise has multiple entities registered under MCA as a social organisation and under the State Bureau of Industry and Commerce (SAIC) as a private company. These two entities usually have independent constitutions but are managed by the same people. The social unit may take the form of foundations, associations, social service centres, and the commercial unit private limited companies.

For example, both CP1 and CP4 started as NGOs and subsequently established a private company to take over their commercial activities. Both CP5 and CP6 set up a foundation to handle funds and donations from the public, while the main organizations mainly operated as private firms; CP6 started as a private company and expanded into a social enterprise group, whereas CP2 started as a programme with the government. CP7 started as a collaborative corporate social responsibility project with a public sector agency, and CP8 is a joint-venture SWE with CDPF. In other words, all cooperative WISEs that register and operate as independent organisations have incorporated some form of hybridity into their structure.

Table 4.3 shows that the younger WISEs, including CP1 and CP2, relied significantly on government funding, but most cooperative WISEs earned the majority of their incomes from the market. Most of the WISEs had established a business model that enabled them to obtain sustainable income through the sales of products and services. The distribution of revenue income shows that the WISEs were well connected with the government and the market. In fact, most of the WISEs under cooperation were leading players in their own terrain. For example, CP1, CP3, and CP4 were among the biggest contractors

Table 4.3 Sources of Revenue for WISEs under Cooperation (Year 2014/15)

WISE	Third Sector (public donationd, funds from foundation, charity sales and events)	Market (sales, investment, loans)	Government (subsidies and grants, procurements, service awards)
CP1	10%	30%	60%
CP2	0	0	100%
CP3	15%	50%	35%
CP4	0	70%	30%
CP5	0	100%	0
CP6	NA	NA	NA
CP7	0	100%	0
CP8	0	90%	10%

Note: WISE = work-integrated social enterprise; NA = not applicable.

for the local government, while CP6, CP7, and CP8 had also established their brand names locally.

4.3.2   *Two Attributes of the Cooperation Relationship*

4.3.2.1   *Political Intervention*

Government intervention with the WISEs involves two major categories: direct subsidies and public–private partnerships. In all cases, the organisations act as strategic partners of the Chinee state in providing work-integration services to local residents with disabilities.

CP1 identified rental subsidies as the most important supportive measure because it 'helped lower the operational costs significantly' (personal communication with the manager of CP1, December 2016). Other subsidies received by CP1 were in the popular form of service procurement, where the local government paid the organisation for every worker with a disability under its care and training programme. The government also coordinated the streaming and selection process by linking individual organisations and agencies together to ensure the smooth transfer of users between programmes. People with special needs who reported to government agencies were sent to CP1 for a thorough health and work capability assessment. They were then streamed to various institutions based on their conditions. Some of these partner organisations include public-sector agencies, such as intensive care centres, and other private organisations providing rehabilitation or employment services. Here, CP1 functioned like a transiting hub for the government. Candidates with employment potential were sent to work in car-washing or packaging shops operated by CP1 or to their business partners. As the manager mentioned, the relationship was 'a mutually reliant and beneficial one' (personal communication with the manager of CP1, November 2016). While the government prioritised the organisation in service procurement and gave them a higher quota compared to their potential competitors (personal communication, November 2016), the

WISE brought expertise and an advanced social enterprise model to the local social service sector.

CP3 had collaborated with the government on various procurement projects. The organisation had been providing employment and training services for graduates from special schools as a contractor for the local government since its establishment. As the manager commented, 'we have received a lot of resources from the government' (personal communication with the manager of CP3, November 2016). The CDPF officer assisted by referring students from special schools to her organisation upon graduation for continuing vocational training. Formal government procurement started in 2010 when the government first expanded its procurement budget. The WISE soon became the leading government contractor in the field of work integration. The government provided subsidies for every local resident recruited into the care centre and the vocational school under the organisation.

Similarly, CP5 recruited and trained people with mental disabilities to work for its bakery shops. According to the manager, the CDPF shared information with the organisation and invited it to public events, thereby publicising the organisation. It also referred potential clients to purchase its products and services (personal communication, December 2016). The manager described the relationship as a 'very important' one, as 'the government has legitimacy … if they [the government] tell the public our food is safe, that is more convincing than our own words' (personal communication, December 2016). In terms of recruitment, the organisation made use of CDPF's database to identify and recruit potential beneficiaries for their services, 'We can use their [CDPF's] database to search for members who fit our criteria, then we go to their training venues to look for them' (personal communication with the manager of CP5, December 2016). CDPF also assisted in connecting CP5 with external parties in training and event hosting.

CP6 recruited people with physical disabilities as software developers and designers. Besides tax benefits for its employees, the organisation also received a specific subsidy for its office building. The local government referred clients, promoted the social enterprise in various charity events and platforms, and purchased services and products from the organisation. The organisation won the China Social Innovation Awards, collectively organised by public-sector agencies, universities, and social organisations in 2010. The organisation has since served as a site for knowledge and information sharing for various social organisations under CDPF and the municipal government. As the manager of CP6 put it: 'We are a name card for the city' (personal communication, April 2016).

In all four cases, the government had offered abundant subsidies in the form of tax benefits, direct stipends and grants, and service contracts. Besides direct financial support, the government also fostered information sharing, organisational learning, and business connections, significantly reducing these organisations' operational costs. Also, these organisations retained their autonomy as the government only played a supportive role and did not interfere with their internal management.

Another common form of government–third sector collaboration is through partnerships. For example, in the *civilian-run, public-subsidised* model, the civilian-run non-profit organisation initiated the project while the government subsidised part or all of the capital.[6] This model was a replacement of the traditional centrally planned economy in China with the aim of reducing state funding in public and social welfare projects. CP4 and CP7 are typical examples of such collaboration. CP4 was set up as a social enterprise pilot project that reallocated women from the poverty-stricken countryside to work as domestic helpers in Beijing. The organisations recruited and transported members to a vocational school in Beijing, where they were trained for a month before being recommended by agents under the organisation to individual local families looking for domestic helpers. Half of the fees were covered in the form of a loan from the school, which they could pay back with their salaries later.

The WISE then collaborated with the government to promote its services and recruited apprentices locally. According to the WISE's director, the collaboration 'saved the organisation' when they could manage the project under the name of the local government. The organisation was facing serious trust issues among the local community before it partnered with the government. The partnership with the government enhanced the public legitimacy of the organisation (personal communication, November 2016). First, the government assisted in the recruitment of beneficiaries by promoting the project as a government project. The officers from the Office of Poverty Alleviation (OPA) and CWF went down to the villages to educate the local villagers together with the organisation. This solved the problem of legitimacy, and the result was imminent, according to the director of CP4: 'Once the local government started to work with us, people all came to sign up and our school had a large group of students right away' (personal communication, November 2016). In terms of subsidies, the government covered the cost of marketing, recruitment, the health check-up, and even transportation to Beijing. The Beijing municipal government provided subsidies based on the number of helpers who had successfully completed the training program and were employed. These subsidies constituted as high as one third of the annual revenue for CP4 and significantly improved the organization's financial status (personal communication, November 2016).

CP7 is under a private manufacturing corporation. The corporation partnered up with a local government social enterprise incubation centre to establish the WISE in the form of an independent entity. The corporation invested in a cafe and a take-away food store in Shunde that exclusively hires staff with disabilities, while the government agency provided the places free of charge (rent-free) and assisted in recruiting staff with disabilities. The corporation injected the initial capital, provided the necessary human resources, and worked with the training centre and the local CDPF in selecting, assessing, and transferring members with a disability to the WISE from other partnering organisations. The training centre also promoted CP7 as one of its undertaking projects in public and connected the WISE with resources from the social sector.

A deepened form of partnership is a joint venture—a business entity created by two or more parties usually with risk and profit sharing of the projects undertaken.[7] Joint ventures may take any form from informal agreements to complex structures. Both CP2 and CP8 were founded with a government agency under this arrangement. A social worker founded CP2 under the CWF, a GONGO founded back in 1949 as the official agency providing support to women in the country; hence the project carried the name of the government right from the start. The organisation was affiliated with CWF as its parental organisation. The government also referred potential business partners to the WISE as a guarantor by signing trilateral contracts with the corresponding parties. The organisation admitted that it was 'never lacking in projects because of their connection with the government' (personal communication with the manager of CP2, May 2016).

CP8 was an SWE founded in 1996 when there were favourable tax policies for SWEs. All SWEs were jointly funded by private enterprises with government agencies (Cheng, 2011), which meant that all SWEs then had close connections with the government. CP8 was founded as a joint venture with CDPF. The SWE enjoyed 100% exemption on value-added tax, with more than 50% of its staff being people with disabilities.[8] It was supervised collectively by the local Social Welfare Office under the MCA as well as CDPF as its joint-venture partner. The government also referred graduates with disabilities from special schools to the organisation and recognised the organisation as an official training base for people with disabilities in the province.

In all cases, the partnership between the WISEs and the local government ensures the smooth collaboration of organisations across sectors under the supervision of the local government. The government provides generous support in funding capital, contracts, and social connections and participates and shares its administrative authority with the organisation. The WISEs obtain public legitimacy by presenting themselves as government service partners. These measures significantly reduce the entry barrier for organisations into the market.

4.3.2.2 *Informal Network*

It is found that all WISEs under cooperation have informal relationships with the government in one form or another. Most of the informal relationships involve some form of personal ties with the government. For example, government officials may take up official positions in these organisations and vice versa.

CP2 and CP3 are examples of organisations with a government background. The founder of CP2 was also a staff of CWF. The manager of CP2 explained that 'the social service centre under CWF helped us set up this organisation' (personal communication, May 2016). Although CWF could not fund CP2 formally, it hosted the organisation inside its office building and shared its facilities and resources with them. As the manager of CP2 explained the role of CWF, 'it shares its resources with us. For example, we can use CWF as our brand name so that we have a parental organisation to rely on' (personal communication, May 2016). CWF also allowed CP2 to access its database so that it could identify and recruit the right members efficiently.

CP3 emphasised during the interview that they were a social organisation with 'red roots' (*Gen Zheng Miao Hong*), which means ties with the Chinese Communist Party (personal communication with founder, November 2016). The founder of the WISE had personal connections with government officials and explained how the organisation was established: 'the [government] official told us that there was a market demand for work-integration services, and he would support us to set up something' (personal communication, November 2016). The founder took up the officer's suggestion and started a vocational training school for local graduates from special schools registered under the CDPF. After the practice for government procurement was standardised, CP3 was given a higher quota for government contracts. The organisation had a budget of *200,000* Chinese dollars, which was twice that of other social organisations (personal communication with founder, November 2016).

Informal ties also occur when the manager or founder of the organisation holds a position in the government, or when a current or former government official sits on the advisory board of the organisation. For example, one of the founders of CP4 was a consultant for the State Council. The model was promoted by the State Council as a poverty-alleviation programme to several under-developed provinces in China. The same type of political linkage was also observed in CP3, CP5, CP6, CP7, and CP8. The founder of CP3 was given an affiliated government position when the organisation was established under CDPF.[9] CDPF also sent an officer to work as the vice chairman in the school during its initial development stage. One of CP5's shareholders was also an officer of CDPF. Its early shareholders included officers from other government departments, such as the Development and Reform Commission (DRC) and the Public Security Bureau.[10] These officials joined the board of shareholders, and 'they introduce their contacts to us when we need it' (personal communication, December 2016). The founder of CP6 was also a member of the national committee of the Chinese People's Political Consultative Conference (CPPCC)—the fourth-largest political body in China in charge of political supervision, consultation, and the discussion and handling of policy agenda and state affairs[11] and a committee member of the Municipal Commission of Information (personal communication, April 2016).

Similarly, CP7 was set up collectively with a government agency as a pilot programme to test the social enterprise model. The manager of CP7 called the government agency 'mother' as it had 'cultivated and nurtured us' (personal communication, December 2016). The manager of CP8 also disclosed that the founder 'knew the officers in CDPF well, so the two decided to invest and set up the SWE together' (personal communication, May 2016).

In some cases, the informal connection is not immediately obvious but is clearly reflected in the exclusive arrangements between the government and the organisation. One example was the priority in service procurement. As the manager of CP1 stated: 'the government always purchases from us first' (personal communication, December 2016). The government also informed and invited the organisation to bid for projects (personal communication, December 2016). Priority was also observed when CP6 was set up in the 1990s by a group of six people with physical disabilities. As the manager put it: 'We managed to register our social association while it was difficult for anyone else to do so ... the government has given us a lot of trial-and-error opportunities so that we can learn from our mistakes' (personal interview, April 2016).

4.3.2.3   *Main Characteristics of the Cooperation Model*

Tsao (1999) claims that the 1998 administrative reform in China matches the basic tenets of New Public Management (NPM) well. Although their claim is controversial, one does witness a significant amount of public functions being transferred to the private sector in the cooperation relationship. The cooperation between the State and WISEs include the discretionary control of organisations with measures such as explicit performance assessment, decentralisation and disaggregation, and the parsimonious use of resource—all fulfilling the principles of NPM.[12] The Chinese state has introduced complicated performance measurement standards to monitor the competency of its contractors. As a policy requirement, social organisations need to report the use of funds and the corresponding outputs to the government. The government then evaluates the financial account and the performance of the organisations annually to ensure the delivery of results.[13] Subsidies and grants still play an important role in the partnerships, but benefits are mostly in the forms of procurement, tax reduction, and political support that strengthens the legitimacy of the organisation.

It is also interesting to note that for all eight case studies, the presence of an informal network was observed in the form of interpersonal ties and exclusive arrangements between the social entrepreneur and government agencies. This includes information sharing, the referral of clients and users, and providing political legitimacy. Although to what extent these informal ties have impacted the organisations is not immediately apparent, it is an indisputable distinctive feature of the cooperation model.

4.4   Complementarity

4.4.1   *Profile of WISEs under Complementarity*

4.4.1.1   *WISEs Interviewed*

Seven WISEs have been included in this section, out of which three were registered as CRNEU and four as private enterprises. Table 4.4 presents the information on the WISEs. The WISEs are labelled as CM1 to CM7.

Table 4.4 Basic Information of WISEs under Complementarity

WISEs	Location	Organisational Status	Business Model	Social Model	Size (full-time staff)	Size (estimated number of beneficiaries)	Founding Year
CM1	Shenzhen	non-profit (CRNEU)	Car-washing service	Provide on-job training and employment to mentally disabled people	7	16	2015
CM2	Guangzhou	non-profit (CRNEU)	Produce and sell handmade canvas bags and laundry bags	Provide employment to women infected with AIDS	4	8	1998
CM3	Shenzhen	non-profit (CRNEU)	Produce and sell handmade retailed products (canvas bags)	Unemployed single mothers and full-time housewives of the migrants	2	30	2015
CM4	Shenzhen	Private company	Produce and sell handmade retailed products (canvas bags)	Women migrant workers	2	20–30	2015
CM5	Shenzhen	Private company	IT company developing commercial apps	People with hearing disability	15	NA	2013
CM6	Shenzhen	Private company	Food and beverage	Migrant workers with physical disabilities	2	8	2010
CM7	Guangzhou	Private company	Provide service consultation and workers' hotline	Factory workers/migrant workers	3	NA	2007

Note: WISE = work-integrated social enterprise; CRNEU = civilian-run non-enterprise unit; IT = information technology; NA = not applicable.

CM1 is an enterprise founded in Shenzhen in 2015 as a car-washing shop. The founding committee comprises 10 parents with children suffering from serious mental disabilities. The shop is founded as an experimental project to explore employment possibilities for their own children. The organisation developed its own special training course for people with serious mental disabilities to follow. The purpose of the organisation is to create a work-integration model to help workers with mental disabilities to be self-reliant and independent.

CM2 was set up by a private foundation from Hong Kong. The foundation has been around since 1998 to provide educational aid to children whose parents were diagnosed with AIDS in rural Chinese villages so that these children can complete their elementary education. CM2 was set up in 2010 in a village in Henan as a workshop for women from families with AIDS to earn extra income through sewing canvas bags. The workshop, which later grew into a full-scale social enterprise under the foundation's support, supplied the bags to hotels, restaurants, and individual buyers.

CM3 is a social enterprise in Shenzhen founded by a full-time housewife with the goal of building a platform for unemployed housewives and training them on cloth art and entrepreneurship so that they could start their own businesses. Quality products were sold through the online store of the social enterprise. The founder was also the local contact person for a national cultural community and used the cultural community as a platform to raise funds and sell products.

The founder of CM4 has been working as a migrant worker for more than 10 years and then as a volunteer in a local NGO for migrant workers. Since factories do not accept female workers over 30 years old, the founder set up the social enterprise as a mutual aid society for female migrant workers to explore their interests and potential. The organisation trained the migrant workers to sew and sell canvas bags and charged them a commission for the products sold. It also organised interest classes and provided legal and daily consultation to the female workers.

CM5 is an information technology start-up developing an app platform that would help people with hearing impairments and deafness to communicate with normal people. The app also plans to serve as a platform to connect users with special needs with available jobs. The social enterprise was founded under the support of a private social venture capital by a team of six professionals, out of which four had hearing disabilities. The social enterprise also organised activities and career fairs tailored to the needs of the deaf community.

CM6 was founded by a migrant worker who lost his left arm in a work-related accident in the factory. After working in an NGO for migrant workers for several years, he realised that the injured workers' main challenge was seeking employment. He then founded a social enterprise in the form of a breakfast shop to train the other workers with disabilities so that they could operate simple catering businesses on their own. The social enterprise also offered accommodation and consultation to the apprentices.

CM7 is a consulting company providing hotline services to migrant workers and management consulting to factory managers on how to improve the working environment and conditions for the workers. The purpose of the consulting firm is to maintain a communication channel between the management board and the factory workers in the absence of an effective union. The workers could seek consultation on work-related or personal issues through the hotline, and this information would be conveyed to the management board by the social enterprise to provide references for future measures. The social enterprise also provided recruitment and employment service for migrant workers who were seeking new jobs in the city.

4.4.1.2 *Organisational Characteristics*

Since most of the WISEs are small in size (from several to no more than 30 members), they usually have a flat organisational structure similar to NGOs. Decisions were made by the administrative committee and sometimes collectively by the members. This means that work relationships within the organisations were based on personal influence rather than hierarchical commands. For example, CM3, CM4, CM6, and CM7 had less than four full-time committee members, while most of their operational and productive work relied on part-time members and volunteers from the local communities. Among all seven WISEs, only CM5, a social business funded by a venture capital fund, had a management board with a clear division of responsibilities. The company is operating like any other commercial business because it 'has to be accountable to its investors' (personal communication with the manager of CM5, May 2016).

The financial conditions of the organisations are shown in Table 4.5. Except for CM7, which was funded by an overseas non-profit foundation, the rest of the organisations had not achieved financial balance. Most of the WISEs relied on other sources of income, such as donations or external investments. The only exceptional case was CM7, which supported its work-integration services with revenues from other projects. Overall, the WISEs were facing severe financial constraints regardless of their ages. All WISEs indicated that they re-invested all revenues back into the organisation and their social programmes.

Table 4.5 Sources of Revenue for WISEs under Complementarity (Year 2014/15)

WISE	Third Sector (public donations, funds from foundation, charity sales and events)	Market (sales, investment, loans)	Government (subsidies and grants, procurements, service awards)
CM1	0%	100%	0
CM2	0	100%	0
CM3	40%	10%	50%
CM4	100% (foundation)	0	0

4.4.2 *Attributes of the Complementarity Relationship*

4.4.2.1 *Political Intervention*

A prominent feature of the WISEs is that they do not benefit from public funding. Out of all WISEs, only CM1 had part of its rental subsidised by the government after they 'attracted attention from the government' (personal communication with the manager of CM1, May 2016). The government officially certified the WISE as a training base for people with disabilities, but the subsidies, as the manager of CM1 put it, were 'still limited' (personal communication, May 2016). The organisation offered cheaper courses than those offered by the CDPF, which show that the subsidies were based on pure economic benefits. CM3 and CM4 obtained part of their development capital by taking part in challenges organised by public-sector agencies, usually through social incubation centres. However, these challenges were open to all social organisations; hence, they were too inconsistent to be considered political intervention.

The absence of political ties was apparent when all seven WISEs indicated that they had tried to approach the government at various stages of development for resources, but they were rejected for various reasons. For example, CM1 was told that the project was too young for the government to provide support, as the organisation needed to 'see some positive results' first (personal communication with the manager of CM1, May 2016). CM4 was rejected because what it offered to the female migrant workers was 'not covered by government procurement' (personal communication with the manager of CM4, September 2016). In the case of CM6, his proposal was turned down due to 'constraints' of the government because priority was given to local residents under the house-registration system (personal communication with the manager of CM6, September 2016).

Interestingly, despite their weak political ties, all seven WISEs hoped for more collaboration with the public sector. The founder of CM1 specified, 'the support must be from the government as it is the best way to maximise social impact' (personal communication, May 2016). The managers from CM4 and CM6 had similar concerns that the government should offer more financial subsidies (personal communication, April–September 2016).

4.4.2.2 *Informal Network*

Although most of the WISEs indicated some informal exchanges with the government, such as attending government-organised public events (CM5), conveying their ideas to local governors (CM1), or joining platform and networking events organised by local government agencies (CM3, CM4, and CM5). However, these events were opened to all social organisations with no personal relationships involved. In general, informal ties between the WISEs and the local government were weak for all complementary WISEs.

4.4.2.3 *Main Characteristics of the Complementarity Model*

A common feature of this relationship model is that the founders of the WISEs had grassroots origins and suffered from the same underlying social issue they sought to address. In the case of CM1, the social enterprise was for his own son; for CM3, the founder was an unemployed housewife herself; for CM4 and CM6, the organisation was founded and run by migrant workers (personal communications, 2016–2017). This means that the WISEs were the result of self-mobilising efforts and based on members' mutual support. This also explained their civil society nature and the absence of political ties. As a result, the WISEs were closely connected with the non-profit sector and received most resource support, such as voluntary services and donations, from the third sector (personal communications, 2016–2017). This shows that WISEs under the complementarity model tended to base their activities and networks on the third sector and local communities the way traditional grassroots NGOs did.

Overall, in a complementary relationship, the government hardly intervenes, and neither does it support the development of the WISEs. Besides official regulation and recognition, the government has demonstrated clear passiveness, sometimes unresponsiveness, to the needs and requests of the WISEs. The organisations are facing not only financial limitations but also the generic constraints that grassroots civil organisations encounter when they try to acquire resources through formal public sector channels. The organisations may apply for grants and awards open to all social organisations or attend business seminars, fundraising, and social-networking events as other NGOs do. However, none of these measures were specially customised for them. The WISEs have to compete with all other social organisations in order to receive these benefits. However, although all the WISEs start with a business model, they still see the government as the most reliable and essential source of support.

4.5 Competition

4.5.1 *Profile of WISEs under Competition*

4.5.1.1 *WISEs interviewed*

Two WISEs, indexed as COMP1 and COMP2, were interviewed in this study. Table 4.6 summaries their profiles.

COMP1 started as a private limited company in 2002 to 'build a sense of respect and dignity among the migrant workers' (personal communication, 2017) in a village in suburban Beijing. The organisation set up a music group in 2002 to perform for the migrant workers, a school for the children of the migrant workers in 2005, and then a charity shop in 2006. A vocational training centre was founded in 2009 to provide skill training to young migrant workers and help them assimilate into urban life. The organisation's founder was awarded the gold prize for young social entrepreneurs in Beijing in 2004,

Table 4.6 Basic Information of WISEs under Competition

WISE	Location	Organisational Status	Business Model	Targeted Socially Disadvantaged Groups	Size (full-time staff)	Size (estimated number of beneficiaries)	Founding Year
COMP1	Beijing	Private company	Charity shops, school and vocational training centre	Migrant workers	50	300–500	2002
COMP2	Guangzhou	Non-profit (CRNEU)	Sheltered workshop, bakery shop	People with mental disabilities	120	300	1990

Note: WISE = work-integrated social enterprise; CRNEU = civilian-run non-enterprise unit.

and the organisation was among the top ten volunteer groups in Beijing in 2005. The organisation has since partnered with various universities, corporations, overseas foundations and government agencies in projects. Besides social activities, it also provided legal and financial consultation to migrant workers.

COMP2 is a sheltered workshop founded in 1990 in Guangzhou and affiliated with an NGO in Hong Kong. It started as a training school for people with mental disabilities and special needs. The organisation adopted a 'community service model' to integrate people with disabilities into everyday communal life. Its parental NGO also owned a school and an elderly care centre and provided services to people with special needs of all ages. COMP2 also founded a bakery shop as a new social enterprise project to provide on-the-job training to people with mental disabilities.

4.5.1.2 *Organisational Characteristics*

COMP1 and COMP2 share a few common and important features. Both organisations started by offering services that appealed to the needs of specific socially marginalised groups. For COMP1 it was the migrant workers, and for COMP2, people with mental disabilities. Over time, both organisations developed multiple service units based on the needs of the social groups they serve and their available resources. Some service units adopted the WISE model as a means to earn extra income by selling their services in the social service market. In both cases, resources from all units were conjoined and allocated by the administrative committee among the different programmes and projects under the organisation. There was no clear division of jobs, and operation was 'flexible, depending on the needs of the members' (personal communication with the director of COMP1, February 2017). As a result of this need-based development, both organisations have internal management like NGOs do with fluid human resources and flat command structures. For example, all units or projects had their own work team led by one or more members from the core administrative committee. For COMP1, its WISE units included a series of second-hand shops selling donated goods that hired migrant workers who could not find jobs in the city, a contracted farm that helped farmers to sell local agriculture products, a school for the children of migrant workers, and a vocational training centre that equipped migrant workers with internet technology skills. Similarly, COMP2 provided a series of services covering all aspects of the needs for people with mental disabilities, ranging from childcare and sheltered workshops to elderly care. The main office of COMP2 was in charge of all administrative and management issues, while the individual projects and organisations beneath received administrative, human resource and financial support from the main office. The sheltered workshop and the bakery shop operated as individual social enterprise units with their own financial accounts.

Table 4.7 summarises the financial condition of the two organisations. Since both organisations earn their income from various projects, the WISEs

Table 4.7 Sources of Revenue for WISEs under Competition (Year 2014/15)

WISE	Third Sector (public donations, funds from foundation, charity sales and events)	Market (Sales, investment, loans)	Government (subsidies and grants, procure-ments, service awards)	Operating expense percentage (%)
COMP1	10%	90%	0	100
COMP2	15%	70%	15%	100

WISE = work-integrated social enterprise.

could sustain on internal capital injections from their parental organisations. The manager of COMP2 stated that both the bakery shop and the sheltered workshop were running on a deficit and needed subsidies from its parental NGO. Similarly, COMP1 was sustaining its social enterprise units with profits from other projects. It is also remarkable that both organisations earned most of their incomes from the market. Overseas partners from the third sector provided another important source of funding for the organisations. COMP2 had collaborated with several overseas foundations and COMP1 had received 'consistent help and support' from a foreign non-profit foundation through-out its development (personal communication, February 2017). Both organi-sations had received little financial support from the government, which shows that the organisations were also highly politically independent.

4.5.2 Attributes of the Competition Relationship

4.5.2.1 Political Intervention

COMP1 was working with several government agencies, including the Communist Youth League and the Beijing Federation of Trade Unions in Beijing. The organisation won a series of awards, such as a prize for the perfor-mance team under the organisation as the 'excellent national folk art perfor-mance group' from the Central Propaganda Department and Ministry of Culture (CPDMC) in 2005. The organisation was also elected as the 'Model Worker's Home' in 2009 by the district office of the Beijing Federation of Trade Unions. This shows there was no antagonism between the organisation and the Chinese state.

However, there was conflict at the township level. Where COMP1 was located used to be a village outside Beijing. Because of its low living cost, the village has attracted a huge population influx of temporary migrant workers. It had quickly grown into a neighbourhood for migrant workers. COMP1 was founded as a mutual society by two migrant workers against this background. The first direct conflict between COMP1 and the township government occurred in 2012 when the village committee sent forklifts to the school to force it to close down. The official explanation given was that the school was illegal since it was not licensed by the Ministry of Education (MOE).

The dispute was resolved after several members of the National Committee of the CPPCC wrote to the MOE to request a special exception for COMP1 to continue to run the school. The privilege was later granted as a non-contractual agreement. However, a second dispute happened in 2016 when the township government issued an ultimatum to the organisation, requesting it to leave the village within a period of two weeks before enforcement actions would be taken with the claim that the organisation had 'potential fire hazards'. The village committee unilaterally terminated the rental contract with COMP1 and cut off its electricity and gas supply, rendering its residency illegal (personal communication, February 2017).

In this case, the government had recognised the contribution of COMP1, reflected in the awards granted to the organisations. The conflict that occurred was mainly between the organisation, the local township, and the village government, which was equivalent to street-level bureaucracy—the level of government the organisations had to deal with directly for daily affairs. The manager of COMP1 ascribed the cause of conflict to different economic interests; 'this didn't happen before urbanisation … but the cost of land [in the village] has been rising, and the local government wanted us to leave' (personal communication with the director of COMP1, February 2017).

This argument was substantiated by comparing the village where the organisation was located with a second village where the organisation had been providing services to. In the second village, the organisation was helping the local farmers to sell their agricultural crops. According to the manager;

> [W]e are welcomed by the township government there because what we are doing is good for the local economy. The village is trying to develop its agriculture so what we offer there coincides with their policies, unlike here [where the organisation is located], the school and the shops don't contribute [to the local economy] at all.
>
> (personal communication with
> the director of COMP1, February 2017)

COMP2 was in a similar situation. The organisation was one of the first organisations to introduce the work-rehabilitation model from Hong Kong to mainland China in the 1990s. The sheltered workshop had operated as a project under its parental organisation for a period of two decades and only became an independent organisation in 2012. The organisation combined work rehabilitation, simple employment skills training, various social activities, and personal care services under one roof for people with special needs.

Managers from the sheltered workshop indicated that the organisation 'has little interaction with the government most of the time' (personal communication, January 2017). Since the sheltered workshop was not independently registered under the MCA until 2012, it was not qualified for government projects and subsidies. It mostly relied on fees for its services and donation. After registration, the organisation started to bid for government projects,

but the attainment rate was very low. Government procurement only constituted 10% to 15% of the organisation's revenue income. This consisted of
social venture funds and service procurement on personal care services for
people with disabilities with no working capabilities and training on social
workers.

The two cases show a multi-array of relationships between the organisation
and different government departments and the organisation. In both cases, the
government has not demonstrated a consistent strategy in managing these
organisations. This can be explained partly by the different levels of administrative power and the lack of an overarching strategy in dealing with the new
organisations. That said, the attitude and actions of the local government
appear to be dependent on economic factors rather than political stand, in
particular, whether the bureau is in direct conflict with the WISEs in terms of
market positioning and services offered.

4.5.2.2   *Informal Network*

For COMP1, running a school for people with special needs without a licence
was an informal arrangement. The school gained this privilege through the
help of some key supporters. This is similar to the cooperation model, in which
the founders have to navigate through environmental obstacles with the help
of their social partners. However, in this case, there is no direct interaction
between the government and the organisation. COMP1 was against the local
township bureau's prior interest in raising tax revenue, while COMP2 was
drawing from the same pool of resources as the local bureaus do in terms of
talents, financial support, and potential customers. As the manager of COMP2
put it, 'We are competitors [with the public-sector WISEs], they are under the
government so all resources go to them, even if we have more comprehensive
training programmes' (personal communication, January 2017).

4.5.2.3   *Main Characteristics of the Competition Model*

Despite these organisations' common goals aligned with the government, the
latter's interest still prevails, and sometimes this crowds out the resources of the
WISEs. The local bureau may not necessarily use political coercion to weaken
the WISEs, but the organisations are oppressed due to asymmetry in power
when they have to compete with the public-sector agents for resources and
markets. The case study suggests that conflicts could occur at various levels
when the market is involved. In both cases, there was minimal direct political
confrontation between the local government and the WISEs; this observation
was confirmed by the various awards and recognitions the organisations have
received. Both types of organisations have aligned their goals with the government, but competition and, hence, conflicts arise inevitably when the two
groups disagree over resource allocation. In both cases, the government still
acts as a regulator and fulfils its administrative and legal functions. The conflict

is an outcome of competing in the same market and having different priorities in how to maximise resources to fulfil the particular social function.

4.6   Summarising the Four Modes of Relationship

Table 4.8 summarises the formal and informal attributes of WISEs under the four modes of relationship.

Table 4.8 demonstrates how the local government manages and interacts with WISEs in the work-integration sector based on the four modes of relationship. In cooptation and cooperation relationships, the government actively supports and promotes the development of the organisations. The government adopts a *laissez-faire* approach (Ho, 2001), or what Young (2000) calls an 'unresponsive government' (p. 22) towards the WISEs under the complementary and competitive relationship. Although legally legitimate, the WISEs rarely interact with the government in practice.

The cooptation relationship is featured by direct government management, supervision and funding. The difference between cooptation and cooperation is that WISEs under the latter are independent entities. Government intervention is mostly through performance measurement and contracts,[14] and direct political control is rare. What is unique about this 'steering' mechanism is the

Table 4.8 Formal and Informal Engagements under the Four Modes of Relationship

Mode of Relationship	Formal Intervention	Informal Network
Co-optation	Direct agenda-setting and management Public funding Endorsement and guarantorship Social security	Re-employment and settlement of past government officials
Cooperation	Financial support (subsidies, grants, allowances) Partnership and service procurement Tax exemption Government affiliation and endorsement	Former government officials sitting on board Promotion and referral through public sector network Information sharing with the organisation
Complementarity	Limited grants and procurement (selective) General certification and regulation	Nil
Competition	General certification and regulation	Nil

informal networks underneath. An important common feature is that all WISEs under cooperation have both formal and informal linkages with the government. Table 4.8 shows that the formal linkages are illustrated by contractual arrangements such as service procurement, contracting, partnerships, or various manifestations of co-management.[15] Informal linkages include personal relationships, private exchange of information, and the exchange of positions in the organisation with current or retired government officers.

As for WISEs under complementarity and competition, the case studies reveal minimal government involvement. The government only serves the role of a passive legislator and regulator. In the context of state–WISE relationships, the government only performs basic regulatory functions such as administration, legislation, and supervision and only imposes controls over or provides assistance to the WISEs based on legal and policy acts. This behaviour of the state is described by Jenkins and Henry (1982) as 'benign neglect' (p. 502).

In reality, neither the organisation nor the government is monolithic. To a large extent, the political and economic dimensions are intertwined since the mobilisation of resources inevitably involves political power. This multi-layered nature of the state-society relationship cannot be ignored. The WISEs and the government demonstrate consistent interaction patterns, which suggests that certain strategies may be present. This is discussed in detail in Chapter 6. Before that, we first look at how institutional effectiveness is measured and the subsequent implications in Chapter 5.

Notes

1 Li Chun (2013) The Development and Implications of the Community Public Service Model in China (Woguo Chengshi Shequ Gonggong Fuwu Moshi de Fazhan Licheng you Qishi), retrieved from http://www.xzbu.com/4/view-4804489.htm
2 Based on the participative observation of the author.
3 For details, refer to the China Charity Law 2016, available at http://www.npc.gov.cn/npc/dbdhhy/12_4/2016-03/21/content_1985714.htm
4 Details of the policy referred to are available at https://hk.lexiscn.com/law/law-chinese-1-3770-T.html
5 Organisation's website, retrieved from http://www.bjlizhi.org/
6 Information retrieved from http://www.mof.gov.cn/zhuantihuigu/2007ysbg/mcjs/200805/t20080519_25679.html
7 Definition retrieved from https://www.inc.com/encyclopedia/joint-ventures.html
8 This was reduced to a maximum amount of total tax exemption of no more than 35,000 Yuan per head for people with disabilities after 2006, retrieved from http://www.cdpf.org.cn/ywzz/jyjyb/jy_229/jyxs/jzjy/201103/t20110304_27403.shtml
9 These positions are given to people employed by state-owned institutions, which are considered affiliated to the public sector but are not part of the government.
10 Note that this information only describes the founding stage of the organisation.
11 Information from the official website of CPPCC, retrieved from http://www.cppcc.gov.cn/

12 The common doctrines of NPM are summarised as followed: entrepreneurial and business-like management, performance measurement and output-based accountability, introduction of competition and market mechanisms, decentralisation and devolution, and replacing bureaucracy with privatisation and contracting (Yang, 2007).

13 From *Guidance on Government Purchasing of Social Work from the Ministry of Civil Affairs and Ministry of Finance* (2012, No. 196), retrieved from http://www.gov.cn/gongbao/content/2013/content_2361580.htm

14 Performance measurement systems are important tools for the government to monitor and select responsible and capable partners to deliver the stated goals (Nanavati, 2007).

15 Co-management can be understood as a process that involves power delegation, continuous problem-solving, and the sharing of institutional networks (Carlsson & Berkes, 2005). The state involves in the management of projects for administrative purposes; only the state has at its disposal the means to ensure that the rules of the schemes are followed (Marine, 1989); hence, having the state as a co-manager significantly enhances the public credibility of the organisation.

References

Alcock, P. (2016). From partnership to the big society: The third sector policy regime in the UK. *Nonprofit Policy Forum*, *7*(2), 95–116. https://doi.org/10.1515/npf-2015-0022

Chen, C. C., Chen, X., & Huang, S. (2015). Chinese Guanxi: An integrative review and new directions for future research. *Management and Organization Review*, *9*(1), 167–207. https://doi.org/10.1111/more.12010

Cheng, H. J. (2011). A study on tax-free policy for the social welfare enterprise (Shehui Fuliqiye Shuishou Youhui Zhengce Wenti Yanjiu). *Policy Analysis*, *4*, 73–78.

Coston, J. M. (1998). A model and typology of government-NGO relationships. *Nonprofit and Voluntary Sector Quarterly*, *27*(3), 358–382. https://doi.org/10.1177/0899764098273006

Defourny, J., & Nyssens, M. (2017). Fundamentals for an international typology of social enterprise models. *Voluntas: International Journal of Voluntary and Nonprofit Organizations*, *28*(6), 2469–2497. https://doi.org/10.1007/s11266-017-9884-7

Franceschini, I., & Nesossi, E. (2018). State repression of chinese labor NGOs- A chilling effect?

Frolic, B. M. (1997). State-led civil society. In B. M. Frolic & T. Brook (Eds.), *Civil Society in China* (pp. 46–67). Routledge.

Gary, I. (1996). Confrontation, co-operation or co-optation: NGOs and the Ghanaian state during structural adjustment. *Review of African Political Economy*, *23*(68), 149–168. https://doi.org/10.1080/03056249608704193

Gronbjerg, K. A. (1987). Patterns of institutional relations in the welfare state: Public mandates and the nonprofit sector. *Journal of Voluntary Action Research*, *16*(1–2), 64–80.

Han, H. (2018). Legal governance of NGOs in China under Xi Jinping: Reinforcing divide and rule. *Asian Journal of Political Science*, *26*(3), 390–409. https://doi.org/10.1080/02185377.2018.1506994

Hasmath, R., & Hsu, J. Y. (2016). *NGO Governance and Management in China*. Routledge.

Helmke, G. S. L. (2004). Informal institutions and comparative politics – A research agenda. *Perspectives on Politics*, *2*(4), 725–740.

Hildebrandt, T. (2012). The political economy of social organization registration in China. *The China Quarterly*, *208*, 970–989. https://doi.org/10.1017/S03057 41011001093

Ho, P. (2001). Greening without conflict? Environmentalism, NGOs and civil society in China. *Development and Change*, *32*(5), 893–921.

Hsu, C. (2010). Beyond civil society: An organizational perspective on state–NGO relations in the People's Republic of China. *Journal of Civil Society*, *6*(3), 259–277. https://doi.org/10.1080/17448689.2010.528949

Hsu, J. Y. J., & Hasmath, R. (2014). The local corporatist state and NGO relations in China. *Journal of Contemporary China*, *23*(87), 516–534. https://doi.org/10.108 0/10670564.2013.843929

Huang, J., Guo, B., & Bricout, J. C. (2009). From concentration to dispersion: The shift in policy approach to disability employment in China. *Journal of Disability Policy Studies*, *20*(1), 46–54. https://doi.org/10.1177/1044207308325008

Jenkins, C. L., & Henry, B. (1982). Government involvement in tourism in developing countries. *Annals of Tourism Research*, *9*(4), 499–521.

Kramer, R. M., Kramer, R. M., & Wilensky, H. L. (1981). *Voluntary Agencies in the Welfare State*. University of California Press.

Lazzarini, S. G. (2004). Order with some law: Complementarity versus substitution of formal and informal arrangements. *Journal of Law, Economics, and Organization*, *20*(2), 261–298. https://doi.org/10.1093/jleo/ewh034

Liu, D. (2020). Advocacy channels and political resource dependence in authoritarianism: Nongovernmental organizations and environmental policies in China. *Governance*, *33*(2), 323–342. https://doi.org/10.1111/gove.12431

Liu, H., & Qiu, M. (2013). Conflicts and cooperation: Analysis on relationship of the government and NPOs in the field of old-age service [Article]. *China Perspectives*, *4*(16), 288–293.

Lowndes, V. (2005). Something old, something new, something borrowed…. *Policy Studies*, *26*(3–4), 291–309. https://doi.org/10.1080/01442870500198361

Lu, Y. (2008). NGOs in China: Development dynamics and challenges. In Y. Zheng & J. Fewsmith (Eds.), *China's Opening Society: The Non-State Sector and Governance*. Routledge.

McFarlane, C. (2008). Sanitation in Mumbai's Informal Settlements: State, 'Slum', and Infrastructure. *Environment and Planning A*, *40*(1), 88–107. https://doi.org/ 10.1068/a39221

Najam, A. (2000). The four C's of government third sector-government relations. *Nonprofit Management and Leadership*, *10*(4), 375–396. https://doi.org/10.1002/ nml.10403

Saich, T. (2010). *Governance and Politics of China*. Palgrave Macmillan.

Skokova, Y., Pape, U., & Krasnopolskaya, I. (2018). The non-profit sector in today's Russia: Between confrontation and co-optation. *Europe-Asia Studies*, *70*(4), 531–563. https://doi.org/10.1080/09668136.2018.1447089

Tsao, J. A. W. K. K. (1999). Reinventing government in China: A comparative analysis. *Administration & Society*, *31*(5), 571–587.

Wiegel, W., & Bamford, D. (2015). The role of guanxi in buyer–supplier relationships in Chinese small- and medium-sized enterprises – A resource-based perspective. *Production Planning & Control*, *26*(4), 308–327. https://doi.org/10.1080/0953 7287.2014.899405

Wu, W. (2019). Adaptive confrontation? Strategies of three women's groups for expanding political space in China. *Issues & Studies, 54*(4). https://doi.org/10.1142/s101 3251118400088

Young, D. R. (2000). Alternative models of government-nonprofit sector relations: Theoretical and international perspectives. *Nonprofit and Voluntary Sector Quarterly, 29*(1), 149–172. https://doi.org/10.1177/0899764000291009

Young, D. R. (2006a). Complementary, supplementary, or adversarial? Nonprofit-government relations. *Nonprofits and Government: Collaboration and Conflict,* 37–80.

Young, D. R. (2006b). Complementary, supplementary, or adversarial? Nonprofit-government relations. In E. T. Boris & C. E. Steuerle (Eds.), *Nonprofits & Government: Collaboration & Conflict* (pp. 37–80). The Urban Institute Press.

Yu, Y. (2012). Cooperation mechanism between NGO and government from resource interdependence perspective. *Communications in Information Science and Management Engineering, 2*(8), 36–42.

5 Measuring Institutional Effectiveness

Introduction

In Chapter 3, I have defined the state–work-integration social enterprise (WISE) relationship model and showed that the Chinese state engages differently with WISEs under different relationship categories. This chapter presents the formulation of institutional effectiveness for WISEs under all four modes of relationship measured by 'mission accomplishment' and illustrates how the model is used to assess and compare the effectiveness of WISEs. This chapter concludes with a comparison of effectiveness across the four relationship modes that link these two factors together.

5.1 The Measurement Framework

5.1.1 The Mission Accomplishment Model

Since social enterprises are defined as 'business-like organisations with a social mission', most approaches in the literature agree on the term *social mission* as a core property of all social enterprises (Duff, 2008; Sanders & McClellan, 2013; Stevens et al., 2015). Certainly, different schools of thought approach the concept of social enterprises differently. Nonetheless, there is consistency as 'for all schools of thought, the explicit aim is to benefit the community or the creation of social value, which is the core mission of social entrepreneurship and social enterprises' (Defourny & Nyssens, 2010a:44). In a nutshell, having a social mission is a core theme of social enterprises and is a reliable factor for determining whether the organisation has fulfilled its social purpose and duties.

A unique characteristic that differentiates WISEs from other social enterprises lies in their social missions and economic activities. WISEs are usually integrated rather than separate units, and their commercial activities usually incorporate the social programmes they offer (Nicholls and Cho, 2006). Because of this correlation between economic activities and social goals, the social missions of WISEs are inevitably related to and depend on their economic health. Since all resources transfer from the commercial unit to the

DOI: 10.4324/9781003231677-5

social programme internally within the organisation, a healthy financial state is vital in delivering the social missions. This renders the mission accomplishment model, which bases its measurement of social effectiveness explicitly on the attainment of social goals, which is a valid and reliable way to assess the institutional effectiveness of the WISEs.

5.1.2   *The Three Levels of Social Mission for WISEs*

This study identifies three levels of social mission based on the latest work of Defourny and Nyssens (2017), which provides a very useful framework to operationalise the mission of social enterprises based on their degrees of 'sociality'. Scholars argue that the 'sociality' of a mission can be divided into three levels (Defourny & Nyssens, 2017). The first level defines social missions as pertaining to the nature of the goods and services provided by social enterprises. The organisations fulfil their social missions given that their operations inevitably address the needs of certain socially marginalised groups, that the public, the market, or the voluntary sector alone fails to address. The second level of social mission relates to new social relationships and networks among social actors. Activities related to empowerment that require broader social participation or the formation of new institutions are also under this category. The third level constitutes broader influence beyond the impacted community, such as policy advocacy and changes in social and political values.

This framework is also applicable to WISEs. In fact, Defourny and Nyssens (2017) have used WISEs as an example to illustrate their framework for social missions, as it is one of the more 'emblematic' (p. 19) forms of social enterprises' missions across the world. Scholars ascribe the first level of the social mission of WISEs as providing employment and professional services to satisfy the unmet needs of the disadvantaged social groups that are involuntarily unemployed (Bidet, 2008; Bode, Evers, & Schulz, 2002; Cooney, 2015; Kuosmanen, 2014). This is usually upgradable to the second level of the work-integration mission (i.e., enhancing social relations and integration). This includes measures that improve job skills (and hence living quality), strengthen social networks, and promote social inclusion for the workers (Defourny & Nyssens, 2017). The third level of social mission concerns broader social impacts and social changes (Defourny & Nyssens, 2017). WISEs that manage to reduce inequality, introduce new values or standards, or induce ecological and social transition have reached this level. The three levels are progressive in terms of service comprehensiveness and social impact; a WISE only moves up to a higher level of mission when it fulfils a more fundamental level to a certain degree.

5.1.2.1   *Evidence of the Three Levels of Mission in China*

A policy paper drafted by the Disabled Persons' Work Committee of the State Council named the *Outline of the 11th Five-Year Plan for the Development of Disabled People in China* (2006)[1] identified the ultimate goals of the government scheme regarding supporting employment for people with disabilities. As part of the country's Five-Year Plan from 2006 to 2010, the policy paper highlighted the direction that the government was heading in supporting the disabled as a socially disadvantaged group. The major goals detailed in the paper include the following:

a. Provide job training and assistance to people with disabilities to increase their employability and skills
b. Further the capacity and service for people with disabilities
c. Integrate people with disabilities into the social security system to ensure their life essentials are fulfilled
d. Improve the social and cultural life of people with disabilities
e. Promote sports activities for people with disabilities
f. Strengthen the legal system and the construction of a barrier-free environment and continue to improve the legal rights and interests of people with disabilities

The first two points focus on the scale, scope, and quality of the services provided to disabled people; points (c), (d), and (e) stress social inclusion and life-quality enhancement, and the last point is on fundamentally improving the social environment for disadvantaged people. The goals emphasized in the policy paper thus cover all three WISEs' social mission levels. These same points were also highlighted in the *Outline of the 12th Five-Year Plan for the Development of Disabled People in China* (2011),[2] in which the main goals for employment-related issues for people with disabilities were to improve further employment-related services, social security, and legal system and promote more equality and rights. The policy paper also emphasized the role of social welfare organisations and encouraged the local governments to support organisations that fulfil these goals through various schemes and measures such as contracting, subsidizing, and collaborative partnerships. The policy documents issued by the State Council set the overall guidelines for mission attainment for the local governments. Although policy implementation may vary in detail at the local level, it could be assumed that the local governments would implement measures and schemes oriented around the three levels of mission as outlined in the Five-Year Plans.

5.1.2.2 *The Measurement*

A study on the existing models of WISEs in the European Union identifies three types of universal objectives for WISEs—production, social, and socio-political (Davister et al., 2004). The production objective concerns the fundamental purpose of WISEs in training and integrating people with physical or mental difficulties. Some WISEs manage to achieve higher social and political objectives for disadvantaged people through various fields of activities, which increases the 'depth' of their impact and influence.

This social mission framework is applied in China too. Table 5.1 summarises the labels collected and grouped based on the interview scripts that illustrate the mission accomplishment of WISEs and divided based on the three levels of social mission previously mentioned. This table was generated using three steps. In the first step, the interview scripts for the 21 WISEs across regions in China, classified under the four modes of state–WISEs relationship, were coded using a qualitative data analysis tool (NVivo) based on the

Table 5.1 Effectiveness Measurement for the Three Levels of Social Missions

Level of Social Mission	*Parameters*	*Codes Used*
Level I: Service Provision	Provide rehabilitation services	Provide occupational rehabilitation
		Provide personal care
		Cultivate independent living ability
	Provide employment services	Provide sheltered employment
		Provide training for employment skills
		Provide on-site work placement
		Provide job recommendation and job matching
		Provide supportive organisational environment
		Continuous follow-ups and assessment for workers
	Provide basic social security and welfare	Provide basic social insurance and welfare
		Increase personal income
Level II: Social Integration and Network Formation	Empowerment of beneficiaries	Promote and protect labour rights
		Provide legal, medical, and miscellaneous consultations
		High user (beneficiaries) participation in workplace and social activities
	Social training and personal development	Cultivate social adaption and communication skills
		Character development and self-value recognition
		Organise extra social activities and interest groups
	Social relations and network formation	Build new social bonds and network formation
		Strengthen integration with local communities
Level III: Policy advocacy and social change	Participate in policy advocacy	Policy research and political consultation
		Participate in policy agenda setting
	Promote positive social values	Reduce discrimination and promote social equality
	Promote social change	Export innovative social service models and set new benchmark for the sector

measurement framework. When a particular achievement was mentioned in the interview, it was coded and 'labelled'. This process was repeated until all the scripts were coded with a list of WISEs delivering each code generated (refer to the Appendix). The second step grouped the labels into parameters that measured mission accomplishment with a higher degree of abstraction. Finally, the number of tasks attained by each WISE under each level of mission was recorded. A higher score indicates that a larger scope of tasks has been achieved under a particular category. This gives a virtual numeric representation of the degree of mission accomplishment for the WISEs with respect to their relationship categories.

5.1.2.3   *Fundamental Service Provision*

Fundamentally, WISEs serve the functions of providing rehabilitation services, employment services, and social security for their users to ensure that their essential needs are met.

- Provide rehabilitation services
  It is common for WISEs to accommodate people with mental and physical disabilities. A European survey conducted in 2013 shows that 31% of the surveyed WISEs employed people with disabilities (Wilkinson et al., 2014). In China, various forms of vocational rehabilitation services in the form of work therapy, enterprise-based sheltered workshops, and daycare centres are provided by the WISEs and supervised by the China Disabled Persons' Federation (CDPF; Yip, 2005). Occupational rehabilitation remains the daily routine for most WISEs, usually providing personal care to disadvantaged workers and cultivating their independent living ability by performing simple manual work as part of the rehabilitation programme.
- Provide employment services
  Experts across different world regions have discussed the contribution of WISEs to employment. Whether in the traditional model of sheltered workshops or as social businesses providing transitional employment, WISEs provide employment-related opportunities for workers typically excluded by the labour market (Bode et al., 2002; Grégoire et al., 2006). Related services include both in-class labour skill development and on-the-job internships and training. The WISEs also provide employment services by engaging in capacity-building for workers, such as building supportive working environments tailored to their members' needs and designing new positions taking into consideration the special needs of workers with disabilities. WISEs that provide job recommendations rather than direct employment may also be considered as providing employment services.
- Social security and welfare
  Most WISEs' member employees receive some form of financial compensation for their manual labour. While job-skill training builds capacity for the members, in the long run, financial compensation increases their personal

income and benefits them immediately. Some WISEs, especially those from the public sector, cover basic social security or subsistence allowances for their members. Some enterprise-based WISEs also offer full salary packages with social insurance and other related welfare for their employees.

5.1.2.4   *Social Integration as Level 2 Mission*

The level 2 mission focuses on social integration. It is related to the nature of the work or the relationships between social actors. For instance, the WISEs may design programs or positions that specifically fit the workers' needs or provide social activities that help the workers assimilate with the social environment better. Here, the organisation is taking on extra responsibilities that prioritise the welfare of the beneficiaries before economic returns.

Some scholars argue that the first and second levels of missions for WISEs are sometimes intertwined. As WISEs provide direct employment and professional training to socially marginalised and disadvantaged people as one of their fundamental services, many of the activities conducted in this process concern social integration that involves the formation and enforcement of social relations and networks between the marginalised groups and the mainstream communities (Defourny & Nyssens, 2017). However, as not all essential services lead to broader social network formation and integration, this study distinguishes between simple service provision and social integration. Only measures designed to promote social integration are classified as level 2 missions.

- Empowerment of employees
  Most of the services concerning empowerment promote social integration in ways such as educating and advocating labour rights, providing legal consultations, and self-governing of the beneficiaries in the workplace and social activities. Better access for marginalised workers in communal life encourages social participation and empowerment of social minorities (Cooney, 2015). Scholars contend that social inclusion through employment contributes to anti-discrimination and sustainable work placement for workers with vulnerabilities (Kuosmanen, 2014). Empowerment is classified as a level 2 mission because it encompasses the nature and the impact of the services offered, and it improves the welfare of the entire local community (Bode et al., 2002).
- Social training and personal development
  Ebrahim (Ebrahim et al., 2014) equates the social activities that WISEs' workers engage in to 'social training' (p. 95). Such activities aim to enable the beneficiaries to acquire the soft skills needed for employability (Battilana & Lee, 2014). This includes cultivating social adaptation and communication skills and helping the beneficiaries in character-building and gaining self-confidence—attributes that are easily overlooked by typical employment agencies but are actually vital for social integration (Vidal & Claver, 2004). These workers are trained to be adaptive to professional work in

terms of job capabilities, communication skills, work manners, and personal conduct (Grégoire et al., 2006).

- Social relations and network formation
  Organisations from the third sector play a key role in informal social net-works and community building (Evers, 1995). One of the benefits of work-ing in WISEs is establishing social networks, an essential element for social inclusion (Vidal & Claver, 2004). Social and supportive networks are built by cultivating a sense of belonging among marginalised people, which is a base for forming social networks among individual members within the community (Ho & Chan, 2010). The WISEs provide a platform for mutual bonding and interaction with the community, generating trust and new communication opportunities. Such interaction is not restricted to benefi-ciaries but expands across other social actors in the same community.

5.1.2.5   Policy Advocacy and Social Change as Level 3 Mission

The third level of social mission concerns the political and public dimensions. The organisations may showcase innovative models to society, new social val-ues, or participate in policy advocacy. This is reflected in the following three aspects.

- Participation in policy advocacy
  Hulgård (2014) points out that social enterprises balance the dual roles of 'autonomous advocacy organisations' and 'providers of services to mem-bers and the wider society' (p. 204). Due to their commercial nature, social enterprises do not usually engage in advocacy activities in the way some traditional non-profits or NGOs do (Borzaga and Defourny, 2001). In pol-icy advocacy with social enterprises, the classical Tocquevillan analysis of representative democracy is less of a concern than the design and provision of goods and services in accordance with the values and demands of the social groups they serve (Hulgård, 2014). The WISEs achieve this by artic-ulating their members' needs through their direct dealings with the group. Advocacy behaviours of the WISEs observed include conducting policy research and dialogues with the government and participating in policy agenda setting through closed-door conferences and policy consultancy to the government.
- Promote positive social values
  As Defourny and Nyssens (2010b) state, the creation of social values is a core mission for social enterprises. Social values usually concern long-term social norms (Fong, 2014); examples are democratic governance, social equality, social inclusion of minorities, and so on (Defourny & Nyssens, 2017). With respect to WISEs, this includes measures to promote social equality, eliminate discrimination, and improve the social status of the dis-advantaged group not only within the organisations but also on a broader social scale.

- Promote social change
  Social change as a mission for social enterprises is linked to social entrepreneurship and social innovation (Defourny & Nyssens, 2010b; Vurro & Perrini, 2006). A key idea for social enterprises is to explore and provide innovative solutions to manage complex social problems (Vurro & Perrini, 2006). Social entrepreneurs are seen as the catalysts for social change, as they are capable of combining public, private, and hybrid approaches with the social enterprise model to create new paradigms of social goods and impacts (Nicholls & Cho, 2006). Nevertheless, not all new measures from WISEs are necessarily innovative. WISES identified as introducing social changes in this study must initiate new methods, processes, or standards in their social services, set new benchmarks in the social sector or introduce genuine solutions to solve persistent social problems.

5.1.2.6 *Comparing Mission Achievement across Organisations*

The institutional effectiveness of WISEs under the four models is compared based on social mission accomplishment, defined by the scope and diversity of missions covered by the organisations. This is measured by the high levels of mission completed and the diversity of missions covered within each category level. A higher level of mission achieved means the WISE has deepened its service from basic employment and training to the integrative needs of its users with its surrounding environment, hence expanding its social impact from the individuals to the local communities, or has further projected its influence onto the political leaders in strengthening labour rights, inducing broader policies and social changes upon reaching the highest level. WISEs with higher levels of mission achievement are therefore seen as more effective.

Diversity as a second parameter indicates NGOs' effectiveness and is recognised by studies as 'multiple programmes with multi-pronged approaches' (Mitchell, 2015). The same measurement could also be applied to WISEs. People with disabilities usually require a broad range of support for their employment and development. A higher diversity of service reflects the organisation's capacity in providing an array of services to meet their needs. The scope of mission accomplishment reflects the WISEs' capability in fulfilling a broad base of objectives across the economic, social, and political dimensions.

5.2 Effectiveness of WISEs under the Four Modes of Relationship

5.2.1 *Co-Optation*

Figure 5.1 shows the percentage of mission accomplishment for WISEs under cooptation.

Figure 5.1 shows that the accomplishments focus almost exclusively on service provision. These include providing training for employment skills, cultivating

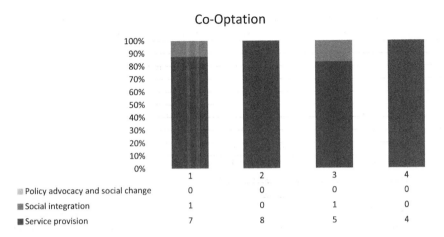

Figure 5.1 Mission Accomplishment (%) for WISEs under Co-Optation

independent living ability, and increasing the members' personal income, sheltered employment, rehabilitation services, and jobs and recruitment services (for all four organisations). Three out of four WISEs (CO1, CO2 and CO3) also offer financial compensation and cover basic social insurance for their members, which is rare among sheltered workshops. Overall, all these WISEs have covered a wide spectrum of basic employment and care services for their members, hence fulfilling their basic duties as WISEs.[3]

However, these WISEs have hardly broached any mission at level 2 and none at level 3. Only CO1 and CO3 had organised some extra activities for their members. For CO1, it was 'taking a walk in the local park' (personal communication with the manager of CO1, November 2016), and for CO3, it was in the form of a group trip organised 'once in a year' (personal communications with the manager of CO3, December 2016). Although these activities promote social integration, they do not involve sufficient interaction with the local communities, and with the reported occurrence rate of occurance, their impact on social integration is assumed to be minimal.

Two members of CO1 were interviewed to solicit their feedback about working in the work-rehabilitation centre (WRC; henceforth user1 and user2). Both members had been working in the centre since it was opened. According to user1, her work was repetitive and demanding. In order to deliver a batch of products on time, the members had to 'sit at the table and work for the entire day, sometimes even staying back after office hours' (personal communication with user2 from CO1, November 2016).

The members worked more slowly than average people due to their disabilities, and according to user1, their workload was heavy:

[T]he work is very stressful to us; I can't feel much joy working here. The workload is heavy and I have to keep myself busy the whole day; if I take time off to drink water, I am behind ... we have no choice because if we can't deliver, the factory can just find someone else and we lose our extra incomes ...

(personal communication, November 2016)

All public-sector WISEs indicated one of their major achievements as increasing the personal income of their members. The members' responses show that this was indeed true and important to them. However, the workload was clearly not tailored to their rehabilitation needs. Also, interviews with the members revealed their dissatisfaction with their pay. The users earned half a cent per bag produced, '*perhaps the lowest in this country*' (personal communication with user1, November 2016).

The pay was similar to the rest of the public-sector WISEs. Interviews with members of CO2 and CO3 reveal that the members were generally paid less than 10 Chinese cents for each item produced manually. While this was partially due to their lack of efficiency and competitiveness, it also showed that these jobs were extremely low in value. As a result, they earned as little as 100 to 200 Chinese Yuan per month with a five-day workweek schedule (personal communication with users of CO1, November 2016). Such findings show that the focus of the WISEs was not to increase personal income. Indeed, CO3's manager confirmed this argument by stating that the paid work was to 'keep them [the members] busy and kill some time' (personal communication with the manager of CO3, December 2016).

The work environment was managed like a factory workshop. The disabled members were divided into different wage categories based on their capabilities and health conditions. They had to report to the centres and check in and out with fixed working hours. According to the interviewees, some of the physically weaker members had difficulty meeting these standards; as a result, their pay was affected. The two members felt 'insulted' by these rules (personal communication with members of CO1, November 2016).

Regarding social activities, extra activities were only organised after work with external social workers; such activities only occurred two to three times a year. Both members were hoping for more outdoor social activities, but both mentioned that improvement would be difficult because 'the teachers' [the managers] had low salaries too (personal communication with members of CO1, November 2016). CO3's manager attested to this as there was 'not enough staff to conduct more activities [for the members]' (personal communication with the manager of CO3, December 2016). Although financial sustainability was never an issue, the use of the budget allocated was inflexible in nature, and they had no discretionary power to hire more staff even when needed. As a result, extra social activities that helped expand the social network of the members were rare.

The interviews indicate that the beneficiaries were not entirely satisfied with the treatments, mostly with the workload, pay, and lack of rehabilitation value the programmes offered. Most of the work was simple and repetitive in nature, offering little personal character development, empowerment, and social inclusion. The members were not formally employed and, therefore, not protected by labour laws and the national social security scheme.

The manager from CO3 highlighted the problem of bureaucracy and lack of clear responsibilities:

> We [the managers] have been working here for ten years; our salaries have not changed much since ... but I don't know who is responsible for this.... When we approached CDPF, they asked us to talk to the subdistrict government, but then the subdistrict government told us it wasn't their responsibility and asked us to go back to CDPF... . I don't even know who is responsible for us.
> (personal communication with the manager of CO3, December 2016)

There is a lack of feedback channels and a clear division of responsibilities within the system. The managers of CO1, CO2, and CO3 all revealed that they had little idea how and where to raise their concerns, so they could not take any active measures to protect their members' welfare. The managers were 'unclear about the status of the organisation' (personal communication with managers of CO1, CO2, and CO3, 2016–2017); they had no idea about the organisation's future direction and development because these things 'depend on the government' (personal communication with managers of CO1 and CO4, 2016–2017). The managers of all WISEs admitted that they had 'never thought about it' (personal communications, 2016–2017). An immediate consequence is that most measures implemented were temporal, and none of the WISEs had planned for long-term benefits for their members, such as more comprehensive social insurance packages or retirement schemes. Clearly, the WISEs' future development depended wholly on the government rather than the strategic direction of their management teams. Unsurprisingly, most of the WISEs focused exclusively on their basic programmes and thought little outside the box to design or suggest measures that cater to the more profound needs of the members.

Since all WRCs have standardised programmes and management structures, the feedback solicited from the interviewed WISEs could be considered as broadly representative. The empirical evidence shows that public-sector WISEs are reliable service providers. With full support from the government, these organisations do not have to compete with other WISEs in the market. Their services are stable and standardised across regions. Since the organisations are operating under the name of the government, there is a low risk of service interruption or budget depletion. The downside is that these WISEs have neither motivation nor capacity to further develop their capacities and upgrade their services to fulfil their members' more sophisticated social and developmental needs. All centres appear to be a monotonous replication of each other within the national social welfare system. The members face the dual problems of social isolation and a lack of participation. It is also interesting to note that although the co-opted WISEs have the closest connections with the government, not one of these organisations has performed at the level of advocacy and social change due to the lack of independent management and the external bureaucracy of the overall system. Despite all their resources and political ties, they have not been able to leverage their ties with the government to optimise their benefits.

5.2.2   *Cooperation*

A distinctive feature of WISEs under cooperation is that while service provision is still the fundamental focus, almost all the WISEs deliver at all three levels of missions, covering a wide array of services at each level (see Figure 5.2). The two exceptional cases, CP2 and CP5, were only established for about two years and are still at their initial stage of development. However, for the majority of the WISEs, service-related activities constitute 30% to 70% of their accomplishments, while social integration accounts for anywhere from 15% to 40%. Level 3 missions make up about 10% to 20% of their total achievement. These WISEs offer standard basic services such as employment skill training, direct job offers, and personal care. All WISEs adopt the model of providing direct employment to socially disadvantaged groups with special arrangements that suit the employee's needs (refer to the Appendix for details).

Also, all the WISEs had accomplished missions at the level of social integration, especially in implementing community integration programmes that boost the beneficiaries' self-esteem. CP2, CP4, and CP7 had organised interest classes such as dancing and reading groups that encouraged the workers to develop their personal talents. CP4, a maid agency, organised public performances for the local

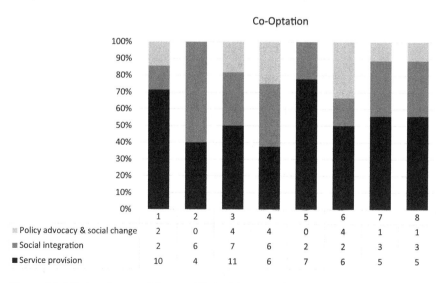

Figure 5.2 Mission Accomplishment (%) for WISEs under Cooperation

residents. CP5 pointed out that it was important to 'make our employees feel useful and needed' (personal communication with the manager, December 2016). In order to achieve this, the WISE tailored all job positions to fit the employees' capabilities. 'We have to assess the needs of our potential employees first and then create jobs that fit their needs' (personal communication with the manager, December 2016). Another emphasis is user participation. For example, CP3 requested that parents participate and contribute to the development programmes for their children and communicated regularly on their progress. The organisation also trained the parents on communication and caring for their children: 'Sometimes we inform the parents about the activities of their children several times a day' (personal communication with the director of CP3, November 2016). Similarly, CP2 and CP4 organised activities based on their members' suggestions: 'when they [the members] want to learn something, they tell us and we make it happen' (personal communication with the manager of CP2, May 2016).

Six out of eight WISEs have stretched beyond social integration towards advocacy and initiating broader social changes. This is a significant achievement. Among them, CP1, CP3, CP4, CP6, and CP8 had collaborated with the government in policy research, open dialogues, and close-door conferences. CP1, CP3, and CP4 submitted a report to the government on the potential development of their social enterprise models. CP4 and CP6 also advocated policy measures and promoted social models that raised the social status of disadvantaged groups and reduced social inequality. The WISEs influenced the government primarily by playing a consultative role with their practical knowledge and first-hand experience about social issues. For example, the founder of CP3 was consulted regularly by the government on relevant new policies before they were announced (personal communication with the director of CP3, November 2016). Through such informal communications, the social entrepreneurs also understood the government's interests better and were able to design programmes that suited the government's needs.

As shown, WISEs that participated in policy advocacy also achieved the mission of promoting their models and setting benchmarks for the sector. CP3 developed its own training curriculum for social workers on work-rehabilitation services (personal communication with the director of CP3, November 2016). CP4 pushed for setting new policy agenda and formalising industrial standards (personal communication, November 2016), and CP6 exported its model to several provinces and mentored other social entrepreneurs using their experience and knowledge (personal communication with the director of CP6, April 2016).

A group of six beneficiaries from CP3 (marked as user1 to user5), who are the parents of the disabled members, were interviewed. All users reported 'significant improvement' in their children's expression, communication skills, and independent living capabilities (phone interviews, November 2016). The organisation provided personal care and rehabilitation and encouraged the members to go out for social activities and work in groups to perform simple daily tasks to train their independent living skills.

It is worth noting that unlike the standardised programmes offered by public-sector WISEs, the director knew the personal character of every member and provided assistance and care based on their individual needs. A user pointed out:

> Our child has aphasia. The teacher designed a programme specifically for him to train his language ability, and he is able to communicate with us in writing now ...
>
> (personal communication with user5 from CP3, November 2016)

The user praised the services from CP3 as being 'highly professional' (personal communication with User5 of CP3, November 2016). The users also recognised that the WISE had spent great effort in promoting social integration for their children. A user mentioned how the WISE had been educating the local communities and taking the members to community activities for social interaction and exposure. The social integration efforts had yielded noticeable effects visible to the parents. A parent reported that his child had gained confidence from the school because 'he has learned that he is not valueless' (personal communication with User1 of CP3, November 2016). Another user's child was placed in an external job position after completing his training in the WISE, and the service was beyond her expectations as she had 'never expected the child to work like a normal person' (personal communication with User2 of CP3, November 2016).

Overall, all five users responded positively regarding their satisfaction with the services (personal communications with users of CP3, November 2016). Four out of five users were highly satisfied with the work-integration services offered. Four out of six users found it 'innovative' (personal communication with users of CP3, November 2013). Three users recognised the social integration effort of the WISE and all five users reported significant improvement in the independence, self-confidence, and social skills of their children (personal communication with users of CP3, November 2013). The responses confirmed the effectiveness of WISE in work-integration missions. The only disadvantage mentioned was the high service fee compared to the free service offered by the public-sector WISEs (personal communication with user3 of CP3, November 2016).

An apparent advantage of the cooperation model is government support. The government is the sole source of political legitimacy in China (Hsu & Hasmath, 2014). All WISEs interviewed had specified that the relationship with the government was one of the determining factors differentiating them from other private players in the WISE sector.[4] This special connection with the government no doubt opens channels for political advocacy since the organisations have higher chances to voice their concerns through informal channels. As the manager of CP6 commented on the role of the organisation in policy-making: 'the relationship is mutually beneficial ... the government needs to see positive examples to guide its public policies' (personal communication with the manager of CP6, April 2016).

5.2.3 Complementarity

Figure 5.3 shows the mission completed by WISEs under complementarity at each level. The WISEs had focused almost exclusively on first- and second-level missions. The most commonly accomplished level 1 missions were direct employment and job skill training, increasing the personal income of the beneficiaries, and developing job positions based on the needs of the disadvantaged workers. These organisations also stressed the importance of user participation and character development for the beneficiaries. Some other level 2 missions attained included building new social relations and networks (CM4, CM5), organising extra social activities (CM4, CM5, CM6), cultivating social adaptation and communication skills (CM1, CM5), and strengthening workers' integration with the community and social environment.

The services offered at the primary level of social missions usually included building supportive work environments and developing job positions based on the needs and skills of the marginalised people. This is not surprising as these WISEs have to generate income through sales of products; hence, it is essential for their business models to suit the needs of their employees. For example, CM1 conducted on-the-job training by breaking down the car-washing process into small and straightforward modular movements so that even people

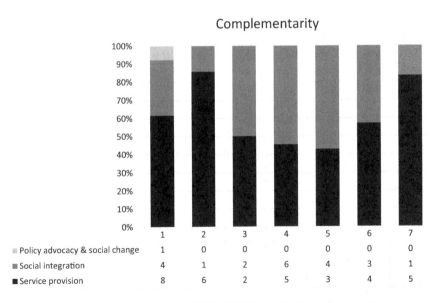

Figure 5.3 Mission Accomplishment (%) for WISEs under Complementarity

with mental disorders could handle the tasks. For CM2, CM3, CM4, and CM6, they offered direct employment and tailored their schedules and tasks to accommodate their members' physical and financial limitations (see the Appendix). CM1 was the only WISE under complementarity involved in advocacy. The social enterprise was invited to produce a report analysing its work-integration model for CDPF and local policy-makers, implying that the organisation had attracted some attention from the local government. However, the political influence of one report was marginal. It could be concluded that the WISEs are far from achieving substantial advocacy or social change.

Three beneficiaries of CM1, who were also the employees' parents, were interviewed to assess the organization's effectiveness from the beneficiaries' perspective. Users reflected that the jobs offered in the WISEs have 'given [the child] confidence', the pay and welfare offered were 'very satisfactory', and the child 'feels at home' in the working environment offered (personal communication with user2, May 2016). All three users of CM1 reported that their children showed improvements in social manners, emotional control, and social communication skills, and all users were fully satisfied with the services offered by the WISE (personal communications, May 2016). It is also noteworthy that these organisations were offering formal contracts and comprehensive social insurance for their employees, which means that workers have full legal protection over their wages and labour rights. This is unusual for WISEs, which usually only provide a minimal income allowance. Although these WISEs are smaller in size (typically ranging from 8 to 30 full-time staff and employees) compared to their peers, they offer better payment schemes and employee benefits in general. This could be a means to building their reputation within their communities.

The WISEs also achieved a high level of user participation, an important feature for social integration. CM1 followed up regularly with the parents on their children's progress at work. The parents were also requested to participate in social activities to understand their children's conditions. The founder also 'attended to all matters personally' (personal communication with users, May 2016) and stressed the importance of 'building self-esteem and personal values' as one of the key missions of the organisation (personal communication with the manager of CM1, December 2016). The organisation focused on creating an open and normal work environment where the employees were 'trained for real-life social skills and interact with clients like in any normal companies' (personal communication, May 2016). Similarly, CM4 also highlighted the importance for their employees to 'feel good about themselves', 'not feeling being discriminated', and 'be proud of their work' (personal communication, September 2016). This bottom-up approach with an emphasis on personal values, development, and empowerment stands out in the interviews with WISEs under the complementarity category.

In general, WISEs under complementarity have fulfilled the fundamental social responsibilities of work-integration organisations. Since the founders themselves are from the same grassroots communities that are marginalised by mainstream society, it is difficult for them to attract public attention and government support, which explains their limited social influence beyond their own communities.

5.2.4 *Competition*

Two WISEs under competition have been included in this study.

Figure 5.4 shows that both COMP1 and COMP2 provided employment-related and social integration services. Both WISEs provided job skills training, direct employment, extra social activities, and personal development programmes. COMP1's basic missions mainly involved providing vocational training, direct employment, consultation, and social insurance for the migrant worker community. For COMP2, the focus was on sheltered employment, building a supportive work environment, and providing work-rehabilitation services and personal care to people with mental disabilities.

Both WISEs demonstrated high user participation, community integration, and network formation. COMP1 emphasised building social networks and fostering the self-esteem of migrant workers. It organised group activities tailored to the developmental and spiritual needs of the migrant workers and provided legal education and consultation on wage and labour rights issues to address their concerns. COMP2 was one of the earliest WISEs that introduced the work-rehabilitation concept to mainland China. Besides basic work-rehabilitation services, the organisation adopted the 'living with local communities' model to promote social integration (personal communications with the manager, January 2017). This means that the members were divided into

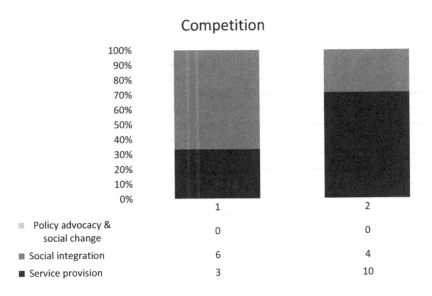

Figure 5.4 Mission Accomplishment (%) for WISEs under Competition

small groups to seek accommodation in the neighbourhood, giving them maximum exposure to normal social lives and interactions (personal communication, January 2017). Neither organisation touched anything at the level of policy advocacy and social change. They also had little engagement with the local government and received limited support from it.

A group interview was conducted with two beneficiaries from COMP2. The organisation consists of several individual units, including a farm, a bakery shop, and a sheltered workshop. Both beneficiaries were working as full-time employees for the bakery shop. According to these beneficiaries, the WISE offered a safe and semi-open work environment. Socialising with people was possible without causing too much stress to the employees. Both beneficiaries indicated that the workload was manageable, and the workplace offered sufficient security and protection against discrimination (personal communication, January 2017). They were also satisfied with the wage, security and support received from the organisation.

In general, both organisations provided suitable employment and social integration services to their beneficiaries. COMP2 reported that its financial difficulty was usually caused by 'conflict between its economic and social missions' (personal communication with manager of COMP2, January 2017). The organisation needed to balance managing members' stress levels and supervising them in their work tasks. It also accepted people with serious mental disabilities that were rejected by other forms of WISEs, demonstrating its priority of putting social missions first.

5.3   Comparison across the Four Modes of Relationship

It has been shown that the four modes of state–WISE relationship vary in effectiveness, and this observation is reflected in their ability and capacity to complete different levels of social mission. Figure 5.2 displayed the number of social missions accomplished for each of the four state-WISEs categories. For a more detailed comparison, the level of mission achievement is divided into three levels: high (H), medium (M) and low (L). The levels are obtained by calculating the median scores of all WISEs under a specific mode of relationship[5] under a representative code and followed by taking the average for a final score under a particular first-level parameter of measurement. A final score between 0 and 0.34 is indicated as 'L', between 0.35 and 0.69 is indicated as 'M', and between 0.7 and 1.0 is indicated as 'H'. Table 5.2 summarises the level of mission achievement for WISEs under all four models.

The table shows that WISEs under co-optation are ranked highly for all basic service functions that they provide to disabled members but are low on all other mission accomplishments. This demonstrates that the public-sector WISEs are achievers in fulfilling the basic needs of the beneficiaries in the employment market. Since they are backed by the state, they offer the best social welfare protection for their members compared to their private counterparts. However, WISEs from the private and the third sector only offer these packages to their full-time employees.

Table 5.2 Mission Accomplishment for the Four Modes of State–WISE Relationship

Social Missions	First Level of Parameters	Co-Optation	Cooperation	Complementarity	Competition
Level I: Service Provision	Provide rehabilitation services	H	L	L	M
	Provide employment services	M	H	M	M
	Provide basic social security and welfare	H	H	H	M
Level II: Social Integration and Network Formation	Empowerment of beneficiaries	L	L	M	M
	Social training and personal development	L	H	M	M
	Social relations and network formation	L	H	L	H
Level III: Policy Advocacy and Social Change	Participate in policy advocacy	L	M	L	L
	Promote positive social values	L	M	L	L
	Promote social change	L	M	L	L

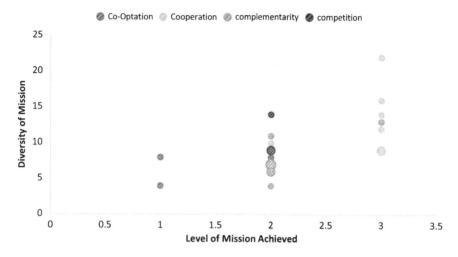

Figure 5.5 Comparing Mission Accomplishment of WISEs across Four Relationships

Figure 5.5 compares the mission accomplishment of all WISEs along the two dimensions of total level of mission covered and mission diversity within a specific level. WISEs under cooperation relations have achieved the highest mission levels and have demonstrated a higher diversity of accomplished missions in comparison to their peers. This shows that WISEs under the cooperation model are more effective in terms of achieving multiple levels of missions and offering a wider range of services. In comparison, there is no significant difference in levels of mission accomplishment for WISEs under both complementarity and competition relations, while the ones under competition in general, demonstrate higher diversity for services offered. Finally, the co-opted WISEs have covered a rather limited range of services, even at the primary level. As government-run organisations, these WISEs are not considered effective based on the mission accomplishment model.

WISEs under the cooperation relationship perform adequately well under all categories. They cover a variety of employment and welfare-related and socially integrative measures. The organisations also perform reasonably well in policy advocacy, promoting positive social values and social changes. It proves that informal social connections between organisational leaders and the party state are key resources for organisations to influence policy implementation and advance their missions (Swanson, Kuhn, & Xu, 2001).[6]

WISEs under the complementarity and the competition relations models are comparable along all three levels of social missions. Both perform decently at levels one and two of social missions with 'Medium' to 'High' achievements. Again, the 'Low' ranking with rehabilitation services for WISEs under complementarity is due to the comparatively larger sample size and lower ratio of rehabilitation service provisions. Note that while both groups of WISEs have taken into account their employees' empowerment and personal development, the WISEs under the complementarity model are underperforming at both social relations and network formation, while those under the competition model prioritise them. Last but not least, both groups are low on all missions concerning policy advocacy and social change due to their resource and political constraints.

This chapter has shown that all WISEs have achieved their production objectives in terms of providing competent social services to their targeted social groups. However, their institutional effectiveness differs mostly along the social and political dimensions. WISEs under co-optation are confined to their basic functions as service providers; those under cooperation demonstrate higher capacity and competency in attaining their social missions and exerting political influence. WISEs under complementarity and competition perform adequately in social work integration but have little political influence. WISEs under the cooperation, complementarity and competition modes perform adequately well for level 2 missions, but the cooperation mode is low on empowerment and the complementarity mode, on network formation. The opinions of the beneficiaries under all four relationships confirm these variations in their performances. Upon establishing the link between the modes of relationship and their corresponding institutional effectiveness, the next chapter discusses the relevant factors and mechanisms.

Notes

1 The policy document is available at http://www.ndrc.gov.cn/fzgggz/fzgh/ghwb/gjjgh/200709/P020150630514120025377.pdf
2 Available at http://www.gov.cn/jrzg/2011-06/08/content_1879697.htm
3 Refer to the Appendix for details.
4 None of the WISEs mentioned any negative political constraints imposed on them. Either the adverse effect is limited or it is rarely discussed by social enterprises.
5 A score of 1 is given to a mission attained by an organisation, whereas a score of 0 is given to the organisation for failing to attain a specific mission.
6 It is worth noting that WISEs under cooptation and cooperation are both low in terms of employee empowerment. Both types of WISE seldom work in the areas of civil rights and legal consultations, neither do they evince high user participation in agenda and programme setting. Most of the policy advocacy actions of the WISEs aim to inculcate problem-solving skills for and improve the economic situation of the socially marginalised people.

References

Battilana, J., & Lee, M. (2014, February 11). Advancing research on hybrid organizing – Insights from the study of social enterprises. *The Academy of Management Annals*, *8*(1), 397–441. https://doi.org/10.1080/19416520.2014.893615
Bidet, E. (2008, July). *The rise of work integration and social enterprise in South Korea*. Paper presented at the 2d EMES-ISTR International Conference, Barcelona, Spain.
Bode, I., Evers, A., & Schulz, A. (2002). *Work integration social enterprises in Germany. Trends and Issues, Liège (EMES Working Papers, no. 02/04)* Quelle. www.emes.net/en/recherche/perse/index.php

Borzaga, C., & Defourny, J. (2001). *Conclusions: Social Enterprises in Europe: A Diversity of Initiatives and Prospects*. Routledge.

Cooney, K. (2015). *Social Enterprise in the United States: WISEs and Other Worker-Focused Models* (ICSEM Working Papers No. 09, Issue). http://iap-socent.be/sites/default/files/USA%20-%20Cooney.pdf

Davister, C., Defourny, J., & Grégoire, O. (2004). Work integration social enterprises in the European Union: an overview of existing models. *Revue Internationale de l'Économie Sociale: Recma, 293*, 24–50.

Defourny, J., & Nyssens, M. (2010a, March 22). Conceptions of social enterprise and social entrepreneurship in Europe and the United States: Convergences and divergences. *Journal of Social Entrepreneurship, 1*(1), 32–53. https://doi.org/10.1080/19420670903442053

Defourny, J., & Nyssens, M. (2010b). Social enterprise in Europe: At the crossroads of market, public policies and third sector. *Policy and Society, 29*(3), 231–242. https://doi.org/10.1016/j.polsoc.2010.07.002

Defourny, J., & Nyssens, M. (2017). Fundamentals for an international typology of social enterprise models. *Voluntas: International Journal of Voluntary and Nonprofit Organizations, 28*(6), 2469–2497. https://doi.org/10.1007/s11266-017-9884-7

Duff, R. R. (2008). Social enterprise as a socially rational business. *International Journal of Entrepreneurial Behavior & Research, 14*(5), 291–312. https://doi.org/10.1108/13552550810897669

Ebrahim, A., Battilana, J., & Mair, J. (2014). The governance of social enterprises: Mission drift and accountability challenges in hybrid organizations. *Research in Organizational Behavior, 34*, 81–100. https://doi.org/10.1016/j.riob.2014.09.001

Evers, A. (1995, July). Part of the welfare mix: The third sector as an intermediate area. *Voluntas, 6*(2), 159–182. https://doi.org/10.1007/BF02353995

Fong, C. W. (2014). *Social values and norms for inclusiveness: A report on dialogues among community leaders*. http://lkyspp2.nus.edu.sg/ips/wp-content/uploads/sites/2/2013/10/WF_Community-Leaders-Dialogue-Report_280116.pdf

Grégoire, O., Campi, S., & Defourny, J. (2006). *Work Integration Social Enterprises: Are They Multiplegoal and Multi-stakeholder Organizations?* Routledge. http://books.google.com/books?hl=en&lr=&id=u6Z_AgAAQBAJ&oi=fnd&pg=PA29&dq=Aiken+(social+enterprise)&ots=tEfAUT04H5&sig=AuoDZQj-apdPThgb7vLxM-BxRdM

Ho, A. P.-Y., & Chan, K.-T. (2010, January 5). The social impact of work-integration social enterprise in Hong Kong. *International Social Work, 53*(1), 33–45. https://doi.org/10.1177/0020872809348950

Hsu, J. Y. J., & Hasmath, R. (2014). The local corporatist state and NGO relations in China. *Journal of Contemporary China, 23*(87), 516–534.

Hulgård, L. (2014). Social enterprise and the third sector: Innovative service delivery or a non-capitalist economy. In J. Defourny, L. Hulgård, & V. Pestoff (Eds.), *Social Enterprise and the Third Sector: Changing European landscapes in a comparative perspective* (pp. 66–84). Routledge.

Kuosmanen, J. (2014). Care provision, empowerment, and market forces: The art of establishing legitimacy for Work Integration Social Enterprises (WISEs). *VOLUNTAS: International Journal of Voluntary and Nonprofit Organisations, 25*(1), 248–269. https://doi.org/10.1007/s11266-012-9340-7

Mitchell, G. E. (2015). The attributes of effective NGOs and the leadership values associated with a reputation for organizational effectiveness. *Nonprofit Management and Leadership, 26*(1), 39–57. https://doi.org/10.1002/nml.21143

Nicholls, A., & Cho, A. H. (2006). Social entrepreneurship: The structuration of a field. *Social Entrepreneurship: New Models of Sustainable Social Change, 34*(4), 99–118.

Sanders, M. L., & McClellan, J. G. (2013). Being business-like while pursuing a social mission: Acknowledging the inherent tensions in US nonprofit organizing. *Organization, 21*(1), 68–89. https://doi.org/10.1177/1350508412464894

Stevens, R., Moray, N., & Bruneel, J. (2015). The social and economic mission of social enterprises: Dimensions, measurement, validation, and relation. *Entrepreneurship Theory and Practice*, 1042–2587. https://doi.org/10.1111/etap.12091

Swanson, K. E., Kuhn, R. G., & Xu, W. (2001). Environmental policy implementation in rural China: A case study of Yuhang, Zhejiang. *Environmental Management, 27*(4), 481–491. https://doi.org/10.1007/s002670010164

Vidal, I., & Claver, N. (2004). *Work Integration Social Enterprises in Spain.* https://www.researchgate.net/profile/Isabel_Martinez12/publication/253653151_WORK_INTEGRATION_SOCIAL_ENTERPRISES_IN_SPAIN/links/53f78f290cf2823e5bd97ce6.pdf

Vurro, C., & Perrini, F. (2006). Social entrepreneurship: Innovation and social change across theory and practice. *Social Entrepreneurship, 23*(1), 57–85.

Wilkinson, C., Medhurst, J., Henry, N., Wihlborg, M., & Braithwaite, B. W. (2014). A map of social enterprises and their eco-systems in Europe: Executive summary. *ICF Consulting Services, European Commission*, 1–16.

Yip, K. (2005). Vocational Rehabilitation for Persons with Mental Illness in the People's Republic of China. *Administration and Policy in Mental Health and Mental Health Services Research, 34*(1), 80–85. https://doi.org/10.1007/s10488-005-0007-1

6 Resource Transfer as a Political Strategy

Introduction

It has been shown that there is a difference in the categorisation of the state–work-integration social enterprise (WISE) relations, and not all WISEs are entitled to the same amount of legitimacy and resources from the state. The attention and support received from the state largely depend on their relationships with the state, thus raising questions on the purposes for these different modes of relationships and what the relevant selection criteria are, in the eyes of the state. The author proposes that the Chinese state engages the WISEs with the tactic of 'resource privilege'. The modes of relationship between the Chinese state and the WISEs reflect the political strategies in selecting qualified partners in social service provision by dominating the organisations' accessibility to political, economic, and social resources.

This chapter analyses the dynamic interaction between the state and the WISEs in order to understand how their relationship leads to different levels of mission accomplishment and social effectiveness of the WISEs. The key argument is that the strategy and behaviour of the state, reflected in its relationship with the WISEs, and the subsequent privilege for resources transfer lead to different levels of mission accomplishment of the WISEs. The state selects its legitimate partners from the service sector based on two major criteria, social stability and economic rationality, assessed through its mutual communication with WISEs and its understanding of them. Social entrepreneurs having informal engagements with the state benefit from advantages in both aspects since they are better trusted by the state, therefore gaining access to all three types of resource privileges—financial support, political legitimacy, and access to a bigger social network—even before they demonstrate their efficacy. Privilege in resource transfer as a strategic preference of the state is correlated to the organisation's capacity for mission achievement. This chapter further argues that the institutional features and effectiveness of the WISEs are constrained by their social positioning, which is linked to the strategic interaction they have with the state.

DOI: 10.4324/9781003231677-6

6.1 State–WISE Relationship as a Political Strategy

To prove that the four modes of relationship are a strategy of the Chinese state, they have to fulfil two conditions. First, the relationships have to demonstrate some identifiable and consistent patterns, and second, the state's strategic preference has to be logically explicable with some clear criteria that divide the organisations apart in terms of resource transfer from the state to the organisations. The second condition is added to prevent reverse causation: the first condition could be counter-argued that the resource transfer results from the relationships; however, this counter-argument will not stand if the resource transfer is, in fact, privileges granted by the state to the WISEs based on certain criteria and if they occur before or at the beginning of the relationships. The fulfilment of both conditions would indicate that the four modes of relationships are the consequences of explicit and consistent strategies of the state to manage the WISE sector.

6.1.1 Privilege as a Political Instrument

6.1.1.1 Resource as a Privilege

Hsu and Hasmath (2014) define 'privilege' granted to non-governmental organisations (NGOs) as the delegation of authority for them to bridge the society and the state in meditating social issues and voicing collective concerns. The establishment and activities of NGOs are usually seen as within the rights of citizens in civil society. However, as Fisher (1996) points out, in many Asian countries, permission from the state and the benefits that come with it are often viewed as 'privileges' rather than rights (Fisher et al., 1996). If the state sees social organisations as a 'transmission belt' (Hsia & White, 2002:4) for its policies, it would only grant access to certain organisations at its discretion. These include government purchases, subsidies, and tax benefits (Fisher et al., 1996).

An added layer of complexity includes the non-monetary support from the government, which might come as privileged statuses such as the permission to operate (Ma, 2002) and the right to engage in certain activities or form collaborative relationships (Najam, 1996). As Townsend and Townsend (2004) claim, partnerships construct 'in a context of power and domination which privileges official discourse(s) over others' (Edwards, Goodwin, Pemberton, & Woods, 2001:293). Hsu and Hasmath describe state–third-sector organisation (TSO) partnerships as a strategy to develop stronger ties selectively with social organisations and to exclude organisations that fail to fulfil their political obligations (Hsu & Hasmath, 2014).

In exchange for this privilege of manoeuvre, the TSOs are obligated to act in accordance with the political interests of the state (Fisher et al., 1996). Najam describes this phenomenon as an NGO–patron relationship (Najam, 1996). Najam (1996) argues that donors may assert financial control by linking conditions and purposes to their funds. Funds might be allocated to the NGOs only when they are committed to the policy goals attached to fund disbursement. Failing to fulfil written obligations with the consequences leading to the withdrawal of support from the patron as 'penalty' is an indicator of patronage (Najam, 1996). The situation of the WISEs fits this description with the disproportional number of resources being transferred. It is logical to deduce that the Chinese state has strategic preferences in supporting the development of the WISE sector. Its choice involves necessary conditions that the WISEs must fulfil in order to be selected as collaborative partners of the state.

These organisations must adhere to the state's political agenda. According to Hsia and White III (2002), this is a strategic move to create vertical control that prevents the formation of a horizontal social matrix of collective class interests. The chosen social organisations would therefore gain a disproportionate amount of power and resources over organisations excluded from these privileges (Hsia & White, 2002), and this specific resource allocation would make them powerful entities for top-down management and control.

6.1.2   Three Forms of Privilege

Since effective and sustainable commercial activities, as well as business models, are fundamental to the survival and development of social enterprises, privileges are in the form of enhancing the competitiveness of these organisations. There are three different resource privileges that the state has granted to WISEs via both formal and informal engagements, and these three forms each reflect the economic, political, and social dimensions of resource transfer. These are the privileges of financial support, legitimacy, and network accessibility.

Table 6.1 summarises how the resource transfer is distributed based on state–WISE relationships. WISEs that receive stronger and more extensive economic and legitimacy support from the government are expected to be bigger in scale. This is consistent with the empirical observations[1] (Table 6.1).

6.1.2.1   Economic Resources

Studies have shown that non-profit organisations perceive funding as their primary resource of interest (Wei, 2017). The various factors of production provided to non-profit organisations increase their productivity, competitiveness, and capacities in the social goods and services sector (Chung, Färe, & Grosskopf, 1997; Maskell, 1999; Sealey & Lindley, 1977). Transfers in economic resources include comprehensive physical, financial, and human resources contributing to the production of goods and services. As shown in the table, the relevant measures include various forms of financial incentives such as grants and subsidies, administrative assistance, contractual partnerships, tax policies, business contracts, and human and technical support that aim to increase revenue or reduce the financial burden for these organisations.

Table 6.1 Factors of Resource Privileges and the Four Modes of Relationship

		Resource Privileges		
		Economic Support	*Legitimacy*	*Access to Social Network*
Mode of Relationships	Co-Optation	Direct funding, subsidies, and allowances Project referrals Social insurance Management and recruitment	Legitimacy as public-sector agencies	Isolated from social network
	Cooperation	Subsidies, grants, and sponsorships Public–private partnership and co-management of projects Government procurement for services and products Tax exemption	Government affiliation Host for party agencies Government endorsement for services and products Former government official joined as shareholders	Business and social partner referrals Information sharing Provide networking platforms
	Complementary	Limited grants and subsides (for NGOs)	Some receive service awards	Nil
	Competition	Limited government procurement	Some receive service awards	Nil

Note: NGO = non-governmental organisation.

Economic assistance is considered a powerful policy tool since the state has an advantage in its treatment of financial issues (Billis & Glennerster, 1998). The direct provision of economic resources lifts financial constraints for the WISEs so that they gain a significant advantage over their private-sector counterparts in the social welfare sector. Formal economic support is also included as a strategy preference of the Chinese state in managing WISEs because the strength and extent of such support were distinctive across various categories of the state–WISE relationships despite the existence of constitutionalised channels which suggests that in theory, support is open to all qualified legal social organisations. As shown in the earlier empirical section, this selection process involves various forms of priority arrangements and special considerations, which primarily depend on the relationship between the WISEs and the local government.

6.1.2.2   Formal Legitimacy

Legitimacy is a perception that 'actions of an entity are desirable, proper, or appropriate within some socially constructed system of norms, values, beliefs and definitions' (Suchman 1995:74). Two forms of organisational legitimacy include formal-procedural legitimacy based on the cultural phenomena and definitive values of the organisation and substantive-purposive legitimacy substantiated by the accomplishment of socially accepted moral values (Flathman, 2017). Kuosmanen (2014) defines these two forms of legitimacy as pragmatic and moral legitimacy, leveraging on utility performance and social values creation, respectively.

There is a widespread concern, especially in developing countries, that NGOs are operating on purse strings considerations rather than by what is appropriate for the beneficiaries (Zaidi, 1999). In the West, where the NGOs are exposed to public scrutiny and inspection by the stakeholders (Conger & Kanungo, 1988; Pierre, 2000), the two types of legitimacy should be mutually enhancing. The accountability of NGOs can be reinforced by their effective performance and social mission accomplishments (Atack, 1999). In China, where the reporting system for NGO transparency is still underdeveloped, the role of the public is largely undermined (Ho, 2001). State–NGO relations in this context is, fundamentally, a question regarding the right of the organisations to be involved in fulfilling public responsibilities, particularly with actions such as organising people, allocating resources, and asserting leadership— behaviours that involve sharing power with the state (Bratton, 1989). When people believe the state has the ultimate responsibility and power in dealing with social problems, association with the state will enhance the symbolic power of the organisation, hence boosting its legitimacy and ability to harness and exploit resources (Hasmath & Hsu, 2016).

Legitimacy is particularly crucial for social enterprises because of their involvement in economic activities (Burt, 2007; Dart, 2004; Smith, Gonin, & Besharov, 2013; Zainon et al., 2014). Sometimes, the clients and beneficiaries are from different social groups, in other cases, the beneficiaries have to pay for the goods and services received. The overlapping roles and multiple goals of stakeholders make them more prone to conflict of interests (Arnesen & Peters, 2018; Smith et al., 2013). Since most WISEs are serving for the benefit of their members or for specific communities, accountability and legitimacy are key issues (Atack, 1999). As shown in the empirical section, the state strengthens the formal legitimacy of the WISEs through partnership collaborations, designations, staff appointments, and awards.

6.1.2.3 *Access to Social Network*

A social network can be interpreted as the sum of interpersonal and social relationships based on trust (Kadushin, 2012; Welter & Kautonen, 2005). It assists in winning support, mobilising resources, gaining legitimacy, and exerting influence for enterprise development (Welter & Kautonen, 2005). In China, social networks are fundamental to economic transactions and societal changes because many interactions involved in this process rely on interpersonal relationships (*Guanxi*), institutional structures, and the distribution power associated with them (Carlisle & Flynn, 2005; Gold, Guthrie, & Wank, 2002; Lin & Si, 2010; Wiegel & Bamford, 2015). Social networks are closely related to resource advantage, as the latter leads to comparative advantage in marketplace positions (Zietlow, 2001). The survival and development of small and medium-sized enterprises (SMEs) depend on their ability to compete in the market (Markelova et al., 2009). In this process, 'barriers to market access' are major obstacles that need to be broken through for enterprises to earn their incomes. It is possible for organisations to enjoy resource advantages, but without access to broader networks, their growth potential and social impact would be impeded.

Access to social networks is crucial for social enterprises because these organisations inherently involve multiple stakeholders from the public, private, and third sectors (Mason, Kirkbride, & Bryde, 2007; Ramus & Vaccaro, 2014). Their spheres of activity inevitably require the participation of different social groups and communities, and this cannot be realised without a network of stakeholders. This is particularly true in China where social networks, or relationships and connections (*Guanxi*), are recognised as crucial factors contributing to business success (Carlisle & Flynn, 2005; Fock & Woo, 1998; Lin & Si, 2010; Wiegel & Bamford, 2015). In China, the government remains the biggest and most dominant player in all economic sectors. It connects the social enterprise to its network by referring third-party partners, members, and users to the organisation, providing a credible social platform for networking, promoting the organisation publicly, and sharing relevant information. Sometimes, individual governors may even act as shareholders for the organisation, and the organisation will get to benefit from their personal network. Government officials also tend to protect particular organisations from economic harm if they have strong ties with the leaders (Swanson, Kuhn, and Xu, 2001). Therefore, deep and

Table 6.2 Level of Privilege Received and Mission Accomplishment for Four Modes of Relationship

		Co-Optation	*Cooperation*	*Complementarity*	*Competition*
Type of Privilege	Economic resources	H	H	L	L
	Legitimacy	H	H	L	L
	Access to social network	L	H	L	L
Level of social mission attained		I	I, II, III	I, II	I, II

extensive social connections are advantageous for organisations competing for clients in the market.

6.1.3 *Linking Resource Privilege with Mission Accomplishment*

The privileges are divided into high and low levels in Table 6.2 based on the intensity and consistency of the support to illustrate how the privileges are related to their level of mission accomplishment. For example, in a cooperative relationship, the level of support is high because of the large scale of funds in the form of procurement and tax reliefs involved. However, WISEs under complementarity and competition receive low levels of resource transfer from the government since the support is limited in scale or random.

State support can be divided into either active or passive approaches. 'Activeness' is defined as the state taking coherent developmental efforts to support the organisations (Bloom & Tang, 1999; Evans, 1996), whereas 'passiveness' refers to the absence of such efforts. It has been shown that the state has taken an active approach towards WISEs under co-optation and cooperation. WISEs, under these two modes of relationship, receive a considerable number of resources through various channels while WISEs under complementarity and competition receive rather generic and limited support. The state recognises their legal existence but has done little to promote their development (Table 6.2).

WISEs under cooperation score high on all three forms of privilege showing that they have received the most comprehensive support from the state. Unsurprisingly, they also achieve a broad scope of missions covering all three levels. The government provides resources, strengthens legitimacy, and connects organisations to social networks that expedite their growth.

However, while the state has taken an active role in both co-optation and cooperation, the co-opted WISEs have not performed beyond their basic roles as service providers. The difference between co-optation and cooperation is that WISEs under co-optation are not connected to either the private or the third sector. The table shows that resources from the state to the WISEs are divided depending on their relationships.

6.1.4 *The Strategic Criteria of the State*

Based on the attributes of the relationships and patterns revealed from the empirical data, the author proposes two underlying criteria for the state's strategy of selecting its collaborative partners in ways that address the political concern of social stability and the economic concern about the social effectiveness of the Chinese state. The first argument is that informal institutions strengthen trust between the state and the organisations and give the former a better understanding of the social activities and political nature of the latter; hence, the state is more likely to collaborate with them. The second argument is that when informal engagement is absent, such as WISEs under complementarity, the state would apply a 'probationary period' to assess the WISEs in order to make effective collaboration decisions.

6.1.4.1 *Social Stability and Economic Rationality as Two Major Concerns*

Huang (2012) argues that the Chinese authoritarian regime's strategy for social welfare reform is 'economic growth with social stability' (Huang, 2012:61). This identifies social stability and economic rationality as two major concerns for the Chinese state when it picks its partners from the private and the third sector. Since the 'privilege' from the state is only granted to certain organisations, it is intuitive to deduce that they must satisfy certain criteria of the state. The political aspect is based on the state's strong desire for social stability in China (Hsu & Hasmath, 2014). Following Hsu and Hasmath's (2014) argument, the state collaborates with social organisations which it understands better in terms of their nature and activities—in other words, when the state perceives the organisations as effective, reliable, and desirable partners both politically and economically. Since partnering up with WISEs inevitably involves power delegation, it is important for the state to understand and trust their political nature and goals before rendering support.

The second condition is derived from policy-making in the public domain: one primary consideration for public policy planning is always economic efficiency (Friedmann, 1987; Innes & Booher, 2010). Government procurement and partnerships are essentially policy tools that help reduce the financial burden and political flaws of the state by utilising the knowledge, skills, and private assets of social partners (Georghiou, Edler, Uyarra, & Yeow, 2014; Kindornay et al., 2014; Selsky, 2005). Economic efficiency is also one of the three basic characteristics of an effective government procurement system (Thai & Grimm, 2000).[2] Even with its unique political concerns, the Chinese state would pursue good practices in government procurement based on economic principles (Chou, 2006). This means that the state will only 'invest' into a collaborative relationship when it makes both political and economic sense to do so, expressed in reality as whether the state fully understands the practices and the nature of the WISE and if the developmental or social values of the WISE justify its cost to the state.

Evidence shows that the first criterion can be satisfied when mutual trust is established through ongoing interaction via informal ties and communications between the organisation and the state. The second criterion explains the performance-based selection strategy of the state. They conjointly explain the strategic preference of the state in selecting WISEs as its social service partners.

6.1.4.2   *The Role of Informal Ties*

Informal institutions refer to North's (1991) idea of 'humanly devised constraints that structure political and social interaction' (p. 97). Studies found that in China, social welfare preferences are made through both formal and informal channels (Huang, 2012). How government agencies and non-profits interact both formally and informally in myriad ways to provide public goods and services has been discussed extensively in the literature (Gazley, 2008; Huang, 2012; Wang, 2016). Some scholars see informal relationships as manipulation and control by the Chinese state over social organisations (Hsu & Hasmath, 2014; Lin & Si, 2010; Spires, Tao, & Chan, 2014).

Where political issues are a concern, the state relies on informal strategies to understand the background and motivation of the NGOs (Hsu & Hasmath, 2014). According to Hsu and Hasmath (2014), the tactic of selective privilege is employed due to 'insufficient epistemic awareness' (p. 936) of the state about the activities and interests of the NGOs; otherwise, the state would have a strong desire to collaborate with NGOs. What is important here is the 'perceived threat' (Najam, 2000:10) towards the NGOs. Theoretically, scholars concord that trust is crucial to collaborative service delivery (Edelenbos & Klijn, 2007; Klijn, Edelenbos, & Steijn, 2010a; Klijn, Steijn, & Edelenbos, 2010b; Romzek, LeRoux, & Blackmar, 2012), as it is a 'safeguard' that enhances cooperative outcomes, especially in complex public–private partnerships and cross-sector networks (Edelenbos & Klijn, 2007, 2016). Since communication is the precursor to trust (Morgan & Hunt, 1994), ongoing informal exchanges based on shared interests enhance trust and common values between collaborative parties and facilitate smooth collaborative actions (Gillespie & Mann, 2004; Romzek et al., 2012).

If the preceding argument is true, one would expect that WISEs having informal ties with the government also have a higher chance to enter collaborative partnerships with it. Informal ties should occur before the formation of a partnership, which would make it an antecedent rather than a consequence of the partnership. Both propositions have been proven to be true by the data. WISEs under cooperation indeed have a higher chance to be considered for financial schemes and partnerships. They also initiate innovative pilot projects and take part in policy agenda discussions with the government.

As further evidence illustrates, the central role of trust as a core factor has been mentioned repeatedly by the WISEs. The director of CP1 explained how their collaboration with the government was formed based on trust: '[T]he government trusted us ... that is why they chose to support us' (personal communication, December 2016). The director of CP3 also identified trust from the government as an advantage over other social organisations: 'Government purchased from us ... because it trusted us' (personal communication with director of CP3, November 2016). Both CP3 and CP6 mentioned that the government would only purchase services from trusted organisations (personal communication with CP3 and CP6, 2016).

Case studies of WISEs that have successfully secured collaborative arrangements with the state show that formal and informal engagements occur interdependently with one another in this process. For example, the founder of CP3 was advised and assisted by the government official to set up the WISE. During the setting up process, the China Disabled Persons' Federation (CDPF) provided consultation on how the WISE should provide its services and incorporated it as its affiliated unit, which further strengthened the formal engagements between the two parties (personal communication with manager of CP3, November 2016). Hence, the WISE provided services that the CDPF could not provide to its registered members because of bureaucratic or financial constraints. Similarly, CP4 was collaborating with the provincial government with which the founder had built personal connections from previous projects. The relationship facilitated smooth communication that helped formalise the model into an enterprise (personal communication with manager of CP4, November 2016).

Both WISEs started with informal communications with the government while developing their innovative ideas into organisations with the help of various partnership schemes. As mentioned in Chapter 4, this pattern was observed for all WISEs under cooperation with the government. In all cases, there was an informal engagement prior to the establishment of the organisations. Access to resources was granted at the start or shortly after the formation of the social enterprises. This differed completely from the treatment towards WISEs under complementarity and competition, which showed that the prior informal engagements had encouraged these contractual collaborations. It is therefore rational to conclude that the connections observed are not a consequence of the contractual relationships but rather that the government preferred to collaborate with these organisations because of these precedent informal interactions.

These instances show that the informal linkages with the government not only construct a private channel of communication between the social entrepreneurs and the government officials but also function as a mechanism for the state to select desirable partners. It ensures that only organisations that share common goals and values of the government gain the special status and the privilege that comes along with it. It also ensures that the right signals can be sent to the government so that the trust is not deterred by information asymmetry between the two partners. As a result, those WISEs with strong government ties are also the same organisations that get to develop and scale up their goods and service production rapidly to become local leaders in the sector.

6.1.4.3 *Selection Based on Economic Rationality*

Much like the traditional NGO sector, most social enterprises are grassroots organisations set up by ordinary citizens without extravagant political and market capital (Hsu, 2010). The majority of the WISEs do not meet the criteria for being strategic partners of the state and are outsiders to the formal 'corporatism' system managed by the state. The empirical evidence showed that most of these WISEs are, by nature, self-organised mutual aid societies, namely organisations that are self-organised and provide exclusive benefits to their own communities. Since the founders of the WISEs and their members are from the same communities, they face common problems and challenges. Social enterprises are set up by social entrepreneurs to provide innovative solutions to the essential issues that they and their peers have to deal with, such as basic needs for employment, security, and personal development.

A dialogue between the manager of CM1 and a local government official confirmed that the government has an open and welcoming attitude towards collaboration with the independent WISEs as the government was 'constantly seeking good projects'. The official expressed the possibility of future collaborations in the form of partial subsidies and service procurement 'if the organisation has proven its value' (personal communication, May 2016). The 'value' in this case means the performance of the organisation, both in terms of the validity of the business model and social effectiveness. The official also explained that the government had already purchased several social projects and was keen to continue, but 'it [the government] is very careful [in offering financial subsidies and forming partnerships]'. In terms of the conditions for this observation, 'the government would only consider purchasing services when things would be taken good care of, and [the organisation] have already shown some effectiveness and future potential' (personal communication with government official, May 2016). Basically, the organisation has to reach a certain stage of self-sustainability and social performance before the government steps in. This is confirmed from the perspective of the WISEs. As CM5's manager mentioned, 'We have to perform well in the market before we could negotiate with the government for more resources' (personal communication with manager of CM5, May 2016). The manager from CM1 shared the same view, 'the government is watching [us] … it would support us if we can prove to them that our model is effective' (personal communication with manager of CM1, May 2016). This WISE had its rental cost subsidised eight months into its operation after it gained a reputation among the users in job training and social integration (personal communication with manager of CM1, May 2016).

The governmental strategy revealed by the governor was based on a combination of political trust and cost–benefit analysis or economic rationality. The government is enforcing a 'probationary period' during which the economic performance and social behaviour of the WISEs are being observed and accessed. Only WISEs showing efficiency, consistency, and social potential would be considered as future partners of the government. This criterion only applies to WISEs under complementarity (and maybe competition) categories. Contrarily, the other two relationship models; namely cooperation and co-optation do not have to get through the same observation and assessment before being granted the privilege to resources. In general, WISEs under the complementarity category seem to be on the periphery of the work-integration system that the government is strategically promoting as a means for providing services and employment to socially marginalised groups. With the government's risk-averse approach, organisations have to find their own way through the initial stage of development before they could expect any tangible support from the government.

6.2   The Social Roles of WISEs

It has already been established that the WISEs differ in their capability in mission accomplishment as a direct consequence and implication of the strategic manoeuvre of the state. This is achieved through the distribution of the different forms of privilege in resource transfers, and the selection criteria of the state have been explained. However, this still does not fully explain the variations in effectiveness among the four relationship categories. The author further argues that the mission focus of the four types of WISEs is fundamentally differentiated by their social roles in the work-integration sector, which is determined by their institutional nature. To understand and explain the institutional effectiveness of WISEs in China thoroughly, one has to investigate in depth the structural factors behind their performances. The following sections explain the differences among WISEs under the four categories of relationship by looking into their fundamental social roles and structural constraints.

6.2.1   *WISEs under Co-Optation: An Isolated Social Safety Net*

From the empirical data presented earlier, we have learned that WISEs under co-optation are inefficient in their internal management due to bureaucracy. There is little motivation for innovation, and the stability of services is paramount. The management system appeared to be confusing and inefficient, with an ambiguous division of responsibilities. Since the WISEs have been operational for nearly a decade, this incompetency is not a result of new institutional development but rather a structural weakness of the system during its formation.

The concept of social safety net fits the situation of the co-opted WISEs. A social safety net describes the social protection policy and the resultant mechanisms and precautionary measures that protect and provide for vulnerable groups against shocks that threaten their livelihoods (Devereux & Sabates-Wheeler, 2004; Kabeer, 2002). The purpose of a safety net is to prevent people from hitting the ground when they fall, that is, to maintain a subsistent level of consumption for those who are unable to do so. To fulfil this purpose, a social safety net should fulfil the conditions of providing livelihood support to targeted groups and ensuring their legal access to economic and social assistance should they be needed (Paitoonpong, Abe, & Puopongsakorn, 2008).

China needed to build a social safety net, particularly for those who lack proper labour skills—the under-skilled, the aged, those in ill health and people with disabilities—after the 'iron rice bowl' was broken as result of the country's structural reform (Cook, 2000). It was an urgent need for the government to construct new social protection schemes as a replacement for the previous centrally planned welfare systems. Scholars have divided the Chinese urban social welfare reform into three dimensions: a payroll-tax-based social insurance system that protects general employees, the privatisation of social services such as health care and education to accommodate and utilise private capital in the social welfare sector, and targeted social protection for urban low-income households, including the unemployed (Huang, 2012). Public-sector WISEs as work-rehabilitation centres and sheltered workshops belong to the last category.

The way co-opted, or public-sector, WISEs are constructed and operated fits the criteria of a national safety net for the unemployed and disabled. As a centrally planned effort, the public sector WISEs are structured in such a way that every sub-district has at least one centre in a location where local residents can conveniently visit. The WISEs are integrated within the public administrative system and are managed like individual departments. The government agency streams potential candidates based on their conditions and capabilities and allocates them to different public-sector service providers. With the provision of the fixed annual budget, the WISEs are responsible for planning the detailed uses of the budget and reporting to the government, which then adjusts the budget accordingly in the typical ways of public-sector budgeting. The internal operation of the organisations also fits their social function as a fundamental unit of a social protection infrastructure that the state has constructed for the socially vulnerable urban residents, where the local state agencies give straight commands, determine the organisational structure and model, and supervise and design the work-rehabilitation programmes under the centralised protocols.

A safety net aims to provide a supportive network for local people with special needs. As *de facto* government agencies, the WISEs rely fully on the government for all management affairs and financial expenses and only need to focus on their social purpose of protecting and providing essential personal care and employment to people with disabilities. The same arrangements have been observed in all three cities (Beijing, Guangzhou, Shenzhen), proving that it is a nationwide political effort. This explains why the public-sector WISEs are effective in providing basic welfare and work-rehabilitation services to the beneficiaries. On one hand, they are perceived as fundamental public-sector units fulfilling basic social responsibilities of the government, as most of the missions that they accomplish such as sheltered employment, rehabilitation, and personal care for disadvantaged workers, overlap with the basic social welfare responsibilities of the state. On the other hand, an over-reliance on the state has restricted their learning opportunities and refrained their capabilities to further develop and upgrade their services. Although organisations enjoy financial stability, the lack of effective management and autonomy has impaired their strategic development. Since the managers have little decision-making power and flexibility beyond daily operations, they have neither the resources nor the motivation to improve organizational effectiveness. As a result, there are minimal attempts at innovation and very limited resources have been invested to promote their social impact beyond delivering basic sheltered employment. In this sense, these WISEs are therefore vehicles for policy implementation rather than third-sector institutions serving diversified social interests.

6.2.1.1   *Bureaucracy as a Structural Constraint*

A vast difference between WISEs under co-optation and cooperation is that the formers are part of the bureaucratic system and are disconnected from the external social environment. The lack of access to social networks could be a major reason why the public-sector WISEs are merely basic service providers despite their abundant economic resources and political ties. Without assessing the market, the employment environment created by the public-sector WISEs is inevitably artificial. The physical and social isolation provides some protection for disabled members, but it also shields them from normal social interaction and reality. As a result, the projects received are usually random, and their rehabilitation value is seldom considered. Bureaucracy is also viewed as opposed to creativity and innovation. Studies have demonstrated that bureaucracy and innovation are inversely correlated (Damanpor, 1996; Kimberly & Evanisko, 1981; Thompson, 1965) as the absence of effective communication channels hinders organisational learning and service improvement.

A second problem caused by bureaucracy is stagnation.[3] Scholars concur that bureaucracy causes institutional stagnation because of its lack of 'cross-functional thinking' and flexibility (Iacovino, Barsanti, & Cinquini, 2017; Kimberly & Evanisko, 1981; Thompson, 1965). Prendergast (2003) ascribes the incompetency to oversight errors, as consumers cannot be relied on to provide effective feedback regarding products or services offered by bureaucrats. It reduces the flexibility of the system in reacting to the changing environment and consumer demands (Prendergast, 2003). There is the argument that delegation always couples with some degree of discretion at all levels of bureaucracy (Hupe & Hill, 2007), but authors debate how far agency officials can pursue personal preferences or act in ways that promote their own agency's growth (Johnson & Libecap, 1994). Here, the public-sector WISEs have little capacity for manipulation. Since they are not dealing directly with their stakeholders, it is difficult for the WISE to plan strategically to combine the interests of its business partners with the needs of its members.

Another issue is accountability. Traditional bureaucracy largely relies on authority to ensure its effective operations (Breton & Wintrobe, 2008). The agencies are held accountable only to their supervisors rather than to their clients and users (Hupe & Hill, 2007). As a result, they are more concerned about the fulfilment of the assessment matrix rather than satisfying their beneficiaries. In addition, given the social vulnerability of the beneficiaries, they would usually be afraid to voice their needs and request improvements. For example, the disabled member from a public-sector WISE recognised that if they did not complete the work on time, the government could easily allocate the project to other centres, and they would end up in a worse situation (personal communication with a member of CO1, November 2016).

In conclusion, the systematic bureaucracy has impeded the independence of the WISEs to develop and upgrade their services. Despite the abundant financial and political resources, the inherent constraints of the institutional system faced by the WISEs because of their social roles have prevented the social enterprises from leveraging on their economic and political resources to expand or upgrade their social programmes, adopt innovative models, or participate in political agenda-making. Unlike private WISEs, co-opted ones are not able to build external social networks on their own. The WISEs are socially isolated, with the government being the only agent bridging them and their external environment. Internally, there is no communication channel for either the beneficiaries or the managers to provide feedback in the form of suggestions and opinions, so any potential improvement is unlikely. There are minimal decisions that could be made and implemented effectively to improve the strategic operations of the organisations or to better meet the beneficiaries' social needs. The overall social isolation of these WISEs, the bureaucratic barriers to effective internal management, and the political constraints of their social roles have largely obstructed their development potential and hindered their ability to innovate and develop. As a result, they function as extended executive units for the government as part of a social safety net designed and constructed for the urban disabled and unemployed.

This 'closed system' (Iacovino et al., 2017:66) has made organisations completely dependent on the government for all resources and administrative measures. A situation of demand significantly outstripping supply has sprung up as only one work-rehabilitation centre is set up per sub-district, and most of these centres can only accommodate up to 30 members at any one time. People have to queue for places in these centres, and those who are in a healthier condition and require less personal care are given priority. This leaves much room for private WISEs to develop as alternative options in the work-integration service sector, as discussed in the forthcoming sections.

6.2.2 *WISEs under Cooperation: Beta Sites for Social Innovation*

In a cooperative relationship, the contribution of the government is supplementary. The state and the WISEs are independent collaborating bodies. The WISEs play leading roles as both the implementer and the resource provider. Transfers from the state are usually project- or per capita–based and do not fund the entire programme. The WISEs would have to raise most of the funds, mobilise both physical and human resources, and design project agendas and business plans independently. Although the government does not directly manage the WISEs under cooperation, it supplies resources along all three dimensions. This privilege significantly escalates the capacity of organisations to expand their influence and achieve higher levels of social and political missions.

One common accomplishment for WISEs under cooperation is the experimentation and introduction of socially innovative methods and models as new solutions to old problems (refer to the table of mission accomplishment in the Appendix). The WISEs perform the social role of generating innovative models and solutions.

6.2.2.1 *WISEs as Social Innovators*

The definition of social enterprise is closely related to the concepts of social innovation and entrepreneurship (Defourny & Nyssens, 2010; Nyssens et al., 2012; Peredo & McLean, 2006), which stresses the role of social entrepreneurs using innovative means such as new configurations and novel governance structures to achieve intended social outcomes and create and sustain social values. Scholars believe that social enterprises are more innovative in nature than other non-profit organisations (Haugh, 2005; Newth, 2016; Vurro & Perrini, 2006). The process of innovation necessarily creates something new or different that adds value to society (Haugh, 2005). With social enterprises, this usually occurs by applying business models to realise new ways of service delivery or utilising resources, new strategies for revenues, or serving new groups of beneficiaries (Haugh, 2005).

An observation is that in all cases, the government leveraged the private and social capital of the social enterprises and provided them favourable and exclusive incentives that significantly lowered the market barriers for these WISEs. The subsidies and grants were usually per capita–based, depending on the size of the beneficiary group served. The WISEs were given policy incentives and privileges in government support to realise their socially innovative ideas or satisfy unmet social needs. In return, the WISEs must contribute knowledge, ideas, and feasible business plans; the necessary human and physical resources; technical skills; and most of the start-up capital required to develop the social innovation models into self-sustainable social enterprises.

First, most of the WISEs have incorporated innovative businesses or social models in tackling old social issues. For example, under the collective support of the overseas non-profit foundation and the local Chinese government, CP1 managed to introduce a more advanced work-integration model to the city to replace the traditional state-run sheltered workshops. The founders of CP3 were economists and they developed the social enterprise to promote their innovative poverty-alleviation model with the Office of Poverty Alleviation (OPA) under the State Council. CP3 and CP8 were providing services that filled an institutional vacuum in the social service market by utilising policy incentives under the supervision of the government. CP2, CP5, CP6, and CP7 were also exploring innovative models to support their beneficiaries. Among them, CP2 and CP7 were experimenting with pilot programmes with local government agencies, while CP5 and CP6 were exploring and promoting their respective social enterprise model as an alternative way to provide work-integration services to the socially marginalised.

It is worth noting that in the preceding cases, the government was actively supporting the pilot programmes from the WISEs. The WISEs not only were strategic partners of the local government in service delivery but also served as the beta site for social innovation. This is particularly apparent when the cooperation is in the form of partnership or co-management, as it is a cost-effective way for the state to test pilot innovation projects and receive prompt feedback. As the director of CP3 commented on their relationship with the local government, 'the government relies on us [for services and advice] ... it consults us on new policies' (personal communication, November 2016). The manager from CP1 pointed out that 'the government supported us because we had external experts from Hong Kong and we knew how the model worked ... the government likes projects that are conceptually advanced but don't cost them much' (personal communication with manager of CP1, December 2016). The manager of CP5 also commented, 'The CDPF is interested to support us ... and why not? We have new ideas and then we try out on our own. If we fail, it won't cost them anything, but if we succeed, they can claim some benefits ... who wouldn't do it?' (personal communication with manager of CP5, December 2016).

The role of the WISEs as social innovators also explains their goal achievements. There are several barriers that social enterprises must overcome to enter the market such as financial accessibility, lack of public awareness and market exposure (Wilkinson et al., 2014). When the government provides economic resources and public legitimacy and connects the WISEs with external resources and social networks necessary for their growth, it significantly reduces the entry barriers they have to overcome. Therefore, the WISEs gain a considerable market advantage over their potential competitors as new players in the social sector. As a result, most of the WISEs under cooperation manage to provide essential work-integration services to their beneficiaries with some degree of social innovation.

6.2.2.2 *WISEs as Policy Advocators*

If the model has been proved effective in fulfilling its social mission, the state would begin to duplicate the model and promote it to other potential social and private organisations as a general policy. The process of policy advocacy usually occurs through formal discussion channels such as closed-door conferences, learning curve for the organisations, collaborative research projects, so on and so forth. On many occasions, the WISEs were also invited by the government to share their experiences and insights with other social organisations and government officials.

The case of CP4 illustrates how policy advocacy happened through formal channels. When CP4 started as a maid agency in Beijing, the market sector was in anarchy. Maids were not protected by labour laws and their working welfare and conditions completely depended on their employers. They had to work seven days a week with no legal and insurance protection and constantly faced discrimination and unfair treatment. The organisation started by promoting the idea of labour protection and pushing for a six-day workweek in the sector through public education, open dialogues, and forums with the government. Concurrently, it upgraded the industrial standard with its quality training and comprehensive social programmes for the maids. The organisation then negotiated specific policies with insurance companies to cover work-related injuries and accidents for the maids. Then the WISE recommended these measures to the Beijing municipal government through conferences and public policy forums and collaborated with universities in research projects and reports that helped promote their role in the sector. The government adopted their advice and imposed the same standard on the entire private maid sector in the city. This significantly improved the welfare and social status of the maids. With these positive records, the WISE took a step forward by advocating its model to the State Council as a tool for poverty alleviation. The model had since been duplicated in several poverty-stricken counties in China (personal communication with director of CP4, October 2016).

This advocacy process was partially expedited through personal networks. Scholars argue that non-state actors utilised informal channels to negotiate with or influence the state in order to discuss their needs or acquire favourable terms (Saich, 2009). One of the founders of CP4 was a consultant of the State Council and he submitted a report directly to the State Council based on his own practices with the social enterprise. The report 'was taken seriously by the senior officials' (personal communication with director of CP4, October 2016), and the director was invited to present in a meeting with senior government officials from the State Council and provincial governments.

The case illustrates how the WISE has successfully influenced policy agenda and initiated social change utilising both formal and informal channels. On one hand, the WISE collaborated with the government and utilised its resources to deliver regular and high-quality social services. On the other hand, the WISE leveraged its connection with the government to attract the latter's attention and further promoted its model as an innovative strategy for the government to address complicated social issues. The WISE subsequently utilised its positive performance as a demonstration and worked with the government to promote the model as a benchmark for latecomers to the social welfare sector. This also shows that even with asymmetric power relations between organisations and the state, social enterprises that gain economy of scale can play consultative roles for the government and expand their influence far beyond their local communities.

The founder of CP6, who was often invited by the government to discuss integration-related welfare policies, illustrated a similar process with his experience of developing the organisation:

> The social organisations are like the nanny and the government is the baby ... bit by bit you must show them your capability, report to them regularly, talk to them about your progress, build your legitimacy ... then over time they will trust you and give you more resources to do bigger things ... you have to understand the policy well, you interpret it well ... then you combine your projects with the interest of the government and with available resources ... now we offer services that the government cannot offer and we solve the problem for the government ... of course it will help us ... then with your experience, you form a model ... we have been promoting our model in many provinces, including Hong Kong. We tour around, meet up with local entrepreneurs and teach them how to do it.
>
> (personal communication with the founder of CP6, April 2016)

If the previously mentioned process is ubiquitous, then both formal and informal channels should be present in all state–WISE collaborations. As discussed in earlier chapters, this is evidence that for all WISEs under cooperation, there are existing channels either in the form of the founder holding official or consultative positions within the government or affiliated agencies (and vice versa) or of strengthening precedent personal ties with certain government officials through formal collaborations. The multiple channels of interaction, alongside concurrent resource transfers, facilitate the development of the organisations and further optimise their social influence.

To sum up, the WISEs under cooperation usually play the role of social innovators. Since the founders of these organisations typically have strong informal ties with the state, they are trusted by the state as reliable partners. These WISEs have their own resources, knowledge, and capital that the state could leverage, so it is also economically rational for the state to work with them as an effective way to run pilot projects and socially innovative programmes. If these projects and programs are successful, these WISEs would then advise the government on future policy issues.

6.2.3   WISEs under Complementarity: Mutual Aid Groups Filling the Institutional Voids

In general, the government demonstrates a passive attitude with no systematic measure or plan to support WISEs under complementarity given that both types of WISEs receive little support from the government for all three forms of resources. In some cases, the government provides formal legitimacy by recognising the legal status and social contribution of the organisations and allowing them to apply for funding schemes or participate in networking events, but these activities are not related to privileges for the organisations. On one hand, the state does not pursue strategies that would benefit the development of the WISEs; neither does it actively facilitate collaborative partnerships with them. On the other hand, there is no apparent suppression, and the organisations are left to survive on their own.

Compared to the other two relationships, WISEs under the complementarity model usually target more challenging social issues. For example, the disabled people accepted by WISEs under complementarity and competition usually suffer from more serious mental disabilities compared to those under co-optation and cooperation.[4] This is because the latter usually have their beneficiaries picked or referred by related government agencies, which usually select candidates in better health conditions, whilst as mutual aid societies, the grassroots WISEs have less choice over the beneficiaries they serve.[5]

As mutual aid societies, WISEs under complementarity often address an institutional vacuum in the social service sector, where effective public and market forces are both absent. Although these organisations receive little support from the state, they manage to gain private support from the communities they serve partly because of the social capital from their community, and also because their services fulfil some existing social demands. Such demands are usually trivial and pertain to specific local social groups, such as families affected by AIDS (CM2), unemployed housewives (CM3), and specific groups of migrant workers (CM4, CM6). These fragmented social issues are difficult to be solved efficiently by public and market institutions, as these issues require certain economies of scale to be productive. Although traditional NGOs are able to fulfil part of the demands, however, they face both political and financial constraints that may seriously impede the service quality. Hence, the social enterprise model offers an alternative option to fill this institutional void for grassroots organizations, as social entrepreneurs emerge from within these communities and mobilise their peers to tackle targeted social issues with their own resources. As a result, the services provided by these WISEs are typically complementary to services provided by the market and the state. Since grassroots social entrepreneurs have resource constraints, they typically operate as SMEs.

6.2.3.1 *Fulfilling Social Needs for the Beneficiaries*

As mentioned above, aside from organizations funded by overseas NGOs, WISEs under these two categories are by nature mutual aid societies. These WISEs bud off as social start-ups or NGOs from socially disadvantaged communities fulfilling a service gap in areas where the public/voluntary sector and the market are unable to fulfil the welfare and the developmental needs of these socially marginalised groups. Weisbrod's (1977) theory of government failure highlights that in heterogeneous communities where the minority's views are not well reflected in public policy, the minorities would organise themselves voluntarily and collectively not only to provide public services for themselves but also to press the government to serve their interests.

In many cases, there is a pressing need for the WISEs under complementarity to promote social inclusion and community integration for their members. Most founders of the WISEs repeatedly stressed the importance of 'personal development' and 'social integration' [of the beneficiaries] as their key missions (personal communications, 2016–2017).

As the founder of CM1 explained:

> We want an exchange of values based on fairness and equity. I serve, you pay. … We want to prove to people the value of our employees, so that they can be respected as a social person, not as someone inferior, begging for kindness and help.
>
> (personal communication, May 2016)

This highlights the fundamental difference between bottom-up social enterprises and public-sector WISEs with their top-down approach. For the public-sector WISEs, work rehabilitation is a social welfare service offering protection to the weak and the helpless while 'employment' is considered by the grassroots WISEs as an empowerment tool for fair exchanges between the beneficiaries and the external world, and to them, this equilibrium forms the basis of their social integration function. This approach was emphasised by all grassroots WISEs with their bottom-up approach. CM6 mentioned that 'boosting the confidence (of the injured workers) is as important as training them' (personal communication, September 2016) while CM3 and CM4 stressed that helping the workers realise the value of their labour is one of the core missions of their organisations (personal communication, May and September 2016). Six out of seven WISEs under complementarity had incorporated these goals into their programmes by building social programmes promoting personal development and social integration of the socially marginalised groups (refer to the Appendix), despite the cost of these programmes taking a heavy toll on their existing limited financial resources.

The disadvantage of the WISEs is also apparent. Their community roots have imposed a constraint on their production efficiency and social impact. Due to their grassroots backgrounds, most of the WISEs under complementarity lack the resources and human talents to form strategic plans for business development. Learning was tough as most of the workers or members do not have the ability and resource capacity to acquire new skills. As a result, all seven organisations adopted simple business models of producing and selling low-value-added goods or services to earn immediate and continuous revenue to sustain their social programmes, which, in turn, exposed them to arduous competition with commercial manufacturers in the open market. They were usually small in size with capacities of no more than 30 permanent members. Compared with some of the cooperative WISEs that have served hundreds to thousands of beneficiaries, their social influence is small. It is challenging for them to scale and upgrade their operations. As a result, they are easily trapped at the bottom of the value chain in terms of business production. Although most of the WISEs fulfil both service provision and social integration missions for their beneficiaries, their social impact is nevertheless concurrently restricted by their own communities.

6.2.4 *WISEs under Competition: Rivalries with Fragmented Interaction*

From the two cases drawn, there is no fixed social role for the WISEs under the competition category. Even within these cases, the relationship between the WISE and the state is marked by fragmentation and inconsistency as different levels and departments of the government have inconsistent and even conflicting interests (Yang & Alpermann, 2014). The relationship of the WISEs with the government therefore depends on its specific business dealings with certain government units and the issues involved, with holistic state involvement as a passive regulator in these dealings.

The awards granted to the organisations by the local municipal governments reflect some degree of approval and recognition from the government on their contributions. Both organisations had been around for more than a decade and were formally registered as NGOs under the Ministry of Civil Affairs. Over the years, both their parental NGOs had expanded into a group of social organisations with considerable sizes and scales and have offered comprehensive ranges of services covering various needs for their beneficiaries.

The examples of the WISEs show that whether economic competition develops into an open conflict is context-dependent. For example, as a migrant workers' NGO, COMP1 had been mindful of its political stances. The prizes and awards it received from the Beijing municipal government were evidence of its attempts to align its interest with that of the government. The NGO was set up in 2002 at a time when China was undergoing rapid urbanisation, which required a continuous influx of migrant workers from the rural areas to work in the cities, and a major concern during this period was the well-being of these migrant workers in the country (Akay, Bargain, & Zimmermann, 2012; Fan, 2002; Zhao, 1999). Since the services provided by COMP1 fulfilled this social demand, its contribution had been recognised by the social elite and government-affiliated officers (personal communication, February 2017). The support it gained from these social elites had assisted in its gaining special permission in setting up unlicensed schools for children of migrant workers who were otherwise not qualified to attend local schools. However, unlike WISEs that had direct ties with the government, this connection through the third parties did not lead to a formal contractual partnership with the state. Such special arrangements were not secured and likely to be easily overthrown by other government departments should direct conflicts of interest occur.

In the case of COMP2, its rehabilitation programs were similar to what the public-sector WISEs and some GONGOs were doing. The WISE was planning to set up a vocational training centre, but since the same training was offered by other government agencies and partners for free, the organisation could not attract sufficient clients. This competition caused a financial loss for the organisation, and it had to give up its programme (personal communication, January 2017). In this case, there was no direct confrontation between the organisation and the state, but the latter overpowered the former and impeded its performance.

Both WISEs were set up as separate entities or departments by their parental NGOs. Their purpose was to fulfil a specific social function or to provide alternative sources of revenue for their parental organisations. In both cases, the conflict was between one or a few of the projects the parental NGO was operating. In such a competitive relationship, both parties did not benefit directly from the services offered by the other party but entered a zero-sum game where one party lost should the other party gain. This occurred in situations of economic resource scarcity or markets of limited sizes. Since the two were asymmetric in power, the NGO either had to purge its project completely or find alternative resources or means to support the project. In both cases, the NGOs managed to sustain the WISE unit on their own, but since such resources were limited, they were only able to provide small-scale services to the local communities.

The two cases show that for the competitive relationship, there is no fixed strategy from the state. The interaction between the two parties is fragmented and largely context-dependent. As COMP1 and COMP2 had not performed at the political level, there was very little collaboration and resource transfer observed between the state and them. In practice, with the resources and political constraints that they are facing, the effects of the organisations are confined to satisfying the personal needs of their immediate beneficiaries.

6.3   Conclusion

In summary, when the state is actively seeking partnerships and procurement with the WISEs, it follows two independent strategies based on its relationship with the organisation. Cooperation is most likely to occur when the state–WISE relationship is a continuity of existing formal partnerships or informal engagements. The case of the WISEs under cooperation shows that information sharing and knowledge exchange occur through the informal channels before the existence of the social enterprises, and the three forms of resource transfers will commence on the establishment of formal institutions. This confirms the proposition that the state is likely to cultivate collaborative relationships with social enterprises connected to it via informal institutions.

The second selection criterion is applied in the absence of informal channels before the social enterprise is established for the state to have an epistemic understanding of the organisation. According to the interview with the government official, the government would evaluate the status and performance of the organisation for a time until it has demonstrated some form of economic and social effectiveness. The government's role, in this case, is to empower the WISE to scale up its services rather than assist and guide it from scratch. Although it was not specified by the governor, one would expect that the political nature of the WISE would have also been assessed during the probationary period to ensure alignment with state policies. Given that only one out of seven WISEs interviewed under complementarity has reached this stage, it could be concluded that the majority of WISEs under this category are still independent.

This chapter takes one step further to explain the variation in effectiveness as a result of the consequences of the institutional characteristics and social roles of the WISEs. WISEs under the four modes of relationship deliver different social functions, either as a strategic choice or as an unintentional result in the process of new institutional formation in China's ongoing social welfare sector reform. The public-sector WISEs are part of the social safety net constructed by the state with the specific purpose to provide basic services to the beneficiaries as a replacement for a state function, whereas WISEs forming collaborative partnerships with the government work as pioneers in social innovation and social entrepreneurship. The remaining WISEs (constituting the majority of the WISE sector) compete in the open social market for private resources as well as limited resources from the government. They fill up the institutional void caused by the withdrawal of the state from the social employment sector as a result of the reform. The complementary and the competitive relationships are differentiated only by the partial conflict of interests between the organisation and local government departments. The characteristics of these different roles and functions that they fulfil inherently lead to the different levels of social mission they are capable of accomplishing.

Notes

1 There are chances when underperformance is due to a list of internal and external factors such as management flaws, geographical disadvantages, and local market preferences. But having a moderate sample size across geographical regions would have reduced the interference of these externalities to a large extent.

2 The other two characteristics, equity and integrity, are based on democratic regimes in Thai's (2000) analysis and therefore are not considered within the scope of this study.

3 In theory, bureaucracy is characterised by the features of managerial hierarchy and rules, professionalism, impersonality, functional specialisation, and technical qualification of staff as described by Weber (1947). Here, it refers to the public administrative structure and nature of the public sector WISEs.

4 This is confirmed both by the personal observation of the inspector and in the interview with COMP2, January 2017.

5 This is concluded from communications with various organisations and practitioners in the sector. Personal communications with CP1, CP5, CP7, CM1, COMP1, and the personal observations of the author in these organisations have also confirmed this statement.

References

Akay, A., Bargain, O., & Zimmermann, K. F. (2012). Relative concerns of rural-to-urban migrants in China. *Journal of Economic Behavior & Organization, 81*(2), 421–441.

Atack, I. (1999). Four criteria of development NGO legitimacy. *World Development, 27*(5), 855–864.

Arnesen, S., & Peters, Y. (2018). The legitimacy of representation: How descriptive, formal, and responsiveness representation affect the acceptability of political decisions. *Comparative Political Studies, 51*(7), 868–899.

Bloom, G., & Tang, S. (1999). *Rural Health Prepayment Schemes in China: Towards a More Active Role for Government.* World Development.

Billis, D., & Glennerster, H. (1998). Human services and the voluntary sector: Towards a theory of comparative advantage. *Journal of Social Policy, 27*(1), 79–98.

Bratton, M. (1989). The politics of government-NGO relations in Africa. *World Development, 17*(4), 569–587.

Breton, A., & Wintrobe, R. (2008). *The Logic of Bureaucratic Conduct: An Economic Analysis of Competition, Exchange, and Efficiency in Private and Public Organizations.* Cambridge University Press.

Burt, E. (2007). Voluntary organizations in the democratic polity: Managing legitimacy, accountability and trust. *Public Money and Management, 27*(2), 157–160.

Carlisle, E., & Flynn, D. (2005). Small business survival in China: Guanxi, legitimacy, and social capital. *Journal of Developmental Entrepreneurship, 10*(1), 79–79.

Chou, B. K. P. (2006). Challenges for China's reform of government procurement. *Journal of Contemporary China, 15*(48), 533–549.

Chung, Y. H., Färe, R., & Grosskopf, S. (1997). Productivity and undesirable outputs: A directional distance function approach. *Journal of Environmental Management, 51*(3), 229–240.

Conger, J. A., & Kanungo, R. N. (1988). The empowerment process: Integrating theory and practice. *Academy of Management Review, 13*(3), 471–482.

Cook, S. (2000). *After the Iron Rice Bowl: Extending the Safety Net in China* (Institute of Development Studies Discussion Paper 377). University of Sussex.

Damanpor, F. (1996). Bureaucracy and innovation revisited: Effects of contingency factors, industrial sectors, and innovation characteristics. *The Journal of High Technology Management Research, 7*(2), 149–173.

Dart, R. (2004). The legitimacy of social enterprise. *Nonprofit Management and Leadership, 14*(4), 411–424.

Defourny, J., & Nyssens, M. (2010). Conceptions of social enterprise and social entrepreneurship in Europe and the United States: Convergences and divergences. *Journal of Social Entrepreneurship, 1*(1), 32–53.

Devereux, S., & Sabates-Wheeler, R. (2004). Transformative Social Protection. IDS Working Paper 232.

Edelenbos, J., & Klijn, E.-H. (2007). Trust in complex decision-making networks: A theoretical and empirical exploration. *Administration & Society, 39*(1), 25–50.

Edelenbos, J., & Klijn, E.-H. (2016). Trust in complex decision-making networks. *Administration & Society, 39*(1), 25–50.

Edwards, B., Goodwin, M., Pemberton, S., & Woods, M. (2001). Partnerships, power, and scale in rural governance. *Environment and Planning C: Government and Policy, 19*(2), 289–310.

Evans, P. (1996). Government action, social capital and development: Reviewing the evidence on synergy. *World Development, 24*(6), 1119–1132.

Fan, C. C. (2002). The elite, the natives, and the outsiders: Migration and labor market segmentation in Urban China. *Annals of the Association of American Geographers, 92*(1), 103–124.

Fisher, J., Heyzer, N., Riker, J. V., & Quizon, A. B. (1996). Government-NGO relations in Asia: Prospects and challenges for people-centered development. *The Journal of Asian Studies, 55*(3), 704–705.

Flathman, R. E. (2017). Legitimacy. In R. E. Goodin, P. Pettit, & T. Pogge (Eds.), *A Companion to Contemporary Political Philosophy* (pp. 678–684). Blackwell Publishing.

Fock, H. K. Y., & Woo, K.S. (1998). The China Market: Strategic implications of Guanxi. *Business Strategy Review, 9*, 33–43.

Friedmann, J. (1987). *Planning in the Public Domain: From Knowledge to Action.* Princeton University Press.

Gazley, B. (2008). Beyond the contract: The scope and nature of informal government-nonprofit partnerships. *Public Administration Review, 68*(1), 141–154.

Georghiou, L., Edler, J., Uyarra, E., & Yeow, J. (2014). Policy instruments for public procurement of innovation: Choice, design and assessment. *Technological Forecasting & Social Change, 86*(C), 1–12.

Gillespie, N. A., & Mann, L. (2004). Transformational leadership and shared values: The building blocks of trust. *Journal of Managerial Psychology, 19*(6), 588–607.

Gold, T., Guthrie, D., & Wank, D. (2002). An introduction to the story of *guanxi.* In T. Gold, D. Guthrie, & D. Wank (Eds.), *Social Connections in China: Institutions, Culture, and the Changing Nature Of Guanxi* (pp. 3–20) Cambridge University Press.

Hasmath, R., & Hsu, J. Y. J. (2016). Conceptualizing Government-Organized Non-Governmental Organizations across Contexts. Presented at the *Development Studies Association Annual Meeting* (*Oxford, UK*).

Haugh, H. (2005). A research agenda for social entrepreneurship. *Social Enterprise Journal, 1*(1), 1–12.

Ho, P. (2001). Greening without conflict? Enviro–nmentalism, NGOs and civil society in China. *Development and Change, 32*(5), 893–921.

Hsia, R. Y.-J., & White, L. T., III. (2002). Working amid corporatism and confusion: Foreign NGOs in China. *Nonprofit and Voluntary Sector Quarterly, 31*(3), 329–351.

Hsu, C. (2010). Beyond civil society: An organizational perspective on state–NGO relations in the People's Republic of China. *Journal of Civil Society, 6*(3), 259–277.

Hsu, J. Y. J., & Hasmath, R. (2014). The local corporatist state and NGO relations in China. *Journal of Contemporary China, 23*(87), 516–534.

Huang, X. (2012). The politics of social welfare reform in urban China: Social welfare preferences and reform policies. *Journal of Chinese Political Science, 18*(1), 61–85.

Hupe, P., & Hill, M. (2007). Street-level bureaucracy and public accountability. *Public Administration, 85*(2), 279–299.

Iacovino, N. M., Barsanti, S., & Cinquini, L. (2017). Public organizations between old public administration, new public management and public governance: The case of the Tuscany Region. *Public Organization Review, 17*(1), 1–22.

Innes, J. E., & Booher, D. E. (2010). *Planning with Complexity: An Introduction to Collaborative Rationality for Public Policy.* Routledge.

Johnson, R. N., & Libecap, G. D. (1994). *The Federal Civil Service System and the Problem of Bureaucracy.* University of Chicago Press.

Kabeer, N. (2002). Safety nets and opportunity ladders: Addressing vulnerability and enhancing productivity in South Asia. *Development Policy Review, 20*(5), 589–614.

Kadushin, C. (2012). *Understanding Social Networks.* Oxford University Press.

Kimberly, J. R., & Evanisko, M. J. (1981). Organizational innovation: The influence of individual, organizational, and contextual factors on hospital adoption of technological and administrative innovations. *Academy of Management Journal, 24*(4), 689–713.

Kindornay, S., Tissot, S., & Sheiban, N. (2014). *The Value of Cross-sector Development Partnerships* (p. 18). The North-South Institute.

Klijn, E.-H., Edelenbos, J., & Steijn, B. (2010a). Trust in governance networks: Its impacts on outcomes. *Administration & Society, 42*(2), 193–221.

Klijn, E.-H., Steijn, B., & Edelenbos, J. (2010b). The impact of network management on outcomes in governance networks. *Public Administration, 88*(4), 1063–1082.

Kuosmanen, J. (2014). Care provision, empowerment, and market forces: The art of establishing legitimacy for Work Integration Social Enterprises (WISEs). *Voluntas: International Journal of Voluntary and Nonprofit Organisations, 25*(1), 248–269.

Lin, J., & Si, S. X. (2010). Can guanxi be a problem? Contexts, ties, and some unfavorable consequences of social capital in China. *Asia Pacific Journal of Management, 27*(3), 561–581.

Ma, Q. (2002). Defining Chinese nongovernmental organizations – Springer. *Voluntas: International Journal of Voluntary and Nonprofit Organizations, 13*(2), 113–130.

Markelova, H., Meinzen-Dick, R., Hellin, J., & Dohrn, S. (2009). Collective action for smallholder market access. *Food Policy, 34*(1), 1–7.

Maskell, P. (1999). Localised learning and industrial competitiveness. *Cambridge Journal of Economics, 23*(2), 167–185.

Mason, C., Kirkbride, J., & Bryde, D. (2007). From stakeholders to institutions: The changing face of social enterprise governance theory. *Management Decision, 45*(2), 284–301.

Morgan, R. M., & Hunt, S. D. (1994). The commitment-trust theory of relationship marketing. *Journal of Marketing, 58*(3), 20–38.

Najam, A. (1996). NGO accountability: A conceptual framework. *Development Policy Review, 14*(4), 339–354.

Najam, A. (2000). The four C's of government third sector-government relations. *Nonprofit Management and Leadership, 10*(4), 375–396.

Newth, J. (2016). Social enterprise innovation in context: Stakeholder influence through contestation. *Entrepreneurship Research Journal, 6*(4), 369–399.

North, D. C. (1991). Institutions. *Journal of Economic Perspectives, 5*(1), 97–112.

Nyssens, M., Defourny, J., Gardin, L., & Laville, J. L. (2012). *Work integration social enterprises and public policy: An analysis of the European situation.* EMES Research Network.

Paitoonpong, S., Abe, S., & Puopongsakorn, N. (2008). The meaning of "social safety nets". *Journal of Asian Economics, 19*(5–6), 467–473.

Peredo, A. M., & McLean, M. (2006). Social entrepreneurship: A critical review of the concept. *Journal of World Business, 41*(1), 56–65.

Pierre, J. (2000). *Debating Governance: Authority, Steering, and Democracy.* OUP.

Prendergast, C. (2003). The limits of bureaucratic efficiency. *Journal of Political Economy, 111*(5), 929–958.

Ramus, T., & Vaccaro, A. (2014). Stakeholders matter: How social enterprises address mission drift. *Journal of Business Ethics, 143*(2), 307–322.

Romzek, B. S., LeRoux, K., & Blackmar, J. M. (2012). A preliminary theory of informal accountability among network organizational actors. *Public Administration Review, 72*(3), 442–453.

Saich, T. (2009). Negotiating the state: The development of social organizations in China. *The China Quarterly, 161*, 124–141.

Sealey, C. W., & Lindley, J. T. (1977). Inputs, outputs, and a theory of production and cost at depository financial institutions. *The Journal of Finance, 32*(4), 1251–1266.

Selsky, J. W. (2005). Cross-sector partnerships to address social issues: Challenges to theory and practice. *Journal of Management, 31*(6), 849–873.

Smith, W. K., Gonin, M., & Besharov, M. L. (2013). Managing social-business tensions: A review and research agenda for social enterprise. *Business Ethics Quarterly, 23*(3), 407–442.

Spires, A. J., Tao, L., & Chan, K. M. (2014). Societal support for China's grass-roots NGOs: Evidence from Yunnan, Guangdong and Beijing. *The China Journal, 71*, 65–90.

Suchman, M. C. (1995). Managing legitimacy: Strategic and institutional approaches. *The Academy of Management Review, 20*(3), 571–610.

Swanson, K. E., Kuhn, R. G., & Xu, W. (2001). Environmental policy implementation in Rural China: A case study of Yuhang, Zhejiang. *Environmental Management, 27*(4), 481–491.

Thai, K. V., & Grimm, R. (2000). Government procurement: Past and current developments. *Journal of Public Budgeting, Accounting & Financial Management, 12*(2), 231–247.

Thompson, V. A. (1965). Bureaucracy and innovation. *Administrative Science Quarterly, 10*(1), 1–20.

Townsend, J. G., & Townsend, A. R. (2004). Accountability, motivation and practice: NGOs North and South. *Social & Cultural Geography, 5*(2), 271–284.

Vurro, C., & Perrini, F. (2006). Social entrepreneurship: Innovation and social change across theory and practice. *Social Entrepreneurship, 23*(1), 57–85.

Wang, Q. (2016). Cooptation or Restriction: The Differentiated Government Control over Foundations in China. Research Infrastructure of Chinese Foundations Working Paper Series. University Press of Colorado.

Wei, Q. (2017). From direct involvement to indirect control? A multilevel analysis of factors influencing Chinese foundations' capacity for resource mobilization. *Voluntas: International Journal of Voluntary and Nonprofit Organizations, 26*(4), 1–17.

Weisbrod, B. A. (1977). *The Voluntary Nonprofit Sector: An Economic Analysis.* Lexington Books.

Welter, F., & Kautonen, T. (2005). Trust, social networks and enterprise development: Exploring evidence from East and West Germany. *The International Entrepreneurship and Management Journal, 1*(3), 367–379.

Wiegel, W., & Bamford, D. (2015). The role of Guanxi in buyer–supplier relationships in Chinese small- and medium-sized enterprises – A resource-based perspective. *Production Planning & Control, 26*(4), 308–327.

Wilkinson, C., Medhurst, J., Henry, N., Wihlborg, M., & Braithwaite, B. W. (2014). A map of social enterprises and their eco-systems in Europe: Executive Summary. ICF Consulting Services, European Commission, 1–16.

Yang, K. M., & Alpermann, B. (2014). Children and youth NGOs in China: Social activism between embeddedness and marginalization. *China Information, 28*(3), 311–337.

Zaidi, S. A. (1999). NGO failure and the need to bring back the state. *Journal of International Development, 11*(2), 259–271.

Zainon, S., Ahmad, S. A., Atan, R., Wah, Y. B., & Bakar, Z. A. (2014). Legitimacy and Sustainability of Social Enterprise: Governance and accountability. *Procedia - Social and Behavioral Sciences, 145,* 152–157.

Zhao, Y. (1999). Labor migration and earnings differences: The case of Rural China. *Economic Development and Cultural Change, 47*(4), 767–782.

Zietlow, J. T. (2001). Social entrepreneurship: Managerial, finance and marketing aspects. *Journal of Nonprofit & Public Sector Marketing, 9*(1–2), 19–43.

7 Conclusion

Introduction

This chapter summarises the study's findings and discusses the applications. It revisits the questions raised in the first chapter. From a supplementary angle, the strategies taken by the work-integrated social enterprises (WISEs) as adaptive responses to the state have been addressed. The last section discusses the limitations of this study, provides policy recommendations, and suggests directions for future research.

7.1 Summary of Findings

This study explores how the modes of relationship between the state and the WISEs impact their effectiveness in social mission achievements. It shows that the relationship directly impacts the institutional effectiveness of the organisations. The two variables are not linearly correlated, as government intervention does not lead to higher institutional effectiveness. The impact is rather categorical and depends on the type of resources being transferred from the government to the organisations, which evince distinctive features in their social mission accomplishment.

Recall that three questions have been raised in the first chapter:

a. Are there distinctive modes of relationship between the state and WISEs in China?
b. How can state–society relationship be related to the institutional features and performance (effectiveness) of the WISEs?
c. How do the findings contribute to our general understanding of social enterprise development in China?

Following an introduction to the typology and related theories, the institutional background and historical development of WISEs in China were outlined in Chapter 3, the first question was answered in Chapter 4. The chapter identifies four modes of state–WISE relationship featured by their formal and informal engagements with the state. Most of the formal interventions involve

DOI: 10.4324/9781003231677-7

resource transfers from the state to the WISEs, while the informal engagements are in the form of interpersonal ties and social networks that grant some sort of exclusivities to the organisations. WISEs under co-optation benefit from direct management and funding from the government but at the cost of managerial autonomy and social isolation. Only WISEs under cooperation benefit from both formal and informal engagements, and WISEs under complementarity and competition receive rather restricted and limited benefits from the state.

Chapter 4 showed that WISEs under different categories exhibit distinctive characteristics in management structure, source of funding, and external network. Chapter 5 showed that WISEs demonstrate distinctive and systematic patterns of effectiveness with the services they provide to the beneficiaries in correspondence to the four modes of relationship identified. A measurement framework with three levels of social mission was constructed to compare and evaluate their effectiveness. All WISEs offer comprehensive essential employment, training, and welfare services to the beneficiaries. Their performances diverge at the social integration and policy advocacy levels. WISEs under cooperation deliver services that cover all prospects, except social empowerment. WISEs under cooptation are suboptimal in social integration and advocacy, although they are consistent and sustainable in sheltered employment and basic care. WISEs under complementarity and competition are comparable in effectiveness—both categories provide responsible and effective social integration services but less so in terms of advocacy.

Following the establishment of a relationship between state–WISE interaction and institutional effectiveness, Chapter 6 emphasised two major points. First, based on the empirical evidence, it explained how the formal and informal engagements dictate resource transfers from the state to WISEs along the political, economic, and social dimensions to affect their capacities in mission accomplishment. Second, it argues that resource transfers are, in fact, a strategic preference of the Chinese state to use privilege as a tactic to select effective and politically reliable partners in the social service sector. By granting privileges to WISEs discriminatorily, the state manages the WISE sector by designating different social roles to the organisations that are tenable to the ongoing social welfare reform in the country.

The current relationships suggest that there are occasions when the government proactively adopts supportive measures to accelerate the development of certain WISEs. The point of difference is the management technique and resulting interactive patterns when these organisations are social enterprises that engage both the market and the third sector in their operation. One advantage social enterprises have over non-governmental organisations (NGOs) is greater financial autonomy due to their ability to tap market resources. In the social enterprise sector, the market should be one of the most important underlying mechanisms to sustain their operation and development (Defourny and Nyssens, 2010; Nyssens & Defourny, 2013). Instead of relying on donors and government funding like many NGOs do, WISEs trade their products and services or charge for their beneficiaries to sustain their operations. As shown in chapter 3, most of the WISEs relied on no less than 20% of their income from market revenues, while 10 out of the 17 private-sector WISEs studied earned more than 50% of their revenue from market activities. It could be concluded that the WISEs are in general commercialised.

This has affected the way organisations interact with the state. Since these WISEs may register and operate as private companies or set up commercial units as independent businesses, direct management and control become less effective. What has been observed in this study is an alternative strategy of selective support based on resource transfer. The state benignly neglects the unselected WISEs unless a conflict of interests occurs. Instead, it grants resource privileges that enhance the market competitiveness of the WISEs that promote them as service partners that take up more important social and political functions while leaving the rest to survive on their own. Upon resource dependency, the different privileges denote the different 'rights' granted by the state to the organisations operating in the social market. The next section briefly discusses the dynamic interaction between the state and the WISEs, in particular how the WISEs adaptively react to the state to maximise their benefits.

7.2   The Adaptive Responses of WISEs

7.2.1   *The Problem with Resource Dependency*

The relationship between the WISEs and the government has been constantly changing and evolving. Organisations react strategically to generate resources for different types of legitimacy, depending on the institutional and cultural context of their environment (Suchman, 1995). The resource dependency theory posits that organisations need to exchange with its external environment for survival (Aldrich & Pfeffer, 1976). In China, the government is the dominating provider for the non-state actors, which means the latter face the risk of losing their autonomy to political discretion, causing an unsymmetrical and dependent relationship (Wang & Yao, 2016). Social organisations have to constantly seek ways to overcome the problem of a shortage of resources and legitimacy without the support of the government (Deng, 2010).

Three strategies have been identified from the interviews conducted as their adaptive responses to their power asymmetry with the state, namely revenue diversification, seeking alternative resources, and building relationships through policy desirability. All three strategies serve the purpose of increasing their resource mobilisation abilities and reducing financial and operational risks. It is also observed that WISEs that are already in collaboration with the state demonstrate different priorities and concerns from those that do not liaise with the state. For WISEs that are already collaborating with the state, the priority is to reduce risks due to resource dependency; therefore, they tend to diversify their sources of revenue and establish across as many sectors as possible to maximise their social networks and influence. For WISEs that are not supported by the government, their critical and immediate need is to acquire sufficient resources for survival. Therefore, they tend to focus on seeking alternative resources and finding ways to gain support from the government by aligning their activities with objectives desirable for the government.

7.2.2 *Revenue Diversification through Hybridisation*

Hybridisation is sometimes used as a strategy by NGOs to circumvent resource constraints (Wang & Yao, 2016). Hybrid organisations are defined as organisations that combine multiple sectoral logics and features, such as a non-profit business venture or an non-profit organisation (NPO) with commercialised operations and products (Zietlow, 2001). Recent development from the angle of institutionalism interprets 'hybridity' as novel combinations of various elements such as capital, knowledge, regimes of justification, innovative practices, and institution logics (Jay, 2012; O'Mahony & Bechky, 2008; Reay & Hinings, 2009; Stark, 2010). Social enterprises typically combine 'multiple organisational identities' (Battilana & Lee, 2014) through their hybrid orgnisational structures. Scholars ascribe the efficiency of social enterprises to their hybrid structure and argue that their ambiguous structures, multiple resources, and steering mechanisms, in fact, enable them to find flexible ways to overcome stubborn obstacles such as the classical principal–agent problem (Billis & Glennerster, 1998; Evers, 2005; Bielefeld, 2012).

Some WISEs employ hybridity as a strategy to utilise resources from multiple sectors. Most of these organisations are combinations of commercial and social units. Through their hybrid network and activities, the WISEs are able to mobilise and integrate resources from all three sectors. Five out of eight WISEs under cooperation adopted a hybrid structure across the private and third sectors. They normally register separately under the Ministry of Civil Affairs (MCA) and the State Administration of Industry and Commerce (SAIC) as two entities under the same brand. While the non-profit unit participates in social projects, the company competes for business deals and provides services and products to the market. This arrangement significantly diversifies the revenue streams and activity scope of orgnisations. The non-profit activities also become more sustainable with profits made by the company.

As an example, the director of CP6 emphasised 'resource integration' repeatedly as a key development strategy for the organisation. Revenue diversification across various sectors through a hybrid organisational structure is a key strategy for the organisation. Its business entities span several sectors, including e-commerce, software development, gaming, and accessible travel, while the non-profit units bid for government projects and promote their social enterprise branding to other non-profits. As the director of CP6 explained:

> The traditional division of three sectors is no[t] only applicable, problems are getting more complicated nowadays. … We have to know how to integrate resources from all three sectors. We set up the primate limited

company so that we could bid for bigger commercial projects. Then we set up the social organisations when we needed social services for our employees, then we started selling these services to other organisations. Then we realised that we had so many different types of resources and activities to take care of, and we set up a foundation to integrate all these resources together to form long-term development strategies … everything we need is out there, and all the policies that we can make use of are out there … but you have to know how to integrate them to serve your needs … integrate as many resources as possible and grow and then the government will notice you … this is how we succeeded.

(personal communication, April 2016)

CP3 has expressed similar concerns over dependency on the government. The organisation received 35% of its revenue from government contracts, and the director thought 'the risk was high because it's unstable' (personal communication, November 2016). The organisation established its brand not only as a public service provider but also as an independent knowledge exporter by selling training courses and curricula. The director explained that independent revenue streams were to be the way to reduce reliance on government funding and to improve the stability of their programme (personal communication, November 2016).

The examples show that WISEs under cooperation utilise a hybrid structure to, first, integrate market mechanisms to strengthen their resource mobilisation abilities and reduce their dependency on government funding and, second, promote their non-profit missions for political and social capital, such as building public reputation and broader social networks. Note that none of the organisations mentioned the lack of political autonomy as an issue. Although this may be partly due to the limitation of interviews as a research method, given that all WISEs under cooperation have positively recognised at the vital role of the government in their development process and anticipated more future government involvement (personal communications, 2016–2017), it is evident that they are looking for more government interaction rather than less. The concern is how to fit themselves into the long-term development plan of the government with changes in policies and funding, which brings unanticipated financial risks.

As a result, the organisations then branched out to multiple services across the sectors as a response to overcome the tension and constraints caused by their external environment. Diversifying and integrating resources and revenues through hybridisation is a sensible tactic for WISEs that are in collaboration with the government.

7.2.3 *Alternative Revenues and Legitimacy*

Pursuing alternative resources is a strategy mostly pursued by WISEs that are not collaborating with the government. Without the support of the government, organisations have to seek alternative sources of legitimacy and economic resources and build social networks on their own. One question raised in the earlier section is how WISEs that do not receive government support manage to achieve high levels of social missions. The answer could be that these WISEs have found alternative resources from either the market or the third sector to sustain their activities and operations. All seven WISEs under the complementarity relationship were actively looking for private partners and investors from either their own communities or the open social service market.

The relationship among local networks, social capital, and legitimacy has been corroborated by Wiegel and Bamford (2015) and Carlisle and Flynn (2005) in their studies about private organisations in China; that is, it is common for non-profits to leverage their social capital to attract resources from their private and public partners. Being part of the community reduced the barriers to member recruitment and programme design for WISEs under the complementary relationship. All community-based WISEs relied heavily on volunteers and philanthropic donations to run their social programmes. For both CM3 and CM4, the volunteers were mostly from the same communities that the WISE emerged from. Even when CM2 was founded by an overseas NGO, it adopted a similar strategy of working with local leaders from the same community they served in order to utilise the local social networks. The manager of CM2 recognised that the success of the project depended on its ability to integrate with local networks, as '*market mechanism alone would be insufficient when you work with the grassroots communities ... people stay with you because of inter-personal relationships*' (personal communication, December 2016; emphasis in the original).

The interpersonal connections also provide essential legitimacy to the WISEs when they are not endorsed by the government. Stressing their effectiveness and contribution to their peers endows the WISEs with substantive legitimacy (Atack, 1999; Flathman, 2017). The WISEs differentiate themselves from other NGOs by stressing their hybrid models and emphasising their community-oriented, civil nature. This strong sense of bonding, mutual help, and community spirit is a unique feature of community-based WISEs. As the director of the CM4 asserted, '*There are many NGOs in this community with the aim to serve and help female migrant workers. We are peers and teammates. We know each other well and we encourage and empower each other, so that we progress together*' (personal communication, April 2016, emphasis in the original).

Since most of the sales were done through local community networks, the market was too limited to support the full operation of the organisations and competitiveness remained a problem. The WISEs usually promote their services and products to potential clients using their social enterprise branding. The managers acknowledged that the social enterprise brand name helped promote the business and justify their charges to the clients (personal communication with CM2, CM3 and CM4, 2016). This increases the bargaining power of the social enterprises by justifying the social values created for the buyers. The WISEs diversify their incomes through multiple channels, including wholesale and retail sales, crowdfunding, and fundraising through their community members.

In contrast, some WISEs completely turned to the market to stress their business capacities rather than social values. CM1 declared that it did not have any contact with other NGOs because it focused exclusively on developing its business brand. The organisation also refused public donations because it would like to project itself as a sustainable business venture rather than one that relies on philanthropic support (personal communication, May 2016). The WISE preferred resources in the forms of market promotion or sponsorships rather than donations to uphold its social enterprise branding. Similarly, the manager of CM5 claimed, 'We prefer people to see us as a commercial company fulfilling a social mission, rather than as a social organisation conducting commercial activities.' (personal communication, May 2016). The organisation started its business with funding from angel investors in 2015, and according to the manager, its business was 'attracting investors right from the start because people saw a future in our model' (personal communication, May 2016). CM6 and CM7 also affirmed that developing their market brand and business model was their priority (personal communication, September 2016). CM7 further stressed that it was trying to keep a diverse revenue portfolio from the first day so that it would not have to depend on the government (personal communication, December 2016).

7.2.4 *Building Ties by Appealing to Political Interest*

Six out of seven WISEs under the complementary relationship have clearly expressed their desire to collaborate with the government, and all grassroots WISEs emphasized how the services they offered aligned with the political interest of the state (personal communications, 2016–2017). The only exception was CM2, which was financially supported by a private foundation in Hong Kong. This shows that the political and economic dominance of the state has clearly resulted in the WISEs' desire to build stronger ties with the government. Strategically, this means aligning their social missions with the political agenda. This is shown when the WISEs claimed that their activities were consistent with the government's policies and that they were offering solutions for social issues the government was concerned about. For example, the director of CM1 proposed to a government officer that its model would '*solve the employment problem for the society and the government*' (personal communication, May 2016; emphasis in the original). The WISE also argued that its innovative working model would satisfy greater social demands if it could be considered by the policy-makers: '*our model can alleviate the employment issue … if this can be turned into a policy … we will be able to achieve more for the government*' (personal communication, May 2016; emphasis in the original). The objective is to demonstrate the political subservience and social effectiveness of the WISE in addressing problems in the social service market in order to attract political attention and support.

It has already been established in the earlier sections that the state selects its private partners based on both political and performance concerns. Although the state has been constantly expanding its procurement budget during its social welfare reform, the economic efficiency and social impact of organisations are not the only factors to be considered. When the organisations have grassroots origins and do not have the channels to communicate with the state, a 'probationary period' is imposed as a window for the state to access and understand the potential of the organisations before any connection can be formed. The adaptive strategies of the grassroots WISEs have catered to these criteria. Besides offering personal development programme and social activities that appeal to the long-term needs of the beneficiaries, the WISEs get through the initial development stage by seeking resources from the third sector and the market. As shown in the interviews, regardless of their capabilities in generating commercial revenues, government procurement and partnerships remain one of the most favourable channels of resources for social enterprises, not only because of the financial assistance but also because of social status, public recognition, and formal legitimacy. Moving closer to the government and climbing up the selective partnership ladder has been an important agenda for the WISEs, shown by the time and efforts they invest in participating in government-backed events and winning awards.

7.3   Linking China with the Broader Literature

In their work with transplanting social enterprise theories in Europe to Eastern Asia, Defourny and Kuan (2011) raise the question whether democratic participation contributes to the better achievement of social mission even in traditional societies that have stronger social hierarchy. Kerlin (2017) raises four major issues the current social enterprise framework has to resolve, one of them being how to understand institutional influence on social enterprises and another being how the diversity in social enterprise at the county-level can be captured. This study responds to these two questions using WISEs in China as a case study.

In a more general picture, two unique factors about East Asia are the Confucius culture and deep regional structural reforms. Ilchman, Katz and Queen (1998) discuss the impact of culture on philanthropic traditions and practices in societies, with Confucianism being a major influencing factor. Traditions and values determine the nature and constituents of philanthropic actions, especially how ethnic Chinese philanthropy and social responsibility are formulated among business leaders in the region (Wang & Juslin, 2009). As Defourny and Kuan (2011) point out, countries in Asia face the same labour market and employment issues as countries in the West do, but they also have a more centralised and dominant state that plays a much more critical role in driving and influencing the social enterprise landscape. Understanding how social enterprises behave against this political economy background is important as many Asian countries are still undergoing structural social reforms and the behaviours and organisational development of social enterprise cannot be separated from this institutional context.

This means more complications in multi-stakeholder relationships and new institutional formations in East Asia. Against this backdrop of a lack of theoretical guidance and empirical rigour, this study contributes to an in-depth understanding of the dynamic power relation and resource transfer between the dominant state and the newly formed institutions in the social context of China. Social enterprise as a new concept is viewed in this study as the result of political strategy as the state makes room for private actors to enter the social service sector. This provides a new angle of viewing not only organisational behaviours but also institutional formation at large during the country's social welfare reform. The most important point is the link between organisational performance and state–society relations—an important stakeholder dynamic that is generally emphasised but rarely explored in detail in organisational studies, especially in social enterprise development. This study hence takes a step towards opening up new prospects for social enterprises in emerging economies.

7.4   Implications, Limitations, and Direction for Future Research

There are important and practical reasons to access and understand how institutional factors affect social enterprise performance, especially in China. China is going through a social change where the traditional concentration employment model for people with disabilities is being replaced by the dispersion model (Huang et al., 2009). This means the work-integration responsibilities have been passed from the state onto the private and non-profit sectors. Since 2007, it has been mandatory for all private business owners to provide employment to people with disabilities.[1] However, this has not fundamentally solved the problem of employment for the disabled because of two reasons. First, many disabled people have not learnt the necessary skills and capabilities to work in a normal workplace environment, and second, these people also have special psychological and social needs that are not catered to by their employers. Therefore, social enterprises specialising in providing on-site job training, employment, and social inclusion services for the disabled and disadvantaged are key to tackling some of these social issues.

Linking social enterprise development to state–society relations has useful implications for revealing the logic behind successful state–social enterprise partnerships and identifying circumstances in which good performance can be expected. By posting the question of what affects institutional effectiveness, it reveals to the readers the sort of policy measures that would promote the accomplishment of the social missions of the WISEs. The three major resources identified as financial support, public legitimacy, and social network are used as gateways to monitor the WISEs. Based on the case studies, the initial round of resource transfers is still mostly through informal channels, which is time-consuming and inefficient. Establishing formal and consistent collaboration channels might be an effective measure to speed up the development of organisations.

It would be useful for policy makers and practitioners to recognise the different patterns and contributions of social enterprises as a result of political interaction. For example, the social function of the grassroots WISEs is to provide complementary services to marginalised communities that have been ignored by mainstream providers. This fills up an institutional void of the social welfare system. In this case, policy measures that help reduce their market and networking costs would be a cost-effective way to enhance their social effectiveness. This study therefore provides a starting point for policy makers, as well as professionals and practitioners in the field, to have a holistic view of the social enterprise development landscape in China and to fully understand their potential.

A limitation of this study is incurred by its small-N samples. Between two and eight organisations were interviewed under each relationship category. A bigger sample size or statistical analysis would provide more insights as substantiative evidence. A positive note, however, is that the case study has demonstrated consistent and distinctive patterns. There is no outliner in the data that cannot be explained, which points to strong evidence supporting the relationship between state–social enterprise relationship and the institutional performance of the organisations.

This study only looks at the state at the local level. The policies and rules for disabled citizens at the municipal and district levels are assumed to be consistent. This assumption is valid to a high degree as the China Disabled Persons' Federation and the MCA have local offices in every district in major cities in China. Selecting WISEs from different cities helped reduce geographical influence and minimise the impact of contextual factors, such as local policies, market openness, and public attitude. This study has also excluded stakeholder behaviours and interests in its analyses. These factors may affect social enterprise performance to different degrees and warrant future investigations.

The problem of 'mission drift' for social enterprises has been a central concern. Economic efficiency is much easier to measure than social impact. As a result, social enterprises may incline to focus more on financial returns, such as production and sales of products for a higher score on performance (Ebrahim & Rangan, 2014). Since the economic and social activities of work integration are highly related, conflicts between economic and social effectiveness are minimised for the WISE sector. However, it is still possible for mission drift to occur when social entrepreneurs spend excessive resources that compromise the social mission. This study put a heavier weight on social missions in measurement; more detailed analyses at the organisational level will reveal if mission drift has occurred.

Further research may be conducted in three directions. First, comparing the WISE sector with a second sector, such as environmental protection, where more international support and advocacy are involved, may reveal new information about state–social enterprise interaction in China. Second, this study included four major cities in China with close levels of economic development to reduce externalities. The rural regions may show different state–society dynamics as they face different local institutions, demographic features, and social issues. The study could be expanded to include cities from less-developed regions or the countryside to investigate the possible existence of an urban–rural divide regarding social enterprise performance and development. Last but not least, this study focused mostly on the institutional factors at the city level, while in reality, a combination of macro- and micro-level components could have played a role. The study could be combined with organisational studies to understand the characteristics and behaviours of social enterprises in greater detail.

Another direction is to consider the social background of the social entrepreneurs as a factor affecting their characteristics and performance. Unlike in developed countries, where informal networks are less influential, this study revealed that informal social networks facilitate collaborations between the state and social enterprises and eventually affect their performance. This, in fact, imposes a criterion on the social background of the entrepreneurs as not all grassroots leaders can build connections with the government. Unlike traditional NGOs, whose activities are usually confined to the non-profit sector and communities, with the market mechanism employed, factors such as business networks, management strategies, and capital investment become crucial to the success of social enterprises. This also means monopolism, a typical market phenomenon, is also possible in the social enterprise sector, especially under the support of the state. These issues and challenges continue to call for further future investigation on this field.

Note

1 According to the *Employment Regulations for People with Disabilities (2007)*, the number of employees with disabilities must be no less than 1.5% of total number of staff in private companies, or a fine will be imposed on the company based on the local average wage.

References

Aldrich, H. E., & Pfeffer, J. (1976). Environments of organizations. *Annual Review of Sociology, 2*(1), 79–105.

Atack, L. (1999). Four criteria of development NGO Legitimacy. *World Development, 27*(5), 855–864. https://doi.org/10.1016/s0305-750x(99)00033-9

Battilana, J., & Lee, M. (2014, February 11). Advancing research on hybrid organizing – Insights from the study of social enterprises. *The Academy of Management Annals, 8*(1), 397–441. https://doi.org/10.1080/19416520.2014.893615

Bielefeld, W. (2012, March 6). Business models of social enterprise: A design approach to hybridity [Word Document]. *ACRN Journal of Entrepreneurship Perspectives, 1*(1), 37–60. http://philpapers.org/rec/MULPWE

Billis, D., & Glennerster, H. (1998). Human services and the voluntary sector: Towards a theory of comparative advantage. *Journal of Social Policy*, *27*(1), 79–98. https://doi.org/10.1017/s0047279497005175

Carlisle, E., & Flynn, D. (2005). Small business survival in China: Guanxi, legitimacy, and social capital. *Journal of Developmental Entrepreneurship*, *10*(1), 79–96. https://doi.org/10.1142/s1084946705000070

Defourny, J., & Kuan, Y. Y. (2011). Are there specific models of social enterprise in Eastern Asia? *Social Enterprise Journal*, *7*(1). https://orbi.ulg.ac.be/bitstream/2268/105732/1/Intro%20to%20SEJ%20special%20issue.pdf

Defourny, J., & Nyssens, M. (2010, March 22). Conceptions of Social Enterprise and Social Entrepreneurship in Europe and the United States: Convergences and Divergences. *Journal of Social Entrepreneurship*, *1*(1), 32–53. https://doi.org/10.1080/19420670903442053

Deng, G. (2010). The hidden rules governing China's unregistered NGOs: Management and consequences. *China Review*, *10*(1), 183–206. http://www.jstor.org/stable/23462247

Ebrahim, A., & Rangan, V. (2014). What impact? A framework for measuring the scale and scope of social performance. *California Management Review*, *56*(3), 118–141. https://doi.org/10.1525/cmr.2014.56.3.118

Evers, A. (2005). Mixed welfare systems and hybrid organizations: Changes in the governance and provision of social services. *International Journal of Public Administration*, *28*(9–10), 737–748. https://doi.org/10.1081/pad-200067318

Flathman, R. E. (2017). Legitimacy. In R. E. Goodin, P. Pettit, & T. Pogge (Eds.), *A Companion to Contemporary Political Philosophy* (pp. 678–684). Blackwell Publishing.

Huang, J., Guo, B., & Bricout, J. C. (2009). From concentration to dispersion: The shift in policy approach to disability employment in China. *Journal of Disability Policy Studies*, *20*(1), 46–54. https://doi.org/10.1177/1044207308325008

Ilchman, W. F., Katz, S. N., & Queen, E. L. (1998). *Philanthropy in the World's Traditions*. Indiana University Press. http://www.worldcat.org/title/philanthropy-in-the-worlds-traditions/oclc/929617652

Jay, J. (2012). Navigating paradox as a mechanism of change and innovation in hybrid organizations. *Academy of Management Journal*, *56*(1). http://amj.aom.org/content/early/2012/07/20/amj.2010.0772.short

Kerlin, J. A. (2017). *Shaping Social Enterprise: Understanding Institutional Context and Influence*. Emerald Group Publishing.

Nyssens, M., & Defourny, J. (2013). *Social co-operatives: When social enterprises meet the co-operative tradition*. http://papers.ssrn.com/sol3/papers.cfm?abstract_id=2437884

O'Mahony, S., & Bechky, B. A. (2008). Boundary organizations: Enabling collaboration among unexpected allies. *Administrative Science Quarterly*, *53*(3), 422–459. https://doi.org/10.2189/asqu.53.3.422

Reay, T., & Hinings, C. R. (2009). Managing the rivalry of competing institutional logics. *Organization Studies*, *30*(6), 629–652. https://doi.org/10.1177/0170840609104803

Stark, A. (2010). The distinction between public, nonprofit, and for-profit: Revisiting the "Core Legal" approach. *Journal of Public Administration Research and Theory*, *21*(1), 3–26. https://doi.org/10.1093/jopart/muq008

Suchman, M. C. (1995). Managing legitimacy: Strategic and institutional approaches. *20*(3), 571–610. https://doi.org/10.2307/258788

Wang, L., & Juslin, H. (2009). The impact of Chinese culture on corporate social responsibility: The harmony approach. *Journal of Business Ethics, 88*(3), 433–451. https://doi.org/10.1007/s10551-009-0306-7

Wang, Q., & Yao, Y. (2016). Resource Dependence and Government-NGO Relationship in China. *The China Nonprofit Review, 8*(1), 27–51. https://doi.org/10.1163/18765149-12341304

Wiegel, W., & Bamford, D. (2015). The role of guanxi in buyer–supplier relationships in Chinese small- and medium-sized enterprises – A resource-based perspective. *Production Planning & Control, 26*(4), 308–327. https://doi.org/10.1080/09537287.2014.899405

Zietlow, J. T. (2001). Social entrepreneurship: Managerial, finance and marketing aspects. *Journal of Nonprofit & Public Sector Marketing, 9*(1–2), 19–43. https://doi.org/10.1300/j054v09n01_03

Appendix

Mission Accomplishment of Work-Integration
Social Enterprises under the Four Modes of
Relationship

Level of Social Mission	First Level of Parameters	Second Level of Parameters	WISEs under Cooptation	WISEs under Cooperation	WISEs under Complementarity	WISEs under Competition
Level I: Service Provision	Provide rehabilitation services	Provide occupational rehabilitation	CO1, CO2, CO4	CP1, CP3, CP5	CM1	COMP2
		Provide personal care	CO2, CO4	CP3, CP4, CP6, CP8	CM6	COMP2
		Cultivate independent living ability	CO1, CO2, CO3	CP3	CM1, CM2	COMP2
	Provide employment services	Provide sheltered employment	CO1, CO4	CP1, CP3	CM1, CM2, CM7	COMP2
		Provide training for employment skills	X	CP1, CP2, CP3, CP4, CP5, CP6, CP7, CP8	CM1, CM2, CM3, CM4, CM5, CM6, CM7	COMP1, COMP2
		Provide on-site workplacement	CO1, CO2, CO3, CO4	CP1, CP2, CP3, CP5, CP7	CM4, CM7	COMP2
		Provide job recommendation and job matching	X	CP1, CP3, CP4, CP7	CM5, CM7	COMP2
		Design business model based on the needs of disadvantaged workers	X	CP1, CP2, CP3, CP5, CP6, CP7	CM1, CM2, CM4, CM6	COMP2
		Continuous follow-ups and assessment for workers	CO2	CP3, CP4	CM7	X
	Provide basic social security and welfare	Provide basic social insurance and welfare	CO1, CO2, CO3	CP1, CP4, CP6, CP8	CM1	COMP1
		Increase personal income	CO1, CO2, CO3	CP1, CP2, CP3, CP4, CP5, CP6, CP7, CP8	CM1, CM2, CM3, CM4, CM5, CM6	COMP2

(*Continued*)

(Continued)

Level of Social Mission	First Level of Parameters	Second Level of Parameters	WISEs under Cooptation	WISEs under Cooperation	WISEs under Complementarity	WISEs under Competition
Level II: Social Integration and Network Formation	Empowerment of beneficiaries	Promote and protect labour rights	X	CP3, CP4	CM4	COMP1
		Provide legal, medical, and miscellaneous consultations	X	CP4, CP8	CM2, CM4	COMP1
		High user (beneficiaries) participation in workplace and social activities	X	CP2, CP3	CM1, CM3, CM4, CM6	COMP1, COMP2
	Social training and personal development	Cultivate social adaption and communication skills	X	CP2, CP3	CM1, CM5	X
		Character development and self-value recognition	X	CP2, CP3, CP4, CP5, CP6, CP7	CM1, CM3, CM4, CM6	COMP1
		Organise extra social activities and interest groups	CO1, CO3	CP1, CP2, CP3, CP4, CP5, CP7, CP8	CM4, CM5, CM6	COMP1, COMP2
	Social relations and network formation	Build new social bonds and network	X	CP2, CP3, CP4, CP8	CM4, CM5	COMP1, COMP2
		Strengthen integration with local communities	X	CP1, CP2, CP3, CP4, CP6, CP7	CM1, CM5, CM7	COMP2

					CM1
Level III: Policy advocacy and social change	Participate in policy advocacy	Policy research and political consultation	X	CP1, CP3, CP4, CP6, CP8	X
		Participate in policy agenda setting	X	CP3, CP4, CP6	X
	Promote positive social values	Reduce discrimination and promote social equality	X	CP3, CP4, CP6, CP7	X
	Promote social change	Export innovative social service models and set new benchmark for the sector	X	CP1, CP4, CP6	X

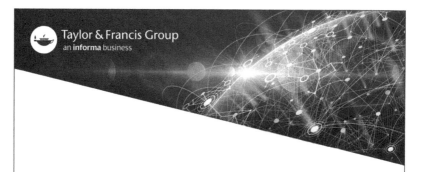